Narrative Inquiry

D. Jean Clandinin

F. Michael Connelly

Narrative Inquiry

Experience and Story in
Qualitative Research

JOSSEY-BASS
A Wiley Company
www.josseybass.com

Published by Jossey-Bass
A Wiley Imprint
989 Market Street, San Francisco, CA 94103-1741   www.josseybass.com

Jossey-Bass books and products are available through most bookstores. To contact Jossey-Bass directly call our Customer Care Department within the U.S. at (800) 956-7739, outside the U.S. at (317) 572-3986 or fax (317) 572-4002.

Jossey-Bass also publishes its books in a variety of electronic formats. Some content that appears in print may not be available in electronic books.

Library of Congress Cataloging-in-Publication Data

Clandinin, D. Jean.
   Narrative inquiry : experience and story in qualitative research / D. Jean Clandinin, F. Michael Connelly.—1st ed.
      p. cm. — (The Jossey-Bass education series)
   Includes bibliographical references and index.
   ISBN 0-7879-4343-6 (alk. paper)
   ISBN 0-7879-7276-2 (paperback)
   1. Education—Research—Methodology.   2. Narration (Rhetoric).
3. Storytelling.   I. Connelly, F. Michael.   II. Title.   III. Series.
   LB1028.C55   2000
   370'.7'2—dc21
                                                                99-6680

FIRST EDITION
HB Printing   10 9 8 7 6 5 4
PB Printing   10 9 8 7 6 5 4

The Jossey-Bass Education Series

⎯ⲧ⎯ Contents

─〰─ Preface

This book, *Narrative Inquiry: Experience and Story in Qualitative Research,* is designed to lead readers to an understanding of the narrative inquiry approach to research—what it is and how it works. We think the stories illustrate the importance of learning and thinking narratively as one frames research puzzles, enters the inquiry field, and composes field texts and research texts. Our approach is not so much to tell you what narrative inquiry is by defining it but rather to show you what it is by creating a definition contextually by recounting what narrative inquirers do. The following chapters are filled with storied examples from narrative inquiries that address a range of research concerns. We start with ourselves and then include representative stories of others' journeys on a narrative inquiry path.

To explain something of the journey that led us to narrative inquiry, we give a brief sampling in Chapter One of some of the influences on our work and discuss how the experiences of others have informed our own views. We begin with John Dewey, the preeminent influence on our work, who believed that examining experience is the key to education. We examine the influence of contemporary work on embodied metaphors and narrative unity. We also discuss the impact of new forms of inquiry in other fields, anthropology, psychology, psychotherapy, and organizational theory, and how these too have influenced our work.

In Chapter Two, we examine the differences between a narrative inquiry vantage point and a grand narrative vantage point by looking at an experience we had on a research team whose assignment it was to revise Bloom's Taxonomy. Our experience illustrates the tensions that are generated when one approach, the narrative inquiry approach, goes head-to-head with a different, more traditional approach.

In Chapter Three, we focus more directly on the area of professional practice. We address the tensions that inevitably arise between narrative inquirers and inquirers who work from different points of view. We identify two boundaries by thinking about inquiries formulated with grand, overarching ideas, concepts, and theories (formalistic) and inquiries formulated in terms of parts, factors, and subprocesses (reductionistic). We explore specific tensions, such as the place of theory and the nature and role of people at each of these boundaries.

In Chapter Four, we begin to demonstrate what narrative inquirers do. It is our intention *not to define* narrative inquiry *but to show* narrative inquiry by recounting what narrative inquirers do. We are interested in the terms of narrative inquiry and how they define and bound the inquiry process, and we discuss the terms that we use to help shape our inquiries. Here, we introduce our research framework, the *three-dimensional inquiry space.* We also provide two examples from our own work that illustrate how narrative inquiry is lived out in practice.

Chapter Five takes us into the field with researchers. We see firsthand how an actual narrative inquiry is a dynamic process of living and telling stories, and reliving and retelling stories, not only those of participants but those of researchers as well. We also look at specific challenges that researchers must learn to negotiate all through the inquiry process.

Chapter Six deals with the challenges associated with writing field texts. It discusses the difficulties inquirers encounter when they think they are losing objectivity and demonstrates how field texts can help clarify their position. Field texts are memory enhancers that fill in the spaces of forgotten occurrences (outward experiences) and feelings (inward experiences).

Chapter Seven describes the many kinds of field texts that can be created by inquirers and participants to represent various aspects of the field experience. We look at how the qualities of the researcher-participant relationship shapes the nature of the field texts as well as the types of field texts that are created. We conclude the chapter with an exploration of how careful and sensitive positioning of the field texts is important to the ultimate integrity of the work.

Beginning narrative inquirers find the move from field texts to research texts one of the most difficult transitions of all. Chapter Eight outlines several topics that need to be carefully considered and skillfully woven into the final "product"—the research text.

In Chapter Nine, we continue examining the complexities associated with writing research texts. We look at how the process brings the researcher back to the reductionistic and formalistic boundaries faced at the beginning of the inquiry process. We explore the feelings of doubt and uncertainty about the purpose of the research text that almost inevitably return for the inquirer at this stage and how it is more than likely that by the time the research text is being written, the researcher will have refined or even changed some of the goals that seemed clear at the outset of the inquiry. The chapter concludes with a discussion of the many considerations around choosing the best narrative form for one's research text.

Finally, Chapter Ten presents issues that must be grappled with on an ongoing basis during the course of the inquiry, from the time that the idea for the inquiry is conceived until the final research text has been composed, issues such as ethics, ownership, and anonymity. We close Chapter Ten by discussing a criterion that for us is of utmost significance for narrative inquirers—maintaining wakefulness.

Edmonton, Canada   D. JEAN CLANDININ
Toronto, Canada   F. MICHAEL CONNELLY
August 1999

⟿ Acknowledgments

Many people traveled with us in our journeys of experience and narrative, and we shall, as best we can, honor and credit these travelers. Some, for reasons of time, place, or academic circumstance, we met only through their writings. Some, perhaps not even narrative inquirers, supported us through related writing that helped us imagine narrative inquiry possibilities. Some were practitioners in schools, universities, colleges, and health care institutions who let us into their professional lives in study after study. Many were students who took our courses and taught us how to teach narrative and how to teach narratively. Many have been master's and doctoral thesis students, people from different cultures and different social and professional niches, writing on a diverse array of topics, all with a narrative inquiry agenda.

Perhaps most important of all to our day-to-day thinking about narrative inquiry are the doctoral students who joined our research team and who blended their work with ours in ways that in the end are impossible to sort out and properly credit. We try throughout the book to acknowledge the significant contributions these others have played in the development of our ideas on narrative inquiry.

Narrative inquiry is, always, multilayered and many stranded. To give a sense of this complexity and the nested quality of stories told, lived, co-composed, and eventually narrated in a research text, we try to place ourselves alongside our doctoral student coresearchers. As we do this, we place ourselves and our research alongside their research with their participants. These nested sets of characters—we as authors of this book, the research team members, and their participants— form a textured space of lives, stories, puzzles, and puzzle-driven narrative inquiry.

As with our other books, we owe a debt of gratitude to Gary Pyper, who carefully worked with multiple drafts, responses, and revisions, making skilled use of the technological resources available.

D.J.C.
F.M.C.

⟿ The Authors

D. Jean Clandinin is professor and director of the Centre for Research for Teacher Education and Development, University of Alberta. She earned a bachelor of arts degree in psychology and history at the University of Alberta, a master of education degree in counseling at the University of Alberta, and a doctorate at the University of Toronto. She is a former teacher, counselor, and school psychologist. She is the author or coauthor of many articles in journals such as *Curriculum Inquiry, Teaching and Teacher Education,* and *Cambridge Journal of Education.* Her most recent books, coauthored with F. Michael Connelly and published by Teachers College Press, are *Teachers' Professional Knowledge Landscapes* (1995) and *Shaping a Professional Identity* (1999). She is a former vice president of the American Educational Research Association (AERA). She is the 1993 winner of the Early Career Development Award for the AERA.

F. Michael Connelly studied at the University of Alberta, Columbia University, and the University of Chicago. He earned a bachelor of science degree, a master of science degree, and a bachelor of education degree at the University of Alberta, and a doctorate at the University of Chicago. He is professor and director of the Centre for Teacher Development, Ontario Institute for Studies in Education at the University of Toronto. He taught secondary school in Alberta and held teaching positions at the Universities of Alberta, Illinois, and Chicago. He coordinated the Canadian component of the Second International Science Study, is editor of *Curriculum Inquiry,* and is a member of the board of directors of the John Dewey Society for Study of Education and Culture. He is codirector, with Clandinin, of a long-term study of teachers' personal practical knowledge and teachers' professional knowledge landscapes. Connelly and Clandinin are coauthors of *Teachers as Curriculum Planners: Narratives of Experience* (1988), as well as numerous articles and chapters in contributed volumes. Connelly was the recipient of the 1987 Outstanding Canadian Curriculum Scholar Award of the Canadian Society for the Study of Education, the 1991 Canadian Education Association-Whitworth award for Educational Research, and the 1999 Lifetime Achievement Award for Division B, AERA.

~~~ Prologue

We were sitting in a meeting room at the University of the Philippines. A year earlier the group had met in Japan; a year later we were scheduled to meet in a wine region of Italy. We finished a fine lunch hosted by the university, and we were looking forward to a series of partial- and full-day trips in Manila and its surrounds. Everyone, it appeared, and certainly Michael, enjoyed the local cuisine and the chance to explore new places.

We were in Manila during our participation in the Second International Science Study of the International Association for the Evaluation of Educational Achievement, an international comparative education study of, at one point, upwards of forty nations. It was the late 1980s.

With the world seemingly opening up and on the brink of a variety of international free-trade agreements, with the world mostly at peace (or at least not engaged in events called world wars), and with a growing recognition (or at least so it seemed to Michael) of the impact of one part of the world on another—German and Japanese manufacturing and marketing success, American political influence, the apparent awakening of China—and the competition that sometimes goes with these recognitions, education—how it is practiced, what schools look like, what people learn in different cultures—had become an interesting topic. News reporters worried about the perceived successes of the Japanese educational system; others wondered about the role of education in the so-called third world and developing countries.

For Michael, someone educated in a one-room country schoolhouse in western Canada, the idea of education and its place in the lives of people who previously only existed in imagination in atlases, world globes, newspapers, and radio was compelling. We visited schools in Manila, schools carefully chosen, as it turned out, for their discipline and rigor. We saw something of contrasting lives, as street children sold trinkets to us as our cars stopped at intersections on the way to and from the schools.

In our meeting room, we buckled down to work and spent the day, two weeks of days, arguing over the correct, most feasible ways to comparatively tabulate and represent student multiple-choice responses to items on tests to be given at three grade levels in participating countries. Michael remembers feeling mildly irrelevant as the meeting wore on, sufficiently knowledgeable to know what was going on, fairly indifferent in an unarticulated way, and all the while glad to be there for the chance to learn something about life and education in another part of the world.

What happened in that room on those days and in other meetings on other days is what happens too often, at least too often for our taste, in educational inquiry—public interest in education turned into manageable, minuscule realities by researchers; researchers' personal interests submerged for the sake of research precision.

Educators are interested in life. Life, to borrow John Dewey's metaphor, *is* education. Educators are interested in learning and teaching and how it takes place; they are interested in the leading out of different lives, the values, attitudes, beliefs, social systems, institutions, and structures, and how they are all linked to learning and teaching. Educational researchers are, first, educators, and we too are interested in people. Educational researchers, with their interest in people, are no different in that sense than anyone pursuing research in the social sciences. These are the sciences of people. People's lives and how they are composed and lived out are what is of interest. We social scientists are gossips on a grand scale, interested in observing, participating with, thinking about, saying and writing the doings and goings-on of our fellow humans. The gossip in that Manila meeting room was deadly boring.

But if our interest as researchers is lived experience—that is, lives and how they are lived—how did our research conversations become focused on the measurement of student responses? How did educational experience come to be seen as something that could be measured in this way?

As with our understanding of all things, people, and events, the reduction of the study of experience to consideration of issues of measurement is part of an ongoing plotline, a powerful plotline for the story of educational research and perhaps for research in the social sciences. Those Manila meetings were not isolated events. They were part of a grand narrative of educational research.

Lagemann (1996) points out something similar in her essay, "Contested Terrain: A History of Educational Research in the United States, 1890–1990," an essay drawn from her book in progress, *John Dewey's Defeat: Studying Education in the Research University 1890–1990*. The book's title itself is telling of how the idea of experience (so key to Dewey's notions of education) has been lost in the study of educational research.

Lagemann notes that in the early 1900s, educational research emerged within a climate of "increasingly common faith in the value of deriving generalizations from empirical data and a widespread disdain toward knowledge based on logic or speculation" (1996, p. 5). The first educational research studies tended, as one would expect within such a climate, to be fairly comprehensive, censuslike investigations. What enabled such early studies were tests and statistical devices that, according to Lagemann, "allowed researchers to measure the achievement of students and the costs of instruction and then, through comparative statistical analysis, to determine which practices were apparently most effective, least costly, and, therefore, most efficient" (1996, p. 6).

The emerging plotline for educational research was set within a context of other social science research with a "reverence for numbers." What was beginning to count for social science research was to lead to research such as that being discussed in that Manila conference room in the late 1980s. The tests and statistical devices made such research possible, and they appealed to government agencies, policymakers, and researchers as a way to engage in research. Experience, life, had begun to be studied in that way long before comparative educational researchers studied student learning in different countries by assessing multiple-choice test results. This was the plotline for education research—the plotline for much research in the social sciences, established in the early 1900s.

If we imagine, as Dewey did, research as the study of experience, what might the plotline for social science research be? The social sciences are concerned with humans and their relations with themselves and their environment. As such, the social sciences are founded on the study of experience. Experience is therefore the starting point and the key term for all social science inquiry.

In our work, keeping experience in the foreground comes about by periodic returns to the writings of Dewey (for example, [1916] 1961, 1934, 1938). For Dewey, education, experience, and life are inextricably intertwined. When one asks what it means to study education, the answer—in its most general sense—is to study experience. Following Dewey, the study of education is the study of life—for example, the study of epiphanies, rituals, routines, metaphors, and everyday actions. We learn about education from thinking about life, and we learn about life from thinking about education. This attention to experience and thinking about education *as* experience is part of what educators do in schools.

Both of us worked as educators in schools. Jean worked for a few years as a school counselor in two elementary schools, where she spent her days listening to children, their parents, and their teachers tell her about their lives and about what was important to them. In the midst of this, she found herself needing to do research for a master's thesis. Her intention was to do something related to what she spent her days doing. Because she was "living her life" as an educator among children and teachers, who were also "living their lives" in school, Jean wondered if it was possible to link the living with the studying of living.

A continuing problem that she faced was how to work with children who were experiencing reading difficulties. Usually, these "reading" problems became apparent to teachers and parents in the later elementary school grades, and a common sentiment expressed was how good it would be to be able to predict which children would experience these problems. It seemed to make sense to study these experiences. The questions were how to study children's experiences and how to begin to work more intensively earlier with children who would face such problems. What became apparent was that the experience of the children needed to be reduced to something that could be measured by tests and statistical devices in order to be researchable. The research, as it turned out, was a study in which children's experiences were measured by a well-known intelligence test and a commonly administered reading inventory. Sure enough, there was a relationship and a way of predicting those who would have a high probability of experiencing reading difficulties.

Although Jean did study those who lived in schools with her, it seemed a long way from life, theirs or hers. Children's experiences were reduced to scores on two tests, scores that were correlated, and based on this correlation, something about how these children would experience school was known. For Jean, something happened as she read and reread the statistical correlations. She knew these children, knew something about their stories as the children told them to her, and knew something about the stories that their teachers and parents told about them. They were much more than their test scores. Their lives were filled with complexities, with hopes, with dreams, with wishes, and with intentions. Though the research community, with its reverence for numbers, focused on the correlations, Jean thought about the children's lives. There was one child whose scores did not work out in the predicted way. He was an "aberration" in the test scores. For the research, he was an exception, outside the standard range. Jean wrote a line about him in the research text that stated this. In life, in school, Jean spent many more hours trying to understand the complexities of his experience.

Both of our stories, coming at different times and in different places, are embedded within the larger story of educational research. In the first story (Michael's), a researcher with personal educational and life interests helps draft multiple-choice items and strategies for a comparative education assessment. In the other story (Jean's), a teacher interested in students' lives learns, through a graduate studies program, to view children's lives as correlations between their test scores. But these stories go well beyond our own personal stories of learning how to translate our teaching and research interests in experience into measurable-manageable strategies with certainty and estimates of error. Our stories resonated across the whole of social science research. This is how researchers were educated; this is how researchers pursued their work; this is how teachers were taught to think about the role of research in their lives.

Lagemann (1989) wrote, "I have often argued to students, only in part to be perverse, that one cannot understand a history of education in the United States during the twentieth century unless one realizes that Edward L. Thorndike won and John Dewey lost" (1989, p. 185). Thorndike was an educational psychologist who popularized the idea of a science of education based on the observation of behavior. According to Cuban (1992), he was a leading figure in North American educational research thought. Doyle (1992) noted that Thorndike provided the psychological basis for the social efficiency movement associated with Rice and Taylor in sociology, business, and professionalization. We see the competition between Dewey and Thorndike as competition between two stories of how to do social science research. The story scripted by Thorndike became so pervasive, so taken for granted, as the only valid story, that we call it a "grand narrative" of social science inquiry.

As we pursued our educational research careers, we were situated within this turning-away-from experience (although we did not realize it at the time). We found ourselves quantifying what interested us, and of course, as we quantified experience, its richness and expression was stripped away. However, for whatever reasons, whether formal education, upbringing, the way we each led our lives, or for other reasons or combinations of reasons, our interest in experience was kept alive. We do know that there was little in our studies of psychology, sociology, administration, or philosophy—fields that look very much like our educational studies—that sustained our continuing interest in trying to understand experience in our lives and in our research.

Eventually, some of which we explain in Chapter One, narrative became a way of understanding experience. Our excitement and interest in narrative has its origins in our interest in experience. With narrative as our vantage point, we have a point of reference, a life and a ground to stand on for imagining what experience is and for imagining how it might be studied and represented in researchers' texts. In this view, experience is the stories people live. People live stories, and in the telling of these stories, reaffirm them, modify them, and create new ones. Stories lived and told educate the self and others, including the young and those such as researchers who are new to their communities (Clandinin and Connelly, 1994).

Narrative Inquiry

CHAPTER ONE

Why Narrative?

Our starting point for this book is our own inquiry into teaching and teacher knowledge. In the past three decades, we have been positioned in different places and in different story lines on the educational landscape—as teachers, as teacher educators, as university teachers, and as educational researchers. Our questions, our research puzzles, have focused around the broad questions of how individuals teach and learn, of how temporality (placing things in the context of time) connects with change and learning, and of how institutions frame our lives.

INTRODUCTION

In this chapter, we review some of the historical influences that have helped shape our views on our journey to narrative inquiry, beginning with our foremost influence, John Dewey. We discuss contemporary influences—Johnson and Lakoff's work on embodied metaphors and MacIntyre's work on narrative unity. We also examine the impact of new forms of inquiry in other fields by reviewing the work of Geertz and Bateson in anthropology, Polkinghorne in psychology, Coles in psychotherapy, and Czarniawska in organizational theory. We conclude the chapter with a broad working concept of what narrative inquiry is for us.

JOHN DEWEY

Our work is strongly influenced by John Dewey, the preeminent thinker in education. Dewey addressed matters that we saw as central to our work, matters to which we continually return. Our research interests over the years shifted from foregrounding students and student learning; to teachers and teaching; to school landscapes of routines, rhythms, values, and people; to school change and reform. However, as we shifted our focus, foregrounding one matter and letting another slide to the background, Dewey's writings on the nature of experience remained our conceptual, imaginative backdrop.

Experience is a key term in these diverse inquiries. For us, Dewey transforms a commonplace term, experience, in our educators' language into an inquiry term, and gives us a term that permits better understandings of educational life. For Dewey, experience is both personal and social. Both the personal and the social are always present. People are individuals and need to be understood as such, but they cannot be understood only as individuals. They are always in relation, always in a social context. The term *experience* helps us think through such matters as an individual child's learning while also understanding that learning takes place with other children, with a teacher, in a classroom, in a community, and so on.

Furthermore, Dewey held that one criterion of experience is *continuity,* namely, the notion that experiences grow out of other experiences, and experiences lead to further experiences. Wherever one positions oneself in that continuum—the imagined now, some imagined past, or some imagined future—each point has a past experiential base and leads to an experiential future. This too is key in our thinking about education because as we think about a child's learning, a school, or a particular policy, there is always a history, it is always changing, and it is always going somewhere. Through the constraints and practicalities of inquiry, one or another specific inquiry might appear to focus on one or another aspect within this broad theory of experience. We tried to hold all these matters in mind as we reflected on the educational puzzles and problems in our inquiry lives. We learned to move back and forth between the personal and the social, simultaneously thinking about the past, present, and future, and to do so in ever-expanding social milieus.

MARK JOHNSON AND ALASDAIR MACINTYRE

In the early 1980s when we were attempting to foreground individual teachers' knowledge, we met Mark Johnson, a philosopher whose work on experiential, embodied metaphors attracted our attention. At that time, we were trying to understand the part that experiential images played in teachers' knowledge and its expression in classroom practice. We had completed a three-year study with two teachers, Stephanie and Aileen. We knew these two teachers, had spent time in their classrooms, in conversations with them, and had written and talked with and about them. Our focus was very much on trying to understand what we called their *personal practical knowledge*. One of our central ways of understanding their knowledge was an inquiry into the nature of their images of teaching. However, as we wrote about the images of Stephanie and Aileen, we were particularly concerned that too much analytic focus on what might be seen as discrete images would lose the holistic sense of an individual person and her experiential knowledge. Our puzzle, at first, seemed one of representation. It was our interest in ways of thinking about experiential knowledge that drew us to the work of Mark Johnson and his collaborator, George Lakoff. Johnson's work with Lakoff on metaphors seemed directly connected to our experiential focus and link—in our minds—to Dewey's work (Lakoff and Johnson, 1980).

With these puzzles in mind, we invited Johnson to spend a day or two with us in Toronto to help us think this matter through. In conversations with Johnson at a local hotel, he challenged us to "say more about how you see knowledge as embodied, embedded in a culture, based on narrative unity" (conversation with authors, February 17, 1983). With these brief words scribbled on a hotel notepad, he introduced Alasdair MacIntyre's work (1981) and the notion of *narrative unity* into our thinking. Narrative unity gave us a way to think in a more detailed and informative way about the general construct of continuity in individuals' lives. Continuity became for us a narrative construction that opened up a floodgate of ideas and possibilities. We turned our attention to other narrative literature and to writers who worked on the links between narrative and life.

We have been pursuing this work under the heading of *narrative inquiry* with a rough sense of narrative as both phenomena under study *and* method of study. We see teaching and teacher knowledge as expressions of embodied individual and social stories, and we think narratively as we enter into research relationships with teachers, create *field texts,* and write storied accounts of educational lives. (Field texts is our term for data collected in the field. This terminology is discussed in Chapter Seven.)

NEW WAYS OF THINKING: THE CONTRIBUTION OF INQUIRY

As we looked back at twenty or so years of work, we had a sense of ourselves in the earlier years as often working at the margins of established inquiry traditions in our field. But now in looking at our field, at educational studies, we are struck by the extent to which narrative inquiry has become part of the discourse. Educational researchers of many different persuasions claim to use narrative, and many who do not use it offer critiques of it.

The same is true in other social science fields. As we look at texts in disciplines such as anthropology, psychology, and psychiatry, we are struck by the fact of similarly reflective pieces on inquiry and on how inquiry and its contribution to knowledge of phenomena in these fields is changing. Clifford Geertz's (1995) *After the Fact,* Mary Catherine Bateson's (1994) *Peripheral Visions,* Norman Denzin's (1997) *Interpretive Ethnography,* Donald Polkinghorne's (1988) *Narrative Knowing and the Human Sciences,* Roy Schafer's (1992) *Retelling a Life,* Robert Coles's (1989) *Call of Stories,* and Barbara Czarniawska's (1997) *Narrating the Organization* are all illustrative.

Though our interest is mainly in the social sciences, something similar seems to be happening in the humanities. For example, consider Donald Spence's (1982) *Narrative Truth and Historical Method,* David Carr's (1986) *Time, Narrative, and History,* and Carolyn Heilbrun's (1988) *Writing a Woman's Life.* These authors also look across their fields to bring in new ways of thinking about changing phenomena and changing inquiry. These relatively recent accounts, some in deliberately historical ways, others more anecdotally and narratively, present a picture of fields in transition with new forms of inquiry coming to the fore. In 1986, Marcus and Fischer wrote (in their title) that this is an "experimental moment" in the life of human science inquiry, an idea echoed by Denzin and Lincoln (1994), who name the present time of inquiry "the fifth moment" (p. 11).

It has been instructive for us to read in other social sciences and in the humanities for insights into these changing inquiries and changing phenomena, which resonate with and inform our own narrative inquiries. We set out to read these texts to get a sense of these authors' accounts of the history of their field of inquiry and what it was that they wished to introduce to their field (if anything) and why.

In the following section, we select certain texts—Geertz and Bateson in anthropology, Polkinghorne in psychology, Coles in psychotherapy, and Czarniawska in organizational theory—and analyze them closely to try to get a picture of what these authors see as happening in their fields. As we do so, we bring forward insights that may inform our narrative inquiries in educational studies.

CLIFFORD GEERTZ, *AFTER THE FACT: TWO COUNTRIES, FOUR DECADES, ONE ANTHROPOLOGIST*

In *After the Fact,* Geertz (1995) reflects on his forty years of anthropological inquiry as he revisits his work in two towns, Pare and Sefrou, in two countries, Indonesia and Morocco. As he conducts this retrospective inquiry, he comments:

> The problem is that more has changed, and more disjointedly, than one at first imagines. The two towns of course have altered, in many ways superficially, in a few profoundly. But so, and likewise, has the anthropologist. So has the discipline within which the anthropologist works, the intellectual setting within which that discipline exists, and the moral basis on which it rests. So have the countries in which the two towns are enclosed and the international world in which the two countries are enclosed. So has just about everyone's sense of what is available from life. . . . When everything changes, the small and immediate to the vast and abstract—the object of study, the world immediately around it, the student, the world immediately around him, and the wider world around them both—there seems to be no place to stand so as to locate just what has altered and how. [pp. 1–2]

What immediately catches our eye in this quote is the tone of instability and *change.* For Geertz, change is the hallmark: not only have the two towns, countries, and world changed, the researcher has also changed. Not only has the discipline changed, the moral basis of it has also changed. It is not only the discipline and its moral basis but also what Geertz calls its "intellectual setting"—what some might call its perspective, point of view, or substantive structure—that has changed. All of this is complicated for Geertz as researcher, for it is no longer clear to him where he should stand in order to understand the changes taking place. The place of the anthropologist in this changing world, and the changing anthropological study of it, is for Geertz uncertain.

Change—change in the world, change in the inquiry, change in the inquirer, change in the point of view, change in the outcomes—is what Geertz notices upon reflection. It is what he calls "the problem." With this problem set, what does Geertz offer for inquiry? To begin with, he says: "What we can construct, if we keep notes and survive, are hindsight accounts of the connectedness of things that seem to have happened: pieced-together patternings, after the fact. . . . It calls for showing how particular events and unique occasions, an encounter here, a development there, can be woven together with a variety of facts and a battery of interpretations to produce a sense of how things go, have been going, and are likely to go" (pp. 2–3).

One reading of these two remarks is that Geertz has an ambiguous sense of what is possible and what one ought to do in inquiry. He wants the anthropologist to be a careful observer gathering a variety of field texts in the hopes of offering accounts of connections among things. Even here, instead of saying that these are things that have happened, he writes "that seem to have happened." Anthropologists work, according to Geertz, "*ad hoc* and *ad interim,* piecing together thousand-year histories with three-week massacres, international conflicts with municipal ecologies. The economics of rice or olives, the politics of ethnicity or religion, the workings of language or war, must, to some extent, be soldered into the final construction. So must geography, trade, art, and technology. The result, inevitably, is unsatisfactory, lumbering, shaky, and badly formed: a grand contraption" (p. 20).

For Geertz, the anthropologist studies things that one is not too sure have happened, establishes connections that might provide links, produces a comprehensive, loosely formed account that, far from having theoretical precision, is "a grand contraption." For Geertz, whatever it is that anthropologists produce is at best "lumbering, shaky, and badly formed."

How are these grand contraptions, these anthropological treatises, constructed? It is here that narrative understandings are important. Photographs, prefaces, and appendixes are "quite inadequate" and, says Geertz, "marginalize what is central. What is needed, or anyway must serve, is tableaus, anecdotes, parables, tales: mini-narratives with the narrator in them" (p. 65).

MARY CATHERINE BATESON, *PERIPHERAL VISIONS: LEARNING ALONG THE WAY*

Bateson's life as an anthropologist overlaps temporally to a large degree with that of Geertz's, and in *Peripheral Visions* (1994), she takes on a task similar to the one taken on by Geertz. She too writes a reflective overview of her life as an anthropologist. Bateson also comes to narrative as a form of inquiry most appropriate for anthropology, and we read her to gather insights for our work on narrative inquiry in educational studies. Bateson's focus is on *learning*, and she carefully weaves her book around themes of continuity and improvisation. She writes about improvisation as characterizing "more and more lives today, lived in uncertainty, full of the inklings of alternatives. . . . Adaptation comes out of encounters with novelty that may seem chaotic. In trying to adapt, we may need to deviate from cherished values, behaving in ways we have barely glimpsed, seizing on fragmentary clues" (p. 8).

For Bateson, improvisation is a response to uncertainties in life, novelties that may even seem meaningless, inexplicable, "chaotic." With this sense of life in turmoil, and with improvisation as a necessary response, how is it possible to see continuity as one of her central themes? Continuity is possible for Bateson because learning is a human endeavor. There is no doubt that for Bateson as for Geertz change is one of the characteristics of lives. For Bateson though, change and continuity are brought together by human agency. Improvisation and adaptation to change allow the past to be connected and to have continuity with the future.

This too is a book about change, change that comes from learning. For Bateson, learning is change. Continuity results because people improvise and adapt, that is, they learn.

It is clear that Bateson's world, like Geertz's, is a world of change. But as they build for the reader an idea of what change is, and its importance to the field of anthropological inquiry, it is clear that they emphasize very different aspects of change. In both Bateson's and Geertz's texts, everything is changing—the phenomena, the discipline, the agent, the methods, and the outcomes. Whereas Geertz emphasizes the changing phenomena, the changing world studied by the anthropologist, Bateson emphasizes the person, participant sometimes, researcher sometimes, always the inseparability of the two. The starting points for the two books highlight their different understandings of change and its role in anthropology. Geertz begins with changes in his anthropological research sites over forty years. He muses about how to describe the changes in those sites. Bateson begins with her daughter in a Persian garden. As she tells a story of how to teach her daughter and how to understand this teaching many years later, she muses about change in her and her daughter's understanding, then and now. Geertz focuses on understanding the changing world; Bateson focuses on understanding how one understands a changing world.

Geertz stays with change as his key term, and he builds his notion of anthropological inquiry and the role of narrative in it on change. Bateson shifts her key term to learning, but she too comes to narrative. She says, "Our species thinks in metaphors and learns through stories" (p. 11). There is a parallel, even an identity, between life as an anthropologist and life generally. For her, anthropological inquiry is meeting difference, adapting, and learning. It is, she says, "a way of being, especially suited to a world of change. A society of many traditions and cultures can be a school of life" (pp. 7–8).

It is narrative that allows Bateson as an anthropologist to learn, narrative that allows all of us to learn. What does she mean by narrative, apart from learning "through stories"? She means much more than do those who simply say that we communicate with one another through stories, that our experiences are recorded and transmitted in story form. To Bateson, it is clear that anthropologists, all of us, lead storied lives on storied landscapes. This perspective on inquiry is a perspective on life, on stories, and their plotlines as everything, the good and the bad, the provocateurs to change. They can "mislead" (p. 83), can change and become "more complicated and ambiguous" (p. 83), and can "have more than one meaning" (p. 11) with no "single true interpretation" (p. 84).

In our exploration of what anthropological inquiry might look like for Bateson, we learn more by her example than by her telling. Her book is vividly narrative in structure and content. It is composed of, to borrow a phrase from Geertz, a series of mini-narratives with the narrator in them.

Bateson also offers lessons in how to go about the work of anthropological inquiry, inquiry that we may call a form of narrative inquiry. Most important is the attitude of the inquirer toward participants, an attitude that will foster learning. Essentially, anthropologists are participant observers, sometimes, she says, more one than the other. She writes, "Sometimes a dissonance will break through and pull you into intense involvement" (p. 5) and sometimes push you away from a participating stance. Always, for learning to occur, the inquirer in this ambiguous, shifting, participant observation role is meeting difference; allowing difference to challenge assumptions, values, and beliefs; improvising and adapting to the difference; and thereby learning as the narrative anthropologist.

Though the route, at least the conceptual route, to final texts, to what it is the inquirer has in the end to say, is different for Geertz and Bateson, there are again similarities. For Bateson, "Ambiguity is the warp of life, not something to be eliminated" (p. 9). Certainty is not a goal. She writes that the anthropologist, indeed everyone, needs to reject the "rhetoric of merely, the rhetoric that treats as trivial whatever is recognized as a product of interacting human minds" and to "accept ambiguity and allow for learning along the way" (p. 235). For Geertz as well, certainty is not a goal, theoretical precision not possible. For Geertz, the anthropologist creates lumbering, shaky, grand contraptions. For Bateson, what is written, finally, is the inquiring agent's construction: it is an *"I" document*. It is "I" who writes the constructions because this authorial voice reduces what she calls the "timeless authority: this is so" (pp. 75–76) and the resistance to a "temptation to be categorical" (pp. 75–76). The narrative anthropologist also offers an "I," the "I" that grows out of the ambiguous, shifting participant observation relationships, the "I" who learns by seeing and telling stories along the way, and who writes stories of relationship. There is a temporality and a situatedness to the anthropologist's writing: relationships to the "I" of the inquirer that imply the biases, perspectives, and particular learnings that the inquirer was able to engage in. Thus, though Bateson does not say so in so many words, there is a comprehensive, loosely formed quality, one might imagine, to the anthropologist's final writing. For Geertz, the anthropologist's edifice rests on the tentativeness of connections among events observed and explanations offered. For Bateson, the anthropologist's edifice rests on the "I" of the agent and all that implies by virtue of the uncertainties of learning.

BARBARA CZARNIAWSKA, *NARRATING THE ORGANIZATION: DRAMAS OF INSTITUTIONAL IDENTITY*

Barbara Czarniawska, an organizational researcher, reflects on the nature and intensity of institutional transformations visible in the early 1990s. She writes, "Things were bursting out of their labels, and words grew short of events. Frantic attempts at interpretation were multiplying" (1997, p. 1). As a researcher, Czarniawska is at a loss to account for these transformations using existing vocabulary, conceptual apparatuses, and metaphors in organization theory. In the face of her changing organizational world and the need for new metaphors, she turns, in an interdisciplinary search, to the disciplines of anthropology, literary theory, and the institutional school within sociology. Unlike Geertz and Bateson—whose approach is to look to the changing phenomena, to themselves as researchers undergoing change, and to the changing discipline for inspiration—Czarniawska's strategy is to borrow and mix metaphors from other disciplines. What she borrows is narrative. Narrative is, for Czarniawska, far from being embedded in the nature of the phenomena, as it is with Geertz and Bateson. For Czarniawska, narrative is a heuristic device, a metaphor useful for understanding organizations.

With narrative in hand as a theoretical frame—at least a metaphorical, metalevel frame—Czarniawska applies the frame to the Swedish public sector. Through applying narrative, she creates three stories of public administration management—"A New Budget and Accounting Routine in Big City," "Tax Reform," and "The Rehabilitation Program." With these as story titles, she conducts an analysis of each story using narrative terms such as *tension-producing devices, paradoxes,* and *interruptions.* She links these stories to the themes of personnel and communication and to the serials of institutional decentralization, "company-ization," and computerization. She calls this entire narrative analytic process *ergonography.*

As with Geertz and Bateson, Czarniawska's researcher changes. However, the change in her researcher is driven by the change in methodology—a narrative inquirer engages differently in her work because she is using a new metaphor. For Geertz and Bateson, the inquirer, along with the phenomena, is already changing because she is embedded in the changing phenomena. For Czarniawska, the researcher is a kind of literary critic, far removed from a systems analyst but distinguished from a novelist. A literary critic pays attention to reality, in this case the reality of life in organizations, whereas a novelist might be free of this constraint.

Nevertheless, Czarniawska says, "Organization researchers thus live forever on shaky ground, insofar as they mediate between the 'organizational authors' and the academic theorists. . . . Practitioners and consultants are busy writing texts and authoring works. The researchers' role is to interpret these texts (although this requires the creation of yet another text). They build worlds; we inspect the construction (although this requires the construction of yet another world)" (pp. 203–204).

The changing organizational world that Czarniawska observes, and the changed role of the researcher (now a narrative researcher), lead to "a redefinition of what research produces" (p. 202). Czarniawska frames the issue in terms of fact and fiction. Borrowing from literary theory means that for her there is "no clear difference between fact and fiction" (p. 203). The documents produced by the narrative organizational researcher are part fact, part fiction, in some inseparable way. For instance, in her story of "A New Budget and Accounting Routine in Big City," there is a strong sense of the application of story structure. A scene is set, a problem is introduced, characters are described, tension is introduced to create an unfolding plot, and there is some kind of climax and resolution. There is a different sense of how she sees research outcomes in her work than did Geertz and Bateson, for whom the structures were tentative, subject to change, and loosely formed. For Czarniawska, the work produced has fictional quality, is smoother, has fewer rough edges, and has a cleaner application of narrative structures.

ROBERT COLES, *THE CALL OF STORIES: TEACHING AND THE MORAL IMAGINATION*

Robert Coles's *Call of Stories* (1989) is a book that blends life, teaching, and the practice of psychiatry. Coles says it is an inquiry into students' responses to literature, a study of teaching and learning. Much like Bateson, somewhat like Geertz, and almost not at all like Czarniawska in their disciplines, the reflection contained in Coles's work unifies psychiatry with life and teaching. Coles learns about life—death, marriage, morality—from his patients and his students. He learns from, and teaches, the same things from literature. Life, teaching, and psychiatry are all interwoven in teaching-learning ways. For our purposes, of course, we keep to our theme by thinking of psychiatry as an inquiry and ask how it is that Coles comes to narrative—a somewhat unidimensional reading of a multidimensional text. Cole's work is richer than is implied by our single question.

Change—the driving force in the reasoning leading Geertz, Bateson, and Czarniawska to narrative—plays no noticeable role in *The Call of Stories*. There is no sense of a changing world nor of once-successful theories and ideas breaking down and needing replacement. In this sense, the temporal, circumstantial quality of the fields of inquiry so evident in our other authors is not an issue for Coles. There is, of course, a persuasive, moral sense that psychiatry "ought" to proceed in harmony with living, a harmony to be contrasted with psychiatry proceeding by the application of psychiatric theories.

Coles comes to narrative through life and through teaching and learning. For him, narrative is not something discovered, as it was for Czarniawska, to be applied metaphorically to his field. Chapter One's opening story is a teaching-learning story that takes place during Coles's psychiatric residency, during which he has two supervisors, Dr. Ludwig and Dr. Binger, whose task it is to help him reflect on the protocols he writes on his work with patients. One supervisor, Dr. Binger, asks for symptoms and the categorization of behavior in terms of syndromes; the other, Dr. Ludwig, encourages Coles to listen. Coles writes, "I was urged to let each patient be a teacher: 'Hearing themselves teach you, through their narration, the patients will learn the lessons a good instructor learns only when he becomes a willing student, eager to be taught'" (p. 22). Dr. Ludwig taught Coles, "What ought to be interesting . . . is the unfolding of a lived life rather than the confirmation such a chronicle provides for some theory" (p. 22). Coles published his book thirty-three years after his residency and believes that Dr. Ludwig, his narratively oriented supervisor, "was actually arguing for a revolution—that the lower orders be the ones whose every word really *mattered*, whose meaning be upheld as interesting" (p. 22). Thus, although change is not the driving force in the thinking that leads him to narrative, Coles believes that narrative represented a revolutionary change in the practice of psychiatry. Narrative for him is not the outcome of change but the origin of it for his field.

What Coles learned in his psychiatric residency was something he had already been taught by his parents. The book's Introduction describes his parents as story readers. Not only was there reading, but equally important for the idea of narrative as it applies to psychiatry were the family discussions that took place around the stories. His mother and father read to each other, discussed what they read, and discussed with Coles not only *what* they discussed but *why* they discussed it. He recalls his father saying "Your mother and I feel rescued by these books. We read them gratefully. You'll also be grateful one day to the authors" (p. xii). What Dr. Ludwig taught Coles about how to engage in psychiatric inquiry was an expression of what he already had been taught and is, in turn, how he describes his own teaching and his work with patients.

What, in detail, is narrative inquiry for Coles? Like Czarniawska, Coles's idea of narrative comes, terminologically, out of literature. *The Call of Stories* from beginning to end discusses relationships among reader, author, text, patient, and life. Specifically, again referring to Dr. Ludwig, Coles writes, "He urged me to be a good listener in the special way a story requires: note the manner of presentation; the development of plot, character, the addition of new dramatic sequences; the emphasis accorded to one figure or another in the recital; and the degree of enthusiasm, of coherence, the narrator gives to his or her account" (p. 23).

From Coles's reliance on literature in teaching and psychiatric practice, one might reasonably imagine that literary theory was an important resource in his thinking about narrative. However, literary theorists play little evident role in the book. Unlike Czarniawska, who draws heavily on existing literary theory terms, Coles appears to construct his own theoretical structure for narrative. Just as Coles wants all of us to learn from life, he learns about narrative from literature, literature which, for him, appears to have originated in the predilections of his parents and in the literature of medicine, especially that of William Carlos Williams. Coles also learns about narrative from the stories told in his psychiatric work and in his teaching. Student stories, patient stories, and stories from literature are Coles's teachers on narrative. William Carlos Williams, for example, is credited with some of these links, when Coles has Williams say, "We have to pay closest attention to what we say. What patients say tells us to think about what hurts them; and what we say tells us what is happening to us—what we are thinking, and what may be wrong with us. . . . Their story, yours, mine—it's what we all carry with us on this trip we take, and we owe it to each other to respect our stories and learn from them" (p. 30).

Thus, it is the *intimacy* of the inquirer and the patient that is the key term for Coles: learners and teachers coming together over their texts, psychiatrists and their patients coming together over their texts—not only the patient's texts but, emphasizes Coles, the psychiatrist's texts as well. For him, none of this is merely in the interest of narrative method; rather, narrative is life, learning, and fiction. It is no mere metaphor for advancing his field.

What is the outcome, the edifice, of narrative psychiatric inquiry? We are, of course, in somewhat different territory with Coles, compared with our other authors. Coles is writing about the practice of psychiatry as an inquiry, whereas Bateson, Geertz, and Czarniawska offer metalevel texts on inquiry in their fields. Coles is not writing a text on how to be a psychiatric researcher of others doing psychiatric work. Nevertheless, parallels are apparent and are important to our purpose. Furthermore, psychiatrists produce things, their own edifices. Professor Ludwig is, again, given credit for telling us what those outcomes, those psychiatric edifices, should be. Coles writes: "I ought to write brief biographies of the patients rather than come to his office with a list of the patients' complaints. I also ought to make a list of 'interesting clinical moments' in the interviews—remarks that I deem important. To what purpose? He wasn't specific or conveniently certain in reply; he simply told me that 'something happened' when we had encouraged our patient to tell a story or two about her life and 'we ought to keep going in that direction,' though he was quick to add, 'not too vigorously or in too organized a way.'" (p. 14).

Thus, a biographical text is created, which—like the texts proposed by Geertz and Bateson but unlike the texts proposed by Czarniawska—have a tentative best-guess-at-the-moment sense about them. These biographies have the quality Coles found himself describing when he came to his question: How do students respond to literature? Thinking at first that medical students might respond to a text one way and business students in another, he found these to be "naive and somewhat absurd generalizations" (p. 190). Instead, he found "an astonishing range of responsiveness" and that the "decisive matter is how the teacher's imagination engages with the text—a prelude, naturally, to the students' engagement" (p. 190). In short, these biographies, written as products, are a kind of starting point—the psychiatrist's "prelude" to engaging the patient in a reflection, a story, a biography.

DONALD POLKINGHORNE, *NARRATIVE KNOWING AND THE HUMAN SCIENCES*

Polkinghorne begins *Narrative Knowing and the Human Sciences* with his "own unsettled feelings about integrating research and practice" (1988, p. ix). As he reflects on his work as an academic researcher and a practicing psychotherapist, he finds that research in his field is out of touch with practical problems of the field. As a clinician, he is unable to make use of research; as a researcher, he finds that social problems are not amenable to the application of social science research methodology and findings. He notices, for example, that funding agencies, following a period of heavy investment in the human sciences in the Great Society, are now turning away from the research enterprise. It is not that the problems are any fewer. He notes that people are increasingly turning to practitioners in the social sciences—to psychotherapists, to counselors, to organizational consultants. This observation leads him to "look at what could be learned from the practitioners about how research should be done" (p. x).

Polkinghorne comes to narrative directly and quickly. Unlike the other authors discussed, who come to narrative slowly and by degrees in their arguments, Polkinghorne looks to practitioners and asserts that narrative is the basis of their work. He says, "They are concerned with people's stories: they work with case histories and use narrative explanations to understand why the people they work with behave the way they do" (p. x). Of course, Coles too began with narrative practice as he learned his profession from Professor Ludwig. But unlike Coles, who begins and ends with practice, Polkinghorne turns from practice to theory in an effort to develop a form of narrative research. He underlines "the importance of having research strategies that can work with the narratives people use to understand the human world" (p. xi). In the end, he wants "our research to be considerably more successful and useful" (p. xi). He wants, in effect, to build a theoretical edifice that is consistent with practice.

In building his version of narrative theory, Polkinghorne, much like Czarniawska in the organizational sciences, borrows from other disciplines, specifically, history, literary theory, and certain forms of psychology. Though Polkinghorne discovers narrative in successful practice, the bulk of his writing in *Narrative Knowing and the Human Sciences* is devoted to these three disciplines and to the task of assembling "a narrative theory for the practice of the human disciplines" (p. 125).

One of the interesting possibilities in Polkinghorne's work is that of constructing a theory of narrative or, perhaps, a theory of narrative practice, based on what practitioners do. The outlines of such an inquiry are seen in Coles's book, in which he learns about narrative from his patients' and his students' stories. Likewise, the careful study of the successful narrative practices of practitioners in interaction with their clients would be, one imagines, a productive avenue for building one's ideas about narrative.

For Polkinghorne, narrative inquiry can be of two types—*descriptive* and *explanatory*. By and large, these two forms of inquiry use the same kinds of narrative data, collected by such means as interview and document analysis. In descriptive narrative, the purpose is "to produce an accurate description of the interpretive narrative accounts individuals or groups use to make sequences of events in their lives or organizations meaningful" (pp. 161–162). In explanatory narrative, the interest is to account for the connection between events in a causal sense and to provide the necessary narrative accounts that supply the connections. Though he has specific suggestions along these lines, Polkinghorne believes that narrative research is research "still in its early stages. Because it includes the temporal dimension in its organizational structure, it is very different from the formal organization that puts 'facts' into categories" (p. 184).

He stops short of (and gives no examples of) what narrative research texts might look like. We are left to wonder whether narrative research, for Polkinghorne, creates the tentative, shambling, personal documents seen in Bateson's and Geertz's work or whether they might have more the polished literary quality of research documents we imagine are produced in Czarniawska's work.

BRINGING THESE AUTHORS TO NARRATIVE INQUIRY

Each of the five authors brought narrative to their work. In so doing, they offered us, as narrative inquirers, new dimensions to consider.

Geertz, in his retrospective look at anthropology and at his own place in it over forty years, offered a metaphor of a parade, his way of capturing change in the whole over time. Geertz reminded us that it was impossible to look at one event or one time without seeing the event or time nested within the wholeness of his metaphorical parade. He introduced tentativeness into our thinking as narrative inquirers in at least two ways. The first sense of tentativeness relates to the way in which one is positioned in the parade. We know what we know because of how we are positioned. If we shift our position in the parade, our knowing shifts. The second sense of tentativeness comes about, says Geertz, because as the parade changes, our relative positions change. What we knew at one point in time shifts as the parade moves temporally forward to another point in time.

Bateson also offers us tentativeness, but hers is a tentativeness related to what we as researchers might write about people and events. What we write is always tentative, always open to revision. Bateson, more explicitly than Geertz, offers researchers links to life. In this linking of life and research, she highlights relational aspects. In effect, she offers us the notion that to do good research, one needs to be a good human being.

Like Bateson, Coles offers us as researchers a trust in life, and he encourages us to listen to our teaching, to the stories that we, and those we teach, tell.

Czarniawska and Polkinghorne offer us the possibility of borrowing theories, metaphors, and terms from other disciplines as a way to bridge our research with practice.

Taken together, these authors offer us, as narrative inquirers, the possibility of disciplinary, homegrown, indigenous narrative concepts (Geertz, Bateson, Coles) and adaptations from other disciplines (Czarniawska, Polkinghorne).

WHY THE TURN TO NARRATIVE?

In our Prologue, and as we opened this chapter, we tried to give a sense of what it was about narrative that led us to turn to it in our own work. We might say that if we understand the world narratively, as we do, then it makes sense to study the world narratively. For us, life—as we come to it and as it comes to others—is filled with narrative fragments, enacted in storied moments of time and space, and reflected upon and understood in terms of narrative unities and discontinuities.

We opened the book by recollecting that we were focused on trying to understand experience. We saw our research problem as trying to think of the continuity and wholeness of an individual's life experience. This research problem in our educational studies eventually brought us to narrative. We then began to reflect on the whole of the social sciences with its concern for human experience. For social scientists, and consequently for us, experience is a key term. Education and educational studies are a form of experience. For us, narrative is the best way of representing and understanding experience. Experience is what we study, and we study it narratively because narrative thinking is a key form of experience and a key way of writing and thinking about it. In effect, narrative thinking is part of the phenomenon of narrative. It might be said that narrative method is a part or aspect of narrative phenomena. Thus, we say, narrative is both the phenomenon and the method of the social sciences.

This was not, however, the reasoning that brought us to narrative. We did not begin with a narrative view of experience. We struggled for years with more intuitive ways of coming to terms with life in classrooms, with life in schools, and with life in other educational landscapes. As with Bateson's participant observation, narrative grew for us into a term for representing what we, and our research participants, saw as healthy, productive, human relationships. Theoretical works like those of MacIntyre's, with his notion of narrative unity, had a cascading effect for us because we could name experience and in the naming, extend research we already had under way.

As we read Geertz, Bateson, Czarniawska, Coles, Polkinghorne, and others, we recognized that much of our own fumbling toward narrative occurs in various ways in other disciplines. Geertz, with his respect for phenomena in all their complexity, gives a sense of having been inexorably pushed toward his narrative version of an *ad hoc* and *ad interim* anthropology. Bateson and Coles, more so than Geertz in *After the Fact*, struggle to build understandings in their disciplines that make sense of life more generally. They too seem to be saying "experience first and narrative because we must." Czarniawska and Polkinghorne have, more than the others, a sense of a methodologist's opportunism. They seem to say that life and narrative are linked because the link seems to work. They too see that narrative brings experience to their fields, but for them it seems more after than before the fact. Czarniawska's organizations, when represented in research texts, are peopled, though we, as readers, are left to wonder how much is life experience and how much is literary construction: How much are people and their places brought forth in the research text? How much are they fictional expressions of literary forms?

Though we thought infrequently of the social science research narrative of which we were a part at the time we began our research, it became important to us as we tried to position our work and the work of others. It is somehow curious, at least from the point of view of a stance that holds that science and its methods are objective and depersonalized, to reflect on the moral tone not only of our own argument but also of the arguments of the other five authors. None of the five merely describes their version of narrative, but rather they say (or at least strongly imply) that things should be done narratively. In our case, we said the grand social narrative of inquiry of which we were a part was reductive of experience and not (we implied) to be favored. Geertz, Coles, and Bateson argue naturalistically along the line that "this is the way the world is, and therefore this is how it should be thought about." Our argument seems much like theirs. Experience happens narratively. Narrative inquiry is a form of narrative experience. Therefore, educational experience should be studied narratively. Czarniawska and Polkinghorne seem more utilitarian in their argument, though of the two, Czarniawska is far more so, as she argues for narrative as literary metaphor for organizational science. Polkinghorne's book is constructed using a similar pattern, although he begins by noting that the public was attracted to psychotherapists who worked narratively, and therefore he believed he could develop a theory of narrative psychology on the basis of what practitioners actually thought and did. However, he does not stay with theory building based on practice and turns instead to importing ideas, as did Czarniawska. Had he continued with his first approach, more of a naturalistic argument might have developed.

As we mentioned earlier, a key term for us is *temporality*. Partially we mean, of course, that an experience is temporal. But we also mean that experiences taken collectively are temporal. We are therefore not only concerned with life as it is experienced in the here and now but also with life as it is experienced on a continuum—people's lives, institutional lives, lives of things. Just as we found our own lives embedded within a larger narrative of social science inquiry, the people, schools, and educational landscapes we study undergo day-by-day experiences that are contextualized within a longer-term historical narrative. What we may be able to say now about a person or school or some other is given meaning in terms of the larger context, and this meaning will change as time passes. Our social science knowledge is, like the things we study, something "in passing." Coles, Czarniawska, and Polkinghorne write little about temporality and leave us more with a feeling that what is said and learned from narrative is simply that. Geertz provides the most forceful sense of temporality. Indeed, it is his key term. Change over time marks Geertz's world, and for him it is this temporal change that is the standout feature of anthropology.

COMING TO RESEARCH NARRATIVELY

In this first chapter, we have tried to highlight why and in what ways some authors in the disciplines of anthropology, psychology, and organizational science came to narrative. We recollected our own story of coming to narrative and tried to answer the question for ourselves: Why narrative?

As a result of such influences as those discussed here and during the past twenty years or so of our work, narrative inquiry has become so integral to our work that we cannot imagine functioning as researchers in any other way. It is that central. Our intention is to come to the "definition" of narrative inquiry slowly in this volume by "showing" rather than "telling" what narrative inquirers do. But for now, here are some characteristics that make up a kind of working concept: narrative inquiry is a way of understanding experience. It is a collaboration between researcher and participants, over time, in a place or series of places, and in social interaction with milieus. An inquirer enters this matrix in the midst and progresses in this same spirit, concluding the inquiry still in the midst of living and telling, reliving and retelling, the stories of the experiences that make up people's lives, both individual and social. Simply stated, as we wrote in the Prologue: narrative inquiry is stories lived and told.

In the next chapter, we begin our exploration of learning to think narratively. Subsequent chapters examine the narrative process in the field, the complexities of the writing process, and the continuing challenges narrative inquirers face at every step along the way.

CHAPTER TWO

Thinking Narratively

A Case at the Boundaries

⌐⌐⌐ In the previous chapter, we explored what it was that led us, and others, to narrative inquiry as a way to understand experience.

INTRODUCTION

In this chapter, we begin to explore specific places where narrative inquiry thinking comes into the intellectual territory of another way of thinking. We call these places *boundaries,* and we illustrate "life at the boundaries" through a vivid experience of our own. Dewey's two criteria of experience, *continuity* and *interaction,* provide a theoretical frame for identifying tension at the boundaries. Tensions pertaining to continuity that were brought up by the experience described in this chapter are *temporality, people, action,* and *certainty.* Tensions pertaining to interaction are *context, people, action,* and *certainty.*

BLOOM'S TAXONOMY

Ten years after the Manila meetings at the University of the Philippines, an invitation to participate in yet another evaluation-related project arrived. This time, the invitation was to join a team working on a revision of what is commonly known in educational studies as Bloom's Taxonomy (Bloom, 1956). The Taxonomy might fairly be said to be a wildly successful achievement within the *grand narrative* of educational research alluded to in our Prologue; that is, the narrative of inquiry Lagemann associated with the struggle between Thorndike and Dewey over the way to conceive of educational research.

To recapitulate, Thorndike was a measurement-oriented psychologist who popularized the idea of a science of education based on the observation and numerical representation of behavior. When this way of looking at educational studies became "the" way, it then became what we call the grand narrative, an unquestioned way of looking at things. Bloom, working within the Thorndike idea, developed a taxonomy of educational objectives built on observable, classifiable behaviors. Sometime later, Bloom, Taxonomy in hand, was the central figure in founding the International Association for the Evaluation of Educational Achievement, an organization that conducts comparative achievement studies and that brought Michael to an international study of science education achievement and eventually to the meetings in Manila. The decade-later invitation was to join a team whose purpose was to upgrade and modernize the Taxonomy.

The nature and status of the Taxonomy is captured in the Preface to the 1994 National Society for the Study of Education Yearbook. The authors wrote:

> Arguably, one of the most influential educational monographs of the past half century is the *Taxonomy of Educational Objectives, The Classification of Educational Goals, Handbook I: Cognitive Domain.* Nearly forty years after its publication in 1956 the volume remains a standard reference for discussions of testing and evaluation, curriculum development, and teaching and teacher education. A search of the most recent *Social Science Citation Index* (1992) revealed more than 150 citations to the *Handbook.* At a recent meeting of approximately two hundred administrators and teachers, the senior editor of this volume asked for a show of hands in response to the question, "How many of you have heard of Bloom's Taxonomy?" Virtually every hand in the audience was raised. Few educational publications have enjoyed such overwhelming recognition for so long. [Anderson and Sosniak, 1994, p. vii]

Even though we were impressed by the citation count, before embarking on this new task, we conducted our own mini-assessment of the extent of use of the Taxonomy and found that general (as opposed to subject-specific) preservice teacher education textbooks and general curriculum textbooks were, as we reported, "loaded" with references to and explications of Bloom's Taxonomy. Interestingly, and perhaps ominously to the new design team, the Taxonomy was cited little in recent educational research handbooks in teaching (Wittrock, 1986), teacher education (Houston, 1990), and curriculum (Jackson, 1992). We concluded that Bloom's theoretical hopes for the Taxonomy had not been realized. He expected the Taxonomy to be the basis for a theory of behavior (Bloom, 1956). However, only his hopes for its practical applications in teacher education and school goal setting appeared to have been realized. Because the Taxonomy seemed to make a difference in the practice, if not the theory, of education, we thought we might make a difference by participating in the revision and we elected to join the team.

The Taxonomy is composed of six levels of cognitive behaviors—*knowledge, comprehension, application, analysis, synthesis,* and *evaluation.* Knowledge, for example, is defined as "those behaviors and test situations which emphasize the remembering, either by recognition or recall, of ideas, material, or phenomena" (Anderson and Sosniak, 1994, p. 18). Synthesis, to give one more illustration, is defined as "putting together elements and parts so as to form a whole" (p. 23). The categories are hierarchically arranged from simple to complex, each category being subsumed in the one above it. The categories are seen as "natural," inherent in the order of things, hence the term *taxonomy* and its justification using a biological taxonomy referent (Bloom, 1956).

We interpreted our invitation to help modernize the Taxonomy as an invitation to introduce narrative thinking into the Taxonomy and therefore into the particular way of looking at goals of education adopted by the Taxonomy. We soon found ourselves rethinking other matters, predominant among them the earlier experience of using the Taxonomy to study science achievement cross-culturally.

At one level, we saw ourselves as taking the task at face value. We saw it as a challenge to rethink Taxonomy categories and their possible uses (as uses were part of the exercise) in terms of narrative. Our task was initially, we imagined, a simple one. For us, narrative is central to our understanding of experience and should therefore be central to documents such as the Taxonomy. We see individuals as living storied lives on storied landscapes. Understanding life, experience, narratively is our research and our life project. So, faced with the invitation, we saw our task as offering an account of behavior and objectives as they would be conceptualized narratively.

As we began, we were vaguely aware of doing something different, but it was not until we were fairly far into the task that we began to see ourselves at the center of a storm—a place where the grand narrative of inquiry in one of its most successful educational expressions—that is, in the construction of a universal set of educational objectives—met an alternative way of inquiry thinking. It was a place where the grand narrative confronted narrative thinking. As an expression of the grand narrative, Bloom's Taxonomy is more than mere application; it is central to it not only via its links to Bloom and Thorndike but also because of its dominance in educational thought.

We recount our story of involvement with the Taxonomy revision team to provide a sense of the context within which narrative thinking inevitably, at this stage of development of the social sciences, takes place. Polanyi (1958), speaking of frames of reference for personal knowledge, used the term "dwelling in" to point toward the necessity for an intellectually safe place for coherent thought to develop. His general idea is echoed throughout the literature on method in various ways—Kuhn (1970), for instance, with his idea of paradigms and paradigm shifts; Dewey ([1916] 1961, 1922), with his idea of doing things by habit or doing things reflectively; and Schwab (1960), with his distinction between fluid and stable inquiry. The person working within a paradigm, by habit, or within a stable inquiry framework proceeds by and large without needing to take account of alternative frames of reference that might generate different inquiry approaches.

But narrative inquiry is not so comfortably located, perched as it is amid a wave of debate and publication over new, "postmodern" ways of inquiring into and representing the social science world. Indeed, at this time, if narrative inquiry is paradigmatic (or at least if it fits within a paradigm), it is a paradigm marked by challenges to accepted inquiry and representation assumptions. Schwab (1960) wrote that when assumptions, presuppositions, and taken-for-granted frameworks gave way to questions, doubt, and uncertainty, a fair amount of travel in attractive blind alleys is to be expected. Students of narrative—especially graduate students who often learn their inquiry practices in supportive graduate studies communities—quickly learn to defend and argue for their work in terms outside their narrative frame of reference. This learning to think narratively *at the boundaries* between narrative and other forms of inquiry is, perhaps, the single most important feature of successful narrative thinking.

WORKING WITH THE TAXONOMY TEAM

We had no trouble in adopting a behavioral language. Narrative is, after all, concerned with doings and goings-on, but somewhat like the alterations effected by wearing or removing stereoscopic glasses, narrative thinking alters what the observer observes. What is a behavior from a narrative perspective? A Thorndike grand narrative inquirer using the word *behavior* means, and therefore sees, something different than does an inquirer thinking narratively. This was our first and most immediate level of query in response to the invitation. What do we mean by behavior? What do we mean by each level? What is seen? By whom? What is recorded? How is it to be interpreted?

We saw our answer to each of these inquiries in terms of narrative. Behaviors, for example, were expressions of an individual's stories within a particular context at a particular time. Because behaviors were narrative expressions, it was important to consider the characters who were living the stories, the characters who were telling the stories, the times at which stories were lived, the times stories were told, the places in which stories were lived and told, and so on.

As we worked through our narrative revision to the newly specified goals (goals set by other members of the team), we struggled not to be caught up in the tentacles of the grand narrative that surrounded us at every turn. These tentacles seemed to find expression in a way to think about behavior—that is, think in a language of objectives, think in terms of observable behavior, think numerically, think causally, think generally with a god's-eye view, think about the here and now. Our struggles to escape these tentacles are struggles we believe are faced every day by narrative inquirers and by students of narrative.

As we worked through our task of bringing narrative thinking to the revision of Bloom's Taxonomy, we began by thinking of objectives as an educational tool. As an introduction to our proposed section on *Curriculum, Instruction and Objectives,* we wrote:

Readers and users of this Handbook may well, indeed surely will, ask what relevance objectives have for their work in curriculum and instruction. Like many tools, objectives are useful in different ways to different people, at different times, in different contexts. Let us take an example of a common woodworking tool, a lathe. A lathe is a tool useful to different people, at different times, in different contexts. It is useful to commercial woodworkers, to hobbyists, to woodworking tool manufacturers, to teachers, to students and so on; in factories, in small home hobby shops, in schools, and so on.

By introducing the metaphor of a lathe as a tool, we attempted to establish common ground between ourselves and our readers. We realized that the central ideas of narrative—*emplotment, character, scene, place, time, point-of-view,* and so forth—would create dissonance for many readers. Our first readers were other members of the Taxonomy revision team, who, for the most part, came out of a non-narrative tradition of inquiry. We chose a lathe because it was as point-of-view free as we could imagine. We were trying to establish several important elements of narrative thinking in such a way that we could all agree on them without interference by the biases of different research traditions. The lathe gave us the possibility to illustrate the notion that a tool could be used by different people, at different times, in different contexts, all fundamentally narrative notions. We hoped the lathe would provide neutral common ground for ourselves and our readers. We needed this common ground because we sensed how different our narrative way of thinking of the Taxonomy was from that of other team members. We were trying to find a way to explain narrative thinking.

We elaborated the metaphor over several pages, drawing attention to the various uses to which individuals might put the lathe, at different times, in different contexts. For instance, with respect to context, we wrote: "Furthermore, the context in which the lathe and shop exist makes a great deal of difference to how it is viewed and used. The reasoning behind the placement of a lathe in a school setting will differ in an isolated aboriginal community compared to a wealthy suburban area or an inner-city setting. Not only will the reasons differ in these different community contexts but the kinds of children will differ, the teachers will differ, and the things made on the lathe will differ. Context makes all the difference."

In narrative thinking, context makes a difference. By drawing attention to how context makes a difference to the use of a lathe in a curriculum context, we assumed we could create shared understanding with our readers. Whether or not one used narrative thinking, we felt the general points made would resonate with educators. At first, it seemed not so difficult. The metaphor worked for us, and we believed that we had established a bridge to the grand narrative, or to put it more prosaically, to the old and to the to-be-revised Taxonomy.

We began to get response. For the most part, responses were transmitted in the midst of phrasings of acceptance and support. But as we read in detail the line-by-line, point-by-point criticisms and suggestions, we soon felt enmeshed. At times, we questioned our own sense of what it was we were trying to do. Had we actually understood the task? Had we done it well or appropriately? The tentacles began to make us feel that our narrative thinking was somehow less than acceptable; somehow weak, effete, and soft; somehow lacking in rigor, precision, and certainty. We shall try to give a sense of the origins of these feelings by quoting sections of the responses, but as we do so, we are aware that the sense of insecurity we experienced by the entrapment is difficult to capture.

RESPONSES TO A NARRATIVE REVISION

One of our central paragraphs that received response was the following: "Recognizing objectives as the most widely used tool for moving between expectations and ends-in-view, we propose to outline a framework for thinking about objectives as used by different people, at different times, in different contexts. We begin to explore the use of objectives by looking at the factors that influence their use."

By this, we wanted to illustrate that a narrative revision of the Taxonomy required a sense of movement over time from expectations to ends-in-view. Objectives, rather than functioning as preestablished givens, could serve as a tool with flexible uses at different times. Later in the paper, we used this narrative notion to construct a framework to show that objectives differed at pre-instructional, instructional, and post-instructional times. Furthermore, we introduced the idea that at each of these times different contexts (such as rural, urban, and inner-city) and different characters (such as book publishers, government officials, administrators, teachers, and evaluators) would use objectives differently. Therefore, dependent on time, context, and character, the narrative into which objectives could or would fit would be different.

The response came back that this was merely a problem of clarity. Our respondent said that if we specified "levels of objectives," the problem would be solved. So, whereas we thought there would be different objectives for the same intention depending on the time, the context, and the characters, *our respondent* translated the concern into a matter of hierarchy of objectives. For our respondent, "expectations" are the top level; "objectives" are the middle level, useful for guiding curriculum; and at the bottom are "very specific objectives" for particular classroom tasks. In this reinterpretation, the respondent removed temporality and replaced it with a time-independent hierarchy of types. Equally as significant, in the respondent's formulation, context is also displaced, and the application of the hierarchy is seen as contextually universal. So, from a notion of applying goals to a particular time, context, and character, our respondent reformulated the notion in a universal, time-free, and context-free way.

In another central explanatory paragraph, we wrote: "Dewey's (1938) notion of 'situation' and 'experience' makes it possible to imagine the teacher not so much as a maker of curriculum but as part of it and to imagine a place for context, culture (Dewey's notion of interaction) and temporality (both past and future contained in Dewey's notion of 'continuity'). In this view ends and means, curriculum and instruction, are so intertwined that designing curriculum for teachers to implement for instructional purposes appears unreal, somewhat as if the cart were before the horse."

In the section in which this paragraph appeared, we were trying to show that the justification for any particular set of objectives is given by its curricular context. The significance of this notion is seen in contrast to the notion of curriculum defined in terms of the grand narrative, in which teachers implement curriculum programs to meet preset objectives and to achieve certain outcomes. In this view, a measure of student outcome behavior is a measure of teaching success. In our narrative rendition, we wanted to show that the idea that ends and means could be easily separated in this way is conceptually flawed. The linear notion that objectives and achievement were mediated by teachers and curriculum was narratively in question. According to a narrative construction, the teacher is not merely a filtering variable or a factor to be considered as either an impediment or a catalyst for the achievement of objectives. Rather, the teacher is part of the curriculum and therefore part of the establishment of the goals in the first place and part of the ensuing achievement. This narrative notion of curriculum was central to our attempt to introduce narrative thinking to the Taxonomy.

Somewhat humorously (humorous because of the rather ponderous weight we attached to these thoughts on curriculum), the response was that the section was more or less fine and could be placed in a footnote. Our respondent said that the section expressed an abstruse reference of interest only to a few special readers versed in academic texts.

INQUIRY LIFE AT THE BOUNDARIES

Our work with the Taxonomy revision team drew us inexorably to the boundaries between thinking according to narrative inquiry and thinking according to the grand narrative. From either side of the boundary, one appears to be communicating with people on the other side—people who are out of focus; not quite able to speak clearly; and who render ideas, thoughts, and suggestions that somehow miss the mark. We were befuddled by the responses of other members of the revision team, and no doubt, they were befuddled by our treatment of objectives. We thought they were slightly intransigent and unwilling to change, whereas they, with the weight of opinion on their side, probably saw us as esoteric and unwilling to compromise. What is it about the boundaries between thinking narratively and thinking in terms of the grand narrative that makes communication so difficult? Our work on the Taxonomy revision team brings some of these matters into the open. We deal with them now.

Temporality

The most apparent tension in our work with the Taxonomy revision team centered on temporality. In narrative thinking, temporality is a central feature. We take for granted that locating things in time is the way to think about them. When we see an event, we think of it not as a thing happening at that moment but as an expression of something happening over time. Any event, or thing, has a past, a present as it appears to us, and an implied future.

From the point of view of the grand narrative, at least in our experience with the Taxonomy revision team, events and things are characterized in and of themselves. They are seen "to be," to have a timeless sense about them. Our respondents sensed something was at issue in our talk about temporality but reframed it in terms of hierarchical levels of objectives and thereby removed the notion of time. This tension between seeing things in time versus seeing things as they are became an issue at the boundary everywhere we turned. There was tension around our notion of the different uses of objectives at pre-instructional, instructional, and post-instructional times; there was tension over our concept of curriculum, with the idea that the teacher's narrative of experience would shape the curriculum; there was tension over the issue of narrative histories of students and teachers and how these histories would influence the interpretation of achievement scores.

People

A closely related tension had to do with people, both students and teachers, a tension closely linked to that generated by temporality. We take for granted that people, at any point in time, are in a process of personal change and that from an educational point of view, it is important to be able to narrate the person in terms of the process. Knowing some of the immediate educational history of a child—for instance, the lessons recently taught, as well as the larger narrative history of each child as that child moves from what was, to what is, to what will be in the future—is central to narrative educational thinking. We assume that the curriculum, the formulation of objectives, and the measurement of achievement will bear these narrative histories in mind.

In contrast, the grand narrative (at least in this case) led our respondents to the construction of essentially people-free notions. For many on the revision team, an objective specified a certain level of thinking and a certain level of content for a certain age or grade level that was to be universally applied. Narrative histories of people were seen as slightly irrelevant and, if not that, wholly impractical for consideration by our revision team.

Action

A third tension centered on how an action was understood. In narrative thinking, an action is seen as a narrative sign. In our case, we intended that curricular actions be interpreted as classroom expressions of teachers' and students' narrative histories. For example, a child's performance at a certain level on an achievement test is a narrative sign of something. It is necessary to give a narrative interpretation of that sign before meaning can be attached to it. Without understanding the narrative history of the child, the significance or meaning of the performance, the sign, remains unknown. Student achievement on a test does not in and of itself tell the tester or the teacher much of anything until the narrative of the student's learning history is brought to bear on the performance. For example, a particular performance might represent the rote application of an algorithm, the application of a set of cues for the solution of certain problems, or a high-level cognitive performance.

In contrast, from the point of view of the grand narrative (in our experience with the Taxonomy revision team), a student's performance on an achievement test is taken as direct evidence of the cognitive level obtained by the student: the more complex the performance behavior, the higher the cognitive level of objective achieved. Thus, for the Taxonomy team, an action is taken as directly evidential. There is an equation connecting action and meaning, connecting performance and cognitive level. In narrative thinking, however, there is an interpretive pathway between action and meaning mapped out in terms of narrative histories.

Certainty

A fourth tension centered on certainty. In narrative thinking, interpretations of events can always be otherwise. There is a sense of tentativeness, usually expressed as a kind of uncertainty, about an event's meaning. For instance, in the measurement of student achievement in the discussion of action above, we showed how a performance could be interpreted in three different ways. Any one interpretation would need to be treated as tentative. Thus, the attitude in a narrative perspective is one of doing "one's best" under the circumstance, knowing all the while that other possibilities, other interpretations, other ways of explaining things are possible. A narrative inquirer creates, in Geertz's terms, an account of teaching and learning that is a "shaky and badly formed" (1995, p. 20) construction.

From the point of view of our experience with the grand narrative on the revision team, causality, with its ensuing certainty, is the hallmark. In the above example of a student's performance on an achievement test, the equation between performance and cognitive level is given by an assumed causality. Thinking at a given cognitive level causes a given test performance. This relationship gives teachers, testers, and others certain knowledge about student performance, and by implication, certain knowledge of the success of curriculum and teaching.

Context

A fifth tension is centered on context. In narrative thinking, context is ever present. It includes such notions as temporal context, spatial context, and context of other people. Context is necessary for making sense of any person, event, or thing. For example, one way we introduced context into our revision of the Taxonomy was by the use of a distinction between the in-classroom and out-of-classroom places on the school landscape. This contextualizing allowed us to show that objectives play a different role for people in a classroom in a teaching setting than they do for people out of the classroom in other settings.

From the point of view of our experience with the grand narrative in the revision team, context was assumed by other members to be everywhere. It was assumed that we all have a context. However, although context was acknowledged, Taxonomy team members proceeded in a context-free way. The important thing was to create a Taxonomy that could be applied in all contexts. For instance, it was assumed that in its application, the cognitive level at which students performed was of prime importance. The contextual circumstances were not. In the grand narrative, more generally, context can be analyzed into variables and measures of certainty attached to the importance of various contextual factors. For example, correlations can be established between performance and the variable, socioeconomic status. In the grand narrative, *the universal case* is of prime interest. In narrative thinking, *the person* in context is of prime interest.

SUMMARY

As we explored the major points of tension at the boundaries between the grand narrative and narrative thinking, we were reminded that a theoretical frame for identifying tension at the boundaries comes from Dewey's two criteria of experience; that is, from *continuity* and *interaction*. Issues of continuity, in work with the Taxonomy revision team, led to tensions of temporality, people, action, and certainty. Issues of interaction led to tensions of context, people, action, and certainty. For Dewey, the two criteria are inseparable, and as we think through the tensions at the boundaries, we see them not as a list of independent factors but as interconnected.

In the next chapter, we begin to explore another boundary between narrative thinking and other forms of inquiry. We deal with these under the broad heading of the boundary between narrative thinking and formalism.

CHAPTER THREE

Thinking Narratively

Reductionistic and Formalistic Boundaries

In Chapter Two, we composed a narrative account of our experience of working at the boundaries, as defined by thinking narratively and thinking according to the grand narrative. For the most part, our main focus so far has been on the tensions between narrative inquiry and the grand narrative. In Chapter Two, however, we moved back and forth between narrative as inquiry and narrative as professional practice and between research according to the grand narrative and professional practice according to the grand narrative. Our example, by and large, takes place on the side of professional practice. As we noted earlier, we justified joining the Taxonomy revision team on the grounds that the Taxonomy is widely used in the professional practice of education.

We have written on this topic in the *Cambridge Journal of Education* (1990) and in the *Handbook of Qualitative Research* (1994).

INTRODUCTION

We want to pick up more directly on professional practice as we begin this chapter because when we look at the matter of boundaries from the point of view of professional practice and its relationship to theory, the grand narrative comes into sharper focus.

The chapter looks at the tensions created when narrative thinking and inquiry life encounter reductionistic and formalistic theoretical boundaries, with the emphasis on the latter. Using our own work as a point of reference, we will identify and discuss four tensions that we have experienced at the boundary between narrative inquiry and formalistic inquiry—the place of theory, the balance of theory, people, and the place of the researcher.

THE IDEAS OF SCHÖN, OAKESHOTT, AND JOHNSON

We use Schön's writings (1983, 1987, 1991) to begin our exploration. Schön created another sense of the boundary generated by the grand narrative in his account of thinking in professional practice. *Technical rationalism* is Schön's name for what we have been calling the grand narrative. Schön, if he had written on the boundaries, would have named the boundary as one between technical rationalism and *reflection-in-action*. He writes, "Once we put aside the model of Technical Rationality, which leads us to think of intelligent practice as an *application* of knowledge to instrumental decisions, there is nothing strange about the idea that a kind of knowing is inherent in intelligent action" (1983, p. 50).

For Schön, that knowing is *knowing-in-action*, and it leads him to an epistemology of practice based on the idea of reflection-in-action. He describes reflection-in-action as research in a practice context in which the researcher in action "is not dependent on the categories of established theory and technique, but constructs a new theory of the unique case. His inquiry is not limited to a deliberation about means which depends on a prior agreement about ends. He does not keep ends and means separate, but defines them interactively as he frames a problematic situation. He does not separate thinking from doing. . . . Thus reflection-in-action can proceed, even in situations of uncertainty or uniqueness, because it is not bound by the dichotomies of Technical Rationality" (1983, pp. 68–69).

Schön's work was rapidly assimilated into educational studies as well as into other professional fields. In education, we like to think that Schön's rapid acceptance resulted from the way his ideas of reflective practice connected with the remnants of practices discredited by the grand narrative or, to put it in Schön's terms, by technical rationalism. These discredited practices had remained in teacher educators' imaginations as a kind of education that was acceptable in the less rationalistic days of teacher education gone by. Schön's books gave modern value to these professional memories.

Schön does not use temporality, history, and memory to make his case. His logic consists of a reasoned case against technical rationalism, combined with the presentation of case evidence of good educational practice in the professions. But the explanation of why his rhetorical influence in education is out of proportion to his argument's substance can be explained narratively. Schön makes it possible for many of us to tell the story of teacher education (and other professional education) in a way that runs counter to the technical teacher education we are encouraged to sponsor and study, and he makes it possible for the story to legitimate our professional memory of reflective practice.

What makes this retelling of the story possible is the sense of reductionism entailed in the idea of technical rationalism. The image of professional practice, held in professional memory and rejected in rationalistic grand narrative discourse, is the thing that has been reduced. A rich whole, the professional memory, has been reduced through technical rationalism to a formulated set of rules that "may then be written in a book" (Oakeshott, 1962, p. 12).

The philosopher Johnson (1987) uses the term *objectivism,* which he metaphorically defines as a "god's-eye-view about what the world really is like" (p. x), to explain the reduction of the whole to a formulated set of rules. This implies that no matter what any particular person happens to believe, there is a correct and true view of the world. It is a depersonalized notion of truth and meaning.

According to Oakeshott and Schön, the god's-eye view has become—in studies of the practical—technical rationalism. Oakeshott tells us that technical rationalism is "the assertion that what I have called 'practical knowledge' is not knowledge at all, the assertion that properly speaking there is no knowledge which is not technical knowledge. The Rationalist holds that the only element of *knowledge* involved in human activity is technical knowledge, and that what I have called 'practical knowledge' is really only a sort of nescience which would be negligible if it were not positively mischievous. The sovereignty of 'reason,' for the Rationalist, means the sovereignty of technique. The heart of the matter is the preoccupation of the Rationalist with certainty" (1962, p. 11).

Johnson sees that the way of reuniting what the god's-eye view and technical rationalism have separated and reduced is to put "the body back into the mind" (1987, p. xxxvi). A disembodied mind permits the certainty needed by technical rationalism. To put the body back into the mind is to wreak havoc with certainty. Emotion, value, felt experience with the world, memory, and narrative explanations of one's past do not stand still in a way that allows for certainty.

Readers will notice that experience, though unmentioned so far, is central to the arguments and positions of Schön, Oakeshott, and Johnson. For Schön, experience is at the heart of his reflective practice theory and proposals for the professions. He writes about reflected-upon experience as becoming knowing-in-action, "the characteristic mode of ordinary practical knowledge" (1983, p. 54). For Oakeshott, people with their prejudices, biases, outlooks, and attitudes (which are the counterparts of experience) are the enemies of certainty. For him, technical rationality is based on the need for certainty. For Johnson, the title of his book, *The Body in the Mind*, shows that he wishes to put experience, which he refers to as "the body," central to his philosophy.

The suspicion of experience in technical rationalism is not born of a scientific mind. As Oakeshott shows, science, no less than art, is incapable of being reduced to technique and taught out of a book. Those who argue against the study of practice—and the imaginative and narratively generated diversity that goes with it—often define practice as the execution of skills. Ironically, they often argue that to discover and name the skills is to *do* science. But that is reductionism, and what Dewey (1929) called (in his title) the "quest for certainty" that marks the technical rationalist and not the doing of science. The doing of science is compatible with narrative and the study of practice in all of its imaginative complexity.

Oakeshott (1962) says, "The rationalist has taken an ominous interest in education. He has a respect for 'brains,' a great belief in training them, and is determined that cleverness shall be encouraged and shall receive its reward of power" (p. 32). It is ominous because the rationalist "has no sense of the accumulation of experience, only of the readiness of experience when it is being converted into a formula: the past is significant to him only as an encumbrance" (p. 2). A person with experience is considered by the technical rationalist to have "negative capability" (p. 2). If the "tabula rasa has been defaced by the irrational scribblings of tradition-ridden ancestors" (p. 5) (and, one might add, by the experiences of life to date), then the first educational task of the rationalist "must be to rub the slate clean" (p. 5). The technical rationalist's interest in education is ominous not because it ignores experience but because experience is seen as a deterrent to the "true" skilled education. In a line that might have been written by Dewey (1938) with respect to his idea of the reconstruction of experience as the foundation of education, Oakeshott writes, "As with every other sort of knowledge, learning a technique does not consist in getting rid of pure ignorance, but in reforming knowledge which is already there" (p. 12).

Schön picks up this theme in his work on professional education by legitimating our professional memory and making it possible to return to experience, not as a black mark on the mental slate but as a resource for the education of professionals.

NARRATIVE THINKING AT THE FORMALISTIC BOUNDARY

Schön and Oakeshott permit us to imagine a Johnson retelling of "the body in the mind," and metaphorically to return "upward" to the whole from the technical rationalist's reduced world. But Schön, Oakeshott, and Johnson keep our attention focused on the boundary between narrative thinking and the grand narrative, with its reductionistic quality.

There is another story at work at another boundary with narrative thinking. This is a story "downward" to the whole from a paradigmatic sociopolitical analysis.

Just as reductionism makes the whole into something lesser, sociological and political analysis can also make the whole lesser through the use of abstraction and formalism. The disputes between narrative inquirers and those promulgating formalistic lines of inquiry are no less dramatic, although far less widespread, than those between narrative inquirers and inquirers within the grand narrative. The latter disputes are more widely known throughout the research literature, partly because narrative inquirers have imagined those within the grand narrative as the only, or at least the main, critics of experience in the study and doing of the social sciences. However, in our view, experience and narrative are as mistrusted in formalism as they are in the grand narrative.

The formalists' argument has been supported from two quite different sources, the study of literature and the philosophy of science. In a discussion of the issues at work, Bernstein remarks, "It has become increasingly fashionable to speak of our time as a 'postera'— 'postmodernity,' 'poststructuralist,' 'postempiricist,' 'postwestern,' and even 'postphilosophic'—but nobody seems to be able to properly characterize this 'postera'—and there is an inability and an anxiety in the naming of it" (1987, pp. 516–517). Bernstein says that this confusion of the theoretical mind is "a reflection of what's happening in our everyday lives where there is a spread of almost wild pluralism" (p. 517). *Wild pluralism* is another way of naming the relativism that troubles Booth (1986) in literary criticism and is an expression of what Popper called the "myth of the framework" (Bernstein, 1987, p. 56). Dewey was opposed to the consequences of the myth of the framework, which "suggests that 'we are prisoners caught in the framework of our theories; our expectations; our past experience; our language'" (Bernstein, 1987, p. 51).

The "framework" is a formalistic view; it is a view that things are never what they are but are rather what our framework or point of view or perspective or outlook makes of them. Further, because nothing is as it seems, the only things worth noticing are the terms, the formal structures, by which things are perceived. One does not teach, one mindlessly reproduces a social structure; one does not have emotionally credited intentions, one has preset expectations; one does not have experiences that are one's own, one merely moves forward by contextual design. Formalists say that the facts of the case, the experience one claims to have, or the data collected by empiricist researchers have little bearing on their claims. Persons, they argue, can never see themselves as they are because they are always something else; specifically, they are whatever social structure, ideology, theory, or framework is at work in the inquiry. Because narrative inquiry entails a reconstruction of a person's experience in relation to others and to a social milieu, it is under suspicion as not representing the true context and the proper "postera" by formalists.

What we have called experience and narrative is, accordingly, as suspect for the formalist as it is for the inquirer within the grand narrative. The difference between the two is the place given experience.

For the inquirer within the grand narrative, experience is a black mark on the slate to be wiped clean; for the formalist, experience is something to be ignored. For the formalist, there is in the end no agency in experience but only in form. For the formalist, a person merely plays out the hegemonies of politics, culture, gender, and framework.

INQUIRY LIFE AT THE FORMALISTIC BOUNDARY

Our consideration of life at the boundary between thinking narratively and thinking formalistically leads us to highlight several tensions. Just as it is with life at the boundary between narrative inquiry and inquiry according to the grand narrative, here, too, from either side of the boundary, one appears to be communicating with people on the other side who are out of focus, not quite able to speak clearly, and who render ideas, thoughts, and suggestions that somehow miss the mark.

The Place of Theory

One of the central tensions at this boundary is the place of theory in inquiry. Formalists begin inquiry in theory, whereas narrative inquirers tend to begin with experience as expressed in lived and told stories. Early in our work in narrative inquiry, Jean was involved in a joint writing venture with a formalist. The task was to write an essay book review. After each of them had read the book, they met to discuss their writing approach. Jean came to the book, and to the meeting, with stories of classrooms and argued that the book review should begin with one or more stories that linked to themes that the book author was trying to develop and that they wished to discuss in the review. Jean's colleague came to the task intent on laying forth, independent of the book, a theoretical frame from a well-known philosopher. Jean had hoped to use the stories to think through the school life possibilities of the book author's ideas. Her colleague wished to use the philosopher to establish an interpretive frame for analyzing the book's ideas. The ensuing tension at the boundary was present throughout the writing task.

We see something similar in our work with beginning narrative inquirers, as they, too, turn to exposition of theoretical frames to position and begin their inquiries. Writers such as those discussed in

Skinner's (1985) *Return of Grand Theory in the Human Sciences—Althusser, the Annales Historians, Derrida, Foucault, Gadamer, Habermas, Kuhn, Levi-Strauss, Rawls* are frequently found in the research of those who come to narrative inquiry from formalistic traditions. Narrative inquiry characteristically begins with the researcher's autobiographically oriented narrative associated with the *research puzzle* (called by some the research problem or research question, discussed in Chapter Eight). The tension this creates for those moving across the boundary from formalistic to narrative inquiry is expressed, in graduate student work, as a tension between the student and the supervisor, and it is expressed in the different advice given by different committee members: Go to the library. What experiences have you had with this? Read Gadamer. Go to a school.

This tension of the place of theory exists not only at the beginnings of inquiry but throughout. The tension appears in discussions on how to write a literature review and over what prominence a separate literature review chapter ought to have in a finished inquiry. Committee members frequently wish theory to appear as a separate chapter designed to structure the inquiry, identify gaps in the literature, outline principal theoretical lines of thought, and generate potential research possibilities. Our own narrative inquiry students, on the other hand, frequently write dissertations without a specific literature review chapter. They weave the literature throughout the dissertation from beginning to end in an attempt to create a seamless link between the theory and the practice embodied in the inquiry.

The former approach to using theoretical literature as an inquiry frame is so ingrained in formalistic research traditions that beginning narrative inquirers are easily shaken when formalists raise questions about the place of theory in their work. We frequently see the uncertainty brought on by this tension in graduate student committee meetings when faculty members with a formalistic approach question a student's interweaving approach to the use of theory in a narrative inquiry. The tension often appears as a tension between literature reviewed as a structuring framework and literature reviewed as a kind of conversation between theory and life or, at least, between theory and the stories of life contained in the inquiry.

The tension appears yet again at the outcome of an inquiry. One outcome of a formalist inquiry is to contribute to the development of a theoretical framework and associated literature. A second outcome is to replicate and apply a theory to the problem at hand, for instance, to a problem of literacy in an inner-city elementary school classroom. Although the first may well be an intended outcome of narrative inquiry, the second rarely is. The contribution of a narrative inquiry is more often intended to be the creation of a new sense of meaning and significance with respect to the research topic than it is to yield a set of knowledge claims that might incrementally add to knowledge in the field. Furthermore, many narrative studies are judged to be important when they become literary texts to be read by others not so much for the knowledge they contain but for the vicarious testing of life possibilities by readers of the research that they permit. This use of narrative inquiry extends the educative linking of life, literature, and teaching earlier seen in Coles's *Call of Stories.*

The literary outcome of narrative inquiry creates one of the more contentious boundary tensions between narrative and formalist researchers. Yet, as our colleague Howard Russell says, these literary uses of narrative in relating to our audience are the narrative inquirer's counterpart to generalization. The narrative inquirer does not prescribe general applications and uses but rather creates texts that, when well done, offer readers a place to imagine their own uses and applications.

The Balance of Theory

A closely related tension is captured in the maxim "Narrative inquiry is not theoretical enough." A few years ago as Michael left on sabbatical, he participated in discussions about what would happen to his narrative inquiry courses. These courses are taught alongside many others that tend toward a formalistic, rich theoretical orientation. In the midst of these discussions, it became apparent that the narrative inquiry courses that Michael had been teaching were seen by some as "not theoretical enough." It was proposed that if his courses were to be picked up, they would be altered in two important ways—in content and in teaching method. His courses began with experiential starting points—students' autobiographical links to their inquiry, field records and memories, critiques of narrative dissertations, and other studies. Course content stressed a diverse narrative literature in biography, autobiography, memoir, narrative ethnography, case study, and so forth, as well as a literature on key terms important to narrative inquiry, terms such as *memory, fact and fiction, interpretation, story, history, context, image,* and *metaphor.* Michael's colleagues proposed course alterations that revolved around a content defined by writers such as those found in the previously mentioned Skinner book. Methodologically, the altered course would start with, and focus on, the reading and analyses of these writers. In retrospect, it is not clear whether or not life events would have formed a part of such revisions to his courses; but what is clear is that if life events were to play a part, they would be seen as illustrative of the theoretical terms produced by the theorists. It is worth noting that in the proposed course revisions, narrative theorists were to be used in formalistic ways. If Propp (1968), for instance, were to appear on the reading list, his work would be read—as one possibility—to show the theoretical link between acts, roles, and narrative structure. If examples were used, literary texts would most likely be preferred over experiential texts and would be analyzed according to act, role, and structure.

As we are discussing ways of thinking, it is worth noting that the work of narrative theorists, such as that of Propp, our own work, indeed any story, could be expressed, reviewed, and taught in formalistic ways. Formalism refers to a way of thinking, as does narrative inquiry.

People

One of the ever-present and strongest tensions is how to understand the place of people in inquiry. One of the simplest ways of saying this is that in formalist inquiry, people, if they are identified at all, are looked at as exemplars of a form—of an idea, a theory, a social category. In narrative inquiry, people are looked at as embodiments of lived stories. Even when narrative inquirers study institutional narratives, such as stories of school, people are seen as composing lives that shape and are shaped by social and cultural narratives. A story of JoAnn Phillion's narrative research (1999) illuminates the tension generated by the place of people in formalistic inquiries and narrative inquiry.

Phillion taught in Japan and more recently taught foreign students in Canada. She undertook graduate work at the master's level in linguistics and multiculturalism. She says of herself, "I always feel I learn the most from people of other cultures." During her doctoral studies, she worked in a university program designed to help immigrant teachers make a transition to their profession in Canada. Her doctoral research began with a proposal to study immigrant teachers' classroom work. As we write this story, she has completed her research with Pam, a teacher of West Indian background.

Phillion feels that some of her most cherished beliefs about culture and about how culture is expressed in teaching have been challenged by her work in Pam's classroom. Phillion held views about West Indian culture, about the West Indian population in Canada, and therefore about how a West Indian teacher would approach inner-city teaching. Culture is, in our terms, a formal category. Phillion began her narrative inquiry with this category in mind and expected Pam to present herself as a role model with particular sympathies for children's learning difficulties. Holding to the formalistic category of culture as a guide to interpreting Pam's practice, Phillion expected Pam to be more aware than other teachers of what it means to be a West Indian living in Canada. She expected Pam to show a keen sense of the deficits and disadvantages children of other cultures would experience in an educational system primarily defined in white middle-class terms.

As she began narrative classroom research with Pam, Phillion was startled to find Pam's classroom practices to be other than she had expected. Students who were late for school, for example, were required to enter the classroom, stand by the door, and announce their reasons for being late. Pam explained to Phillion her philosophy that students need to take responsibility for themselves and for their actions. Phillion observed many instances of the expression of Pam's philosophy in Pam's relationship to children and their learning, as Pam insisted that individual children figure things out on their own without strong guidance from her. Her philosophy was also expressed in class activities when Pam required students to develop class projects.

From Phillion's perspective, Pam tolerated what appeared as unproductive activity on the grounds that students needed to work things through on their own. One of Pam's rules is that students need to be quiet before they are dismissed from the classroom to go, for example, to physical education class, to swimming, or to recess. Pam waits for students to quiet down even if they sometimes miss most of a scheduled activity. Phillion found the expression of this rule uncomfortable, and especially so one afternoon when a parent came for an after-school meeting. The parent found it necessary to talk to Pam amid a noisy room full of children who, following Pam's rule, were not allowed to leave. Phillion reports that (had she been the teacher) she would have found it embarrassing and difficult to tolerate the noise with the parent present. Her impulse probably would have been to dismiss the children, but Pam appeared unperturbed.

Phillion's surprise at Pam's practices, and her sense at having her views about the practices of West Indian teachers overturned, highlight the difference between thinking narratively and thinking formalistically. Particularly at issue is the place of people. Phillion, fully committed to a narrative inquiry, also began with a formalistically driven notion of how cultures interact in a teaching setting. She began with the view that Pam would be an exemplar of her culture and with a view of how that culture would be expressed in classroom practice. In Phillion's narrative inquiry, Pam as a person, as an embodiment of lived stories, replaces Pam as an exemplar of culture. It is the person, rather than the formal category, that is important to Phillion's inquiry.

In addition to culture, other formalistic inquiry terms in common usage are *race, class, gender,* and *power.* Narrative inquirers, in developing or explaining their work with other researchers, find themselves almost inevitably at the formalistic inquiry boundary, as other researchers read through their work for the formalistic terms that apply: a person is a member of a race, a class, a gender, and may be said to have varying degrees of power in any situation. Part of the tension for a narrative inquirer is to acknowledge these truths while holding to a different research agenda.

The Place of the Researcher

The story of Phillion's research with Pam highlights a closely related tension, the place of the researcher in inquiry. We saw that Phillion was startled as she realized the practical significance of what she knew in her head—that Pam is much more than the expression of a formalist category. She is a person. But Phillion was also startled by the discovery of the tension within herself. She saw herself undertaking a narrative inquiry in which she was trying to understand the experiential personal practical knowledge of an immigrant teacher. She wished to do this over a long period of time, with many hours of conversation about teaching and about life in general. The surprise comes in finding that she is initially uncomfortable with where this narrative process leads her, and she discovers a boundary within herself—a boundary created by her own narrative history with respect to formalistic thinking on matters of culture and her purpose in undertaking a narrative inquiry.

Phillion's experience of tension at the boundaries is important to all of us as we think through our narrative inquiries and become autobiographically conscious of our own reactions to our work. We all, novice and experienced researchers alike, come to inquiry with views, attitudes, and ways of thinking about inquiry. These histories, these personal narratives of inquiry, may coincide with or cross a boundary to varying degrees with the actual inquiries that we undertake. Almost all of us—it is almost unimaginable that we could not—come to narrative inquiries with various versions of formalistic and reductionistic histories of inquiry. To the extent that this is true, we are forever struggling with personal tensions as we pursue narrative inquiry. Michael's own struggles are with tensions at a reductionistic boundary. It was no accident, but rather a resulting expression of his own inquiry history, that he found himself in Manila on an international science achievement research study and, again, engaged in a Bloom Taxonomy revision task. The most general lesson to be learned from Phillion's story is that narrative inquirers need to reconstruct their own narrative of inquiry histories and to be alert to possible tensions between those narrative histories and the narrative research they undertake.

SUMMARY

In Chapters Two and Three, we have set out to explore the question of what it means to think narratively. We did this by exploring the rough edges, the places where narrative inquiry thinking comes into the intellectual territory of other ways of thinking. We refer to these places as boundaries and have described two main boundaries given by reductionistic and formalistic ways of thinking. Using Lagemann's historical work on the comparative roles of John Dewey and Edward Thorndike, we have developed the reductionist way of thinking in terms of the grand narrative. We have explored the boundaries of our own thinking with the grand narrative as we worked with the Bloom Taxonomy revision team. We have described five resulting tensions at the boundary—temporality, people, action, certainty, and context. In Chapter Three, we have used several examples drawn from various aspects of our work over the years to identify four tensions at the boundary between narrative inquiry and formalistic inquiry—the place of theory, the balance of theory, people, and the place of the researcher.

We do not mean to suggest that these tensions are exclusively at one or the other boundary. They reflect how we have experienced narrative inquiry at the boundaries over the years. We also know that the terms and distinctions are not so sharp and clear as to make it possible to provide a fixed list—five tensions with the reductionistic boundary and four with the formalistic boundary. Our discussion of the tension with respect to "people" at both boundaries is illustrative. People, of course, have a special place in narrative inquiry, but then people are at the heart of all social science inquiry. Furthermore, we do not intend the list of tensions to be read as an exhaustive list. These tensions are the ones that we have experienced most frequently both in our own work and in our work with graduate students undertaking narrative inquiry. They are tensions that throw into relief important aspects of thinking narratively. Unlike Czarniawska and Polkinghorne who borrow theoretical terms from other fields to understand narrative, we, in ways similar to Coles, learn most about narrative inquiry from the doing of narrative inquiry. Doing narrative inquiry, frequently at the boundaries, is the principal source of our thinking about what constitutes thinking narratively in narrative inquiry.

One final observation before moving to more specific matters having to do with working in the field is to note that none of the tensions and associated ways of thinking are isolated and stand-alone items. These matters all take their place in any narrative inquiry and need to be thought of as related matters coming in and out of focus depending on circumstance.

CHAPTER FOUR

What Do Narrative Inquirers Do?

B efore we go on to explain what narrative inquirers do, we offer a parallel. It is always useful to establish a context of purpose. To do this, it is necessary to clarify what one is *not* going to do in order to clarify exactly what one *is* going to do. We use the work of Joseph Schwab to illustrate this point.

Schwab's article entitled "What Do Scientists Do?" (1960) was part of an intense debate about scientific method. Schwab pointed out that much of the discussion about scientific method and the nature of science was without reference to the doing of science but, rather, tended to be built on considerations of scientific logic and the coherence of scientific concepts. Analytic philosophy with its abstract emphases on language construction played a large role in the scientific method literature of the time. Schwab, by his title, signified his intention of entering the discussion by providing an account of what scientists actually did. In the article, Schwab specifically did not want to deal with what people *thought* scientists should do, nor did he wish to offer metalevel logical or analytic and linguistic *interpretations* of what they did, nor even to expand philosophically derived notions of what science was. He wanted to study scientific thinking as expressed in what scientists actually did.

INTRODUCTION

Likewise, in this chapter, and throughout the book, we wish to address the topic of what narrative inquirers do. We do not deal with the huge literature—some modern, much postmodern—that talks about narrative. An example of what we are *not* doing is what Richardson does in her chapter on narrative and sociology in a section entitled "What Is Narrative?" (1995, p. 200), in which she defines narrative. Just as Schwab made clear that he was not setting out to define science nor even the methodology of science, we wish to make clear that we are *not* setting out to define narrative.

We see our task as similar to Schwab's, as one of trying to provide an answer to the question, *What do narrative inquirers do?* As with Schwab, we are interested in inquiry terms and the spaces these terms create for inquiry. We are interested in exploring how these terms define and bound narrative inquiries—how they bound the phenomena, shape what passes for evidence, and determine what makes defensible research texts.

We discuss the terms that we choose to use in our inquiries, which derive from the Deweyan view of experience (particularly *situation, continuity,* and *interaction*). This leads into an examination of our research framework, the *three-dimensional narrative inquiry space* and the "directions" this framework allows our inquiries to travel—*inward, outward, backward, forward,* and *situated within place.* Finally, we demonstrate how our inquiry process is used with two examples from our work.

NARRATIVE INQUIRY TERMS AND NARRATIVE INQUIRY SPACES

What are the terms for narrative inquiry? Readers familiar with the narrative literature might imagine an array of terms derived from modern and postmodern writing and from literature studies. So numerous are the terms that there is even a dictionary of narratology (Prince, 1987). Our terms emerge not from this literature but from our concern for experience and from our purpose—which is to think through the doing of narrative inquiry. As discussed in earlier chapters, our terms for thinking about narrative inquiry are closely associated with Dewey's theory of experience, specifically with his notions of situation, continuity, and interaction. Our terms are not rigorous extrapolations of Deweyan theory. Indeed, a Dewey scholar might find much to criticize. Dewey's work on experience is our imaginative touchstone for reminding us that in our work, the answer to the question, Why narrative? is, Because experience. Dewey provides a frame for thinking of experience "beyond the black box," that is, beyond the notion of experience being irreducible so that one cannot peer into it. With Dewey, one can say more, experientially, than "because of her experience" when answering why a person does what she does.

With this sense of Dewey's foundational place in our thinking about narrative inquiry, our terms are *personal* and *social* (interaction); *past, present,* and *future* (continuity); combined with the notion of *place* (situation). This set of terms creates a metaphorical *three-dimensional narrative inquiry space,* with temporality along one dimension, the personal and the social along a second dimension, and place along a third. Using this set of terms, any particular inquiry is defined by this three-dimensional space: studies have temporal dimensions and address temporal matters; they focus on the personal and the social in a balance appropriate to the inquiry; and they occur in specific places or sequences of places.

Elsewhere (Clandinin and Connelly, 1994), we wrote about two of these dimensions, following Dewey's notion of interaction, by focusing on what we call four directions in any inquiry: *inward* and *outward, backward* and *forward.* By inward, we mean toward the internal conditions, such as feelings, hopes, aesthetic reactions, and moral dispositions. By outward, we mean toward the existential conditions, that is, the environment. By backward and forward, we refer to temporality—past, present, and future. We wrote that *to experience an experience*—that is, to do research into an experience—is to experience it simultaneously in these four ways and to ask questions pointing each way. Thus, when one is positioned on this two-dimensional space in any particular inquiry, one asks questions, collects field notes, derives interpretations, and writes a research text that addresses both personal and social issues by looking inward and outward, and addresses temporal issues by looking not only to the event but to its past and to its future.

In this earlier work, we included the dimension of place within the environment. We now believe it is preferable to see place as a third term, which attends to the specific concrete physical and topological boundaries of inquiry landscapes.

A STORY OF WORKING IN A THREE-DIMENSIONAL NARRATIVE INQUIRY SPACE WITH MING FANG HE

Unbeknownst to either of them when Ming Fang He knocked on Michael's door and asked if she could be a member of his research team, she was beginning a doctoral journey that would carry them both back in time, her to her origins in precultural revolution times in China and Michael to growing up in a rural cattle-ranching community in western Canada where Long Him ran Long Him's General Store in the nearest two-store town. The ranching area had been settled primarily by British Isle immigrants, though by the time Michael attended the one-room country school, central Europeans were in evidence. Still, they all seemed and spoke like Michael and being a second-generation Canadian, he grew up in what now appears to him to have been a mostly homogeneous cultural community. Long Him was, to Michael's 1990s adult recollection, the only person who did not fit easily into the cultural landscape. Long Him could speak enough English just to conduct business. As a child, Michael accompanied his parents to town for bimonthly, sometimes weekly, shopping trips, and though his parents patronized the other store (the owners being longtime friends), they usually managed to visit Long Him's.

Thinking back, Michael knew almost nothing about Long Him, and his guess is neither did his parents. Michael had no sense of Long Him's being integrated into community life. When a traveling preacher started up a once-monthly Anglican church service, mostly everyone attended, but not Long Him. Michael does remember what seemed to him then to be an exotic story unfolding, as Long Him showed off a Chinese bride one Saturday. The arrival of this mysterious bride, who spoke no English, was explained by an equally mysterious "mail-order" process. She did not last through the first winter. Michael also recalls being fascinated by a chest-high water pipe that Long Him would smoke, especially if asked to do so by Michael's parents to please the children. Michael recalls the store, full of dark, secret hiding places as a marvelous place for a favorite childhood game of hide-and-seek.

Meeting Ming Fang and working through her thesis led Michael to wonder where Long Him had come from. Moreover, his encounter with Ming Fang led Michael to wonder about himself, his family, and his community life and how his story of himself in relation to other cultures was shaped by family and community stories on the rural landscape. Long Him was no doubt dropped off at Lundbreck, as the railroad was built with stations every four miles. Canada was knit into a country by the railroad, a railroad built on the backs of labor brought from China.

Michael has begun to puzzle, now that Ming Fang has finished her thesis, over who she and he are, relative to Long Him. Long Him was, as far as Michael can remember, his first multicultural experience. In his memory, there were no others until he attended a residential high school, where members of the Peigan Indian reserve of the Blackfoot Nation attended. Ming Fang brought Michael back to these experiences, and only now is he beginning to puzzle over his own attitudes, sympathies, and outlooks toward people from other settings. Both Ming Fang and Michael journeyed back to their childhood beginnings through *her* inquiry. Her completed dissertation on who she is helped Michael start to wonder who he is in a multicultural world. But she too is faced with a new puzzle as Michael's stories of Long Him are brought forward, and Ming Fang wonders about the place of Chinese in Canada.

Ming Fang He is a mainland Chinese woman who went through the cultural revolution as a young girl, spent time on a reforming farm, received her bachelor's degree in China and her master's degrees in English and in linguistics at two different universities in Canada. She took out landed Canadian immigrant status and as her dissertation work began was a citizen of two countries. She and her women friends with similar backgrounds were deeply puzzled and confused over who they were. At the time her dissertation proposal took shape, this confusion was expressed as one of experiencing a variety of culture shocks. She found community and university support networks inadequate in helping her attain a strong sense of self. She partially supported herself by teaching English as a second language to immigrants, many of whom were Chinese. She found little to clarify her sense of dislocation in this teaching and in the literature supporting it. This literature is essentially based on the notion of cultural adaptation through language acquisition. Her experience of Chinese and Canadian culture, and her movements back and forth between them, led her to think that much more was at stake than language and culture adaptation.

It was out of this cluster of experiences and considerations that she articulated her thesis proposal, which she ultimately conceptualized in her completed dissertation abstract as "a study of identity formation and cultural transformation of three Chinese women teachers as they moved back and forth between Chinese and Canadian cultures" (He, 1998). The thesis is an intensive study of the lives of three Chinese women, Shiao, Wei, and Ming Fang, tracing their lives from the late 1950s through a series of political and cultural upheavals in China, their move to Canada, and the further upheavals they experienced in living in Canada and in the study of higher education in Canada. Due in part to ongoing political sensitivities in China, and in part to the limitations of biography and autobiography, she created a method she calls *composite autobiography* to narrate each woman's identity formation and cultural transformation.

As Michael read and reread Ming Fang's, Shiao's, and Wei's stories of growing up in China, he came to understand something of how that time and place shaped their lives and the stories they tell of them. The more Ming Fang worked to understand the relationship between her memories of her life and the landscape on which the lives of the three Chinese women were played out, the more Michael realized how limited his knowing of Long Him was, and how what little he did know was milled by the peculiar cultural qualities of his childhood landscape. In her dissertation, Ming Fang traveled back to a place where her stories first unfolded. Though Michael too traveled back to a place where his stories first unfolded, he realized there was no Chinese place in his story of Long Him. Long Him was, in Michael's story, almost wholly constructed from Michael's experience of him as he appeared on Michael's rural Canadian landscape. Michael had a distant observer's stereotypical sense of China, in which his childhood stories of Long Him were embedded. Michael remembers two things in this regard. The first is his mother's admonition that they should clean off their plates because, she would say, "Think of the starving children in China," as if his eating were linked somehow to their starvation. The second thing he remembers is the entrancing thought that if he could dig down far enough, he would come out in China. He has no re-membered links of how these stories were connected in his mind to Long Him's experiences of growing up in China.

Ming Fang's narrative inquiry carries Michael to the place of these experiences. He is—through Ming Fang's thesis—a "world traveler" in Lugones's (1987) sense. It has taken a lifetime for him to even won-der about becoming a world traveler to Long Him's world. Ming Fang's long-ago China stories and present-day Canadian ones help us, as Blaise (1993) suggests, "live in their countries, speak their language, negotiate their streets on their buses and turn our keys in their locks" (p. 201).

THREE-DIMENSIONAL
NARRATIVE INQUIRY SPACE

We earlier created a metaphor of a three-dimensional space, in which narrative inquirers would find themselves, using a set of terms that pointed them backward and forward, inward and outward, and lo-cated them in place. We saw these dimensions as directions or av-enues to be pursued in a narrative inquiry. As we come to Ming Fang's and Michael's inquiries, we might think of these terms in sev-eral different ways.

In terms of the grand narrative, we might imagine the terms as an analytic frame for reducing the stories to a set of understandings. For instance, looking backward would be illustrated by Ming Fang's sto-ries of the cultural revolution, and looking inward would be repre-sented by her feelings of culture shock as she entered Canada and began her dissertation studies. If we persisted in developing the terms as an analytic frame, we might go on to state findings developed for each set. For example, at the intersection of place and time, we might claim that the China of Ming Fang's early life is a construction that now only exists in her remembered stories. At the intersection of look-ing inward and place, we might claim that Ming Fang experienced cul-ture shock as she moved from one place, China, to another place, Canada. At the intersection of looking outward and place, we might claim that it was the difference between the two places that caused the culture shock.

To turn the use of the terms more toward their experiential origins, we could think of them not so much as generating a list of under-standings achieved by analyzing the stories, but rather as pointing to questions, puzzles, fieldwork, and field texts of different kinds appropriate to different aspects of the inquiry. Thus, we might see Ming Fang collecting memory records of the cultural revolution through conversations and interviews with her participants or, perhaps, reviewing posters, slogans, and news accounts of the era. As she focused on the personal, we might see how, perhaps through letters with her parents, she reconstructed a sense of how she felt about herself and her family during the cultural revolution. This use of the terms is how we develop the remainder of this chapter.

What is unsaid, a third use of the terms (and not possible to say with the stories so far presented), is the ambiguity, complexity, difficulty, and uncertainties associated with the doing of the inquiry. These doings, the "stuff" of narrative inquiry, can only be sensed and understood from a reading of the full-blown inquiry. Though we do not explore this complexity here, we will come back to it in these and other stories.

To return, then, to the second use, namely to the use of the terms to show how an inquiry is structured by the inquirer—that is, to see what the narrative inquirer does—we pick up on the temporal dimension. Ming Fang began, in her present time, with a feeling of culture shock. She described this feeling as personal, situated in the present time, and located in her Canadian place. She looked backward in time to her feelings in China. She remembered a calm, intellectual childhood interrupted by the turmoil of the cultural revolution. As she engaged in this process, she remembered not only the personal but also the intersection of the personal with the social. Her research text, minimally described above, constitutes a dual personal and social narration. Throughout her narrative inquiry, she remains in her Canadian place while traveling back in time and place, in memory, to a China that no longer exists. The three-dimensional space in which her research is situated creates an ongoing sense of dislocation as she moves from a remembered past in one place to a present moment in another, all the while imaginatively constructing an identity for the future.

To return to Michael's remembered stories of childhood, he realizes that the terms also structure his (unexpected) narrative inquiry. He began in the present time with his work with Ming Fang. In telling stories of Ming Fang to Jean, he moved to recollecting memories from his childhood, then to memories of the first Chinese Canadian, Long Him, he had ever met. In so doing, he moved backward in time and place, composing new stories for his present time and place. Thus, Michael composed yet untold stories of visiting Long Him's store. But he also recollected stories his mother had told him. Both kinds of stories were lived in his childhood place and time. Both were told from his adult place and time, and in the bringing forward, both were placed alongside his present-day story of Ming Fang and her long-ago stories.

In composing Michael's stories of another place and time, he was called to consider how he felt. Here, he began an imaginative process based on faint memories of an environment—a dark store, a water pipe, a Chinese wife briefly seen. But as he located himself within the three-dimensional inquiry space as we wrote this research text, Michael began to awaken to how Long Him had "world traveled" to his place and to the significance of the fact that he had not "world traveled" to Long Him's Chinese place and to Long Him's inner conditions. Michael composed his relationship with Long Him from his place on the rural western landscape, from his child's time, with his child's feelings, all milled and crafted by the landscape of childhood. As Michael composes this research text, he sees new possibilities as he restories his knowing of Long Him, Ming Fang, and himself in relation to them. Being in this space is complex for the narrative inquirer because all of these matters are under consideration all of the time.

In this story, we play within the three-dimensional narrative inquiry space. Place shifts from Ming Fang's long-ago China to present-day Toronto, from Michael's long-ago western Canadian place shared with Long Him to Toronto. Time shifts from childhoods in western Canada and China to present days in Toronto. Inner and existential conditions for Michael as a child, for Ming Fang as a child, and for both of them as adults are recounted. Long Him remains as partial memory, as partial imaginative construction, a figure in Michael's puzzling over who Ming Fang and he are in this modern world broth of cultures and ideas. He wonders what Ming Fang's written words of living in between, and either belonging nowhere or belonging everywhere, might mean on the inside. He wonders at what Long Him made of his own life in the two-store ranching community town, and he wonders what his parents would think to hear their son, a generation later, question the community's sensitivity to people of other cultures. He can only imagine they would be shocked and offended because, as he remembers them, they were so conscientiously egalitarian.

In the next story, we play again within a three-dimensional narrative inquiry space, but this time we locate the place within schools, as we move temporally backward and forward. We work again with field texts of memory relationships and field texts of research transcripts.

A STORY OF WORKING IN A THREE-DIMENSIONAL NARRATIVE INQUIRY SPACE WITH KAREN WHELAN

There are five people gathered at the table in the Centre on a cold, crisp, sunshine-filled day in winter. It is Saturday and the light filters in the window. The sky is an unbelievable blue but they hardly notice. This is one of their research Saturdays. Chuck and Annie have driven up from Calgary to meet with Janice, Karen, and Jean to talk about and share their research. The tape recorder hums softly in the middle of the table. They are intent on their conversation even though they have been sitting for several hours.

They are part of an ongoing research group—teachers, principals, and teacher educators—who are trying to understand their places on the professional knowledge landscapes on which they live. In what follows, Jean shares a fragment of the transcript made from that conversation (as picked up by the tape recorder), in which Karen Whelan speaks:

I think sometimes when you do feel strongly about things though, that marginalizes you. I can remember the first year with that principal. I just got red faced arguing with him over these report cards because he wanted every kid to be evaluated the same way. Like we're going to say that, you know, a kid in your class is operating at a grade-one level, and a kid is operating at a grade-three level in a grade-three classroom. We're going to evaluate them the same on the, we're going to, we're going to check off for the kid operating at a grade-one level always failure, failure, failure because they are not working at grade level, so they're always on the bottom, and I mean I can remember, I was in hysterics almost that he could even be thinking this way. How can you always mark a child as failing? And when I get upset about those things, I tend to get really passionate about them. Like I get tears in my eyes and I'm almost like incredulous, how can this be happening? [group conversation, January 18, 1997]

The conversation goes on, as they weave their talk across their own childhood memories, their student stories of remembered classrooms, their teacher stories of remembered classrooms, their sharing of transcripts from ongoing research projects, one story calling up another from one or another of them, from their pasts, from the data they had collected. The tape recorder continues to record their talk, some of it memory relationships and some of it sharing of research field texts, such as school board documents and transcripts of research groups.

The day ends, transcripts are made, and some months later Jean is studying them. She studies them at her desk, reading and rereading them, stopping at this passage, for she is reminded of what she remembers thinking that day. She searches the transcript for it, but there is no record that she had spoken the words. She stops reading and begins to write. This is what she wrote:

> In the midst of a project meeting discussing transcripts of conversations with participants and field notes of school classroom meetings, a story of my own long-ago surfaces in my mind. I remember a classroom of my childhood: the smell of floor wax, gestetner fluid, and wet woolen mittens and scarves. I remember the sounds of desks scraping on hard wood and her voice as she called out spelling words. The knot of anxiety clutches at my stomach, a feeling called forth by discussions of children's experiences of being graded on report cards in standardized ways. The smells, the sounds, the sights, the feelings create a picture and a story comes quickly to mind.

Jean is a child in the classroom, a classroom of the early 1950s in an old brick school situated in the small town to which she is bused each day. Donnie and Daryl, two big boys, ride on her school bus. They command respect on the school bus, and they always sit at the back of the bus. But when they come into the school, they come to Jean's grade-four classroom. And it is from within that classroom that she remembers the day of that spelling test.

As Jean sits at her university professor's desk, reading the transcript, she remembers herself as a child in that school, a child taking a test. She remembers a teacher standing tall in the center of the room, moving between the rows of desks. Is she marching? Do her high heels click on the floor? Does she stop at Jean's desk to observe her writing a word? Does she pause at Daryl's desk? Is Daryl really a bad boy? Does Donnie take the test? Does Jean remember that Donnie and Daryl are fifteen and just putting in time in that grade-four classroom, waiting to turn sixteen so they can legally drop out of school? These wonders surface for Jean as she writes about the remembered day.

Still later, as we write this research text, we think about inquiry spaces. On that January day of the conversation, Karen took Jean and the others in the research group backward in time as she told her story. Karen described, from her vantage point of narrator, the conversation with her principal. She described herself as red faced, as hysterical. She felt passionate, she recalled, in the encounter. She described her talk with the principal, who wanted to have all students graded with reference to their grade level. She took the group back to that moment and pulled them forward into the future as she made the connection between that moment and how she now sees herself as marginalized on the landscape where standardized testing and grading is now the accepted story of school. She situated them in a place—a school in an urban center—where new policies on grading have come down the conduit, relaying from policy to principal, to Karen, as teacher.

Jean was, at first, a listener but Karen's story evoked a memory for her. She knows that she did not speak, for if she had, her words would have been captured in the transcribed conversation. It was only as she read the transcripts that she remembered that Karen's story had evoked a memory for her, which she had then written down. Jean recalled the long ago brought forward, first as a response to Karen's telling and subsequently by Jean's reading of the transcript.

Jean went backward to her long-ago classroom and forward to her present-day research and to questions of what it means to be a narrative inquirer on the professional knowledge landscape. All of this takes place within a place—her present-day place within a research university, where she does research and writes about her work with teachers, and her long-ago place, where she is a country child educated in a small-town school.

These are story fragments now stitched together in Jean's memory. When she was a child in that long-ago classroom, she was not a narrative inquirer. There was no intention to keep notes of those experiences. She now re-creates the narrative through memory relationships. From a temporal and spatial and bodily distance, she tells a story from the now: spinning a story of a teacher, of two boys, of a small girl, of a classroom. There are no field texts, no careful notes, no photographs, no transcribed conversations of the events in that classroom.

Our purpose in giving this example is to demonstrate the use of terms that structure our three-dimensional narrative inquiry space. We began in the present with a segment of transcript from an inquiry group meeting in which Karen describes a year-ago encounter with her principal. Karen's words take Jean further back along the temporal dimension to her own childhood. But as we slide backward and forward temporally, it is clear that we stay rooted in a place called school, a place where grading is practiced, and children's experiences are sorted according to those grades. We go inward to Karen's intense feelings and outward to the conversation with her principal, who is describing the mandated report cards and the grading system. Jean too goes inward to old feelings of anxiety produced by a spelling test and to stories of classmates who were visible evidence, to her child's-eye view, of what happens when tests are failed. What starts to become apparent as we work within our three-dimensional space is that as narrative inquirers we are not alone in this space. This space enfolds us and those with whom we work. Narrative inquiry is a relational inquiry as we work in the field, move from field to field text, and from field text to research text.

A REFLECTIVE NOTE

As we worked within our three-dimensional spaces as narrative inquirers, what became clear to us was that as inquirers we meet ourselves in the past, the present, and the future. What we mean by this is that we tell remembered stories of ourselves from earlier times as well as more current stories. All of these stories offer possible plotlines for our futures.

Telling stories of ourselves in the past leads to the possibility of retellings. We saw this in Michael's story in his relations with Ming Fang and Long Him. We saw it again in Jean's story with Karen and Jean's grade-four classroom. It is not only the participants' stories that are retold by a narrative inquirer. In our cases, it is also the inquirers' (Michael's and Jean's) stories that are open for inquiry and retelling.

As narrative inquirers, we share our writing on a work-in-progress basis with response communities. By this, we mean that we ask others to read our work and to respond in ways that help us see other meanings that might lead to further retelling. We shared this chapter and received, among the responses, some that were surprising to us, especially with respect to Michael, Ming Fang, and Long Him's story. Among the responses was one that suggested that Michael was racist in his portrayal of Long Him. The response seemed to suggest that racism was apparent in the use of stereotypical language, such as water pipe, mail-order bride, and exotic. In this response, our language was taken as representative of our present-day tellers' point of view. We have reworked the text to strengthen the narrative links between then and now.

This response made us stop and wonder, for we had intentionally chosen the language to represent, as memory would have it, the attitudes at work in Michael's childhood landscape. As tellers of the story, we deliberately embedded what we realized were cultural stereotypes and insensitive attitudes available in his childhood landscape. We are now clearer in our thinking for having taken the response seriously. Why do we portray Michael's childhood as we do? Partly, we use the language we do to make it clear that these were our stories. We did live out what we now call cultural stereotypes. This telling of ourselves, this meeting of ourselves in the past through inquiry, makes clear that as inquirers we, too, are part of the parade. We have helped make the world in which we find ourselves. We are not merely objective inquirers, people on the high road, who study a world lesser in quality than our moral temperament would have it, people who study a world we did not help create. On the contrary, we are complicit in the world we study. Being in this world, we need to remake ourselves as well as offer up research understandings that could lead to a better world.

We could have left Michael's story out or glossed over what seemed less than proper in our current view of the world. We could have created a script that suggested Michael's first encounter with Chinese Canadians was with Ming Fang, a script that would have left him as a wise present-day inquirer without a humbling narrative past. His place in this unnarrated script is present-day Toronto, a city the United Nations calls the world's most multicultural city, a place from which Michael could readily claim unparalleled insight on cultural matters. But such a script removes Michael from the world, as if he were not also part of the phenomenon, as if he were not a person with narrative blinders like any other.

What this response has highlighted for us is that as narrative inquirers we work within the space not only with our participants but also with ourselves. Working in this space means that we become visible with our own lived and told stories. Sometimes, this means that our own unnamed, perhaps secret, stories come to light as much as do those of our participants. This confronting of ourselves in our narrative past makes us vulnerable as inquirers because it makes secret stories public. In narrative inquiry, it is impossible (or if not impossible, then deliberately self-deceptive) as researcher to stay silent or to present a kind of perfect, idealized, inquiring, moralizing self.

CHAPTER FIVE

Being in the Field
Walking into the Midst of Stories

A s we worked within the three-dimensional narrative inquiry space, we learned to see ourselves as always *in the midst*—located somewhere along the dimensions of time, place, the personal, and the social. But we see ourselves in the midst in another sense as well; that is, we see ourselves as in the middle of a nested set of stories—ours and theirs.

INTRODUCTION

In this chapter, we take a look at several researchers' experiences in the midst. We examine the complexities they must negotiate. Specifically, we explore key areas that researchers must learn to work through in their fieldwork—negotiating relationships, negotiating purposes, negotiating transitions, and negotiating ways to be useful.

BEGINNING IN THE MIDST

As researchers, we come to each new inquiry field living our stories. Our participants also enter the inquiry field in the midst of living their stories. Their lives do not begin the day we arrive nor do they end as we leave. Their lives continue. Furthermore, the places in which they live and work, their classrooms, their schools, and their communities, are also in the midst when we researchers arrive. Their institutions and their communities, their landscapes in the broadest sense, are also in the midst of stories.

Geertz (1995) felt this way about his anthropological work in Sefrou. He wrote: "Entry of this sort into an entr'acte where all the really critical things seemed just to have happened yesterday and just about to happen tomorrow, induces an uncomfortable sense of having come too late and arrived too early, a sense which in my case never afterward left me . . . it always seemed not the right time, but a pause between right times" (p. 4).

Kerby (1991), though he had something else in mind, might have said that to enter the field of inquiry was to carry with us, and meet as we entered, prenarratives—lives in motion, structured narratively, the retelling still to come via the inquiry.

The stories we bring as researchers are also set within the institutions within which we work, the social narratives of which we are a part, the landscape on which we live.

BEGINNING IN THE MIDST AT BAY STREET SCHOOL

In Chapter One, we wrote of our work with two teachers, Stephanie and Aileen. Our work with them was part of a two-decade study of teacher knowledge. We worked in one school, Bay Street, for much of this time. Here is a sampling of the Bay Street School story as it began for us back then:

> A school known around the board as one with racial problems. That's the school where they had some kind of fight in the yard a few years ago. Everyone thought it had some racial basis. There were stories about fighting in the hallways and on the playgrounds. This was a tough school.
>
> A school with declining standards. We heard that from some people in the community. We heard it from the staff at a neighboring school, and they told us that parents choose to send their children to that school because they have higher standards. After all, Bay Street

was named a project school because there is such poor achievement. Lots of teachers want to transfer out of there.

A school where you can send kids who can't make it in other schools. We heard it is a place to send kids who are too troubled or not achieving or too much of a problem to keep in school.

Those were the stories that came flashing to mind as we first arrived at the nineteenth-century brick building in downtown inner-city Toronto on that first day when we arrived to meet the school principal and a number of teachers. We met in the school staff room, and we felt the oldness of the school and the ways the problems of the years of neglect hung in the air. The couches were old, the hallways dark, and there was little sign of student work. Still, we sensed, as people talked with us, possibility, feelings of hope for being able to change what had been to something else. It was after school hours when we arrived, and we thought the school was empty of children. However, after our meeting we went upstairs for tea with one of the special education teachers and met some students there. These students, we noted in our field texts, appeared to feel cared for by their teacher.

We walked away from the school with feelings of hope for being able to work with the school in the research project but also with feelings of apprehension. What kind of school were we becoming part of? Would we be able to work in that school with the intensity that our research called for? What were we, two people from rural Alberta, doing in trying to learn about the problems of inner-city children and teachers? But we sensed, even as we asked the questions, the imagination and hope of the principal and teachers who saw possibility for things to be otherwise.

We had two senses of being in the midst—being in the midst of a three-dimensional narrative inquiry space, and being in the midst of a temporal, storied flow. These two senses came together and helped create mixed feelings of apprehension and hopeful possibility. As we prepared to work in Bay Street School in that first meeting with the principal and teachers, our apprehension was not so much one of being in the right place at the wrong time but more a question of our appropriateness for the place. We sensed how different the lives of the children in this school must be from our own lives in our childhoods, growing up on vast unpopulated rural landscapes. Could we, with our journeys from there through academic halls in Chicago and Toronto, meaningfully connect with the students, teachers, and parents with whom we would work if this project were to go forward?

Right now as we write this book, what do we make of these different narrative trajectories? Does one have to be one of "them" to do the research? Can we reach across a narrative space to work meaningfully with participants? What do we narrative inquirers do with our diverse backgrounds? Had we been asked these questions directly following our meeting in the school, we probably would have answered with the doubts that appeared in our notes on the visit.

But as our stories of Chapter Four with Ming Fang He, Michael, and Long Him show, reaching across autobiographically storied boundaries is possible, perhaps even necessary, for the creation of narrative insight. Bateson (1994) wrote that quite apart from the researcher's wishes on the matter, participants sometimes draw one in and sometimes hold one at a distance. It is like this as we explore this question of different narrative histories coming together in the inquiry field. Sometimes there is sensitive observation and sometimes intimate coparticipation in the intermingling of narratives. Over the years, we have experienced some of both, at different times, with different people, at Bay Street School.

Curiously, perhaps we feel a kind of intimacy with the school building and its institutional narrative. People have come and gone, and we have observed, and merged, narrative histories with them. But the school building remains and so does its neighborhood, though both go on and have their own stories.

In the cartoon strip, "For Better Or For Worse," a grandmother sometimes appears with the ghostly outlines of a deceased grandfather hovering over her and a grandchild asking, "Why are you talking to yourself grandma?" Perhaps the intimacy we experience toward the building and its community is partially like that of the grandmother. It is impossible for us to talk of Bay Street School without a cascade of ghostly memories of people and happenings flooding into our consciousness. This too is perhaps one of the things that narrative inquirers do, at least those in it for the long haul. Their places—for us Bay Street School, its classrooms, halls, grounds, and community— become *memory boxes* in which the people and events of today are retold and written into the research texts of tomorrow. Once this narrative process takes hold, the narrative inquiry space pulsates with movements back and forth through time and along a continuum of personal and social considerations. The school and community, and the people that come in and out of them, take on a dynamic interactive sense. The community is experienced as infusing the school and the school as infusing the community. Histories too have this sense. The opening date, bricked in relief on the school tower, is not merely something to be photographed, but like the hovering grandfather in the cartoon is something that speaks to the school in its present conditions.

The school and the community, the landscape in its broadest sense, have taught us that they too have narrative histories. We entered the school in the midst of a series of inquiries on teacher knowledge, and in so doing were tuned to individual persons' narrative histories. But the financial support that brought us to the school was a U.S. National Institute of Education (NIE) grant on school reform. Our topic was institutional, and our focus was people. The institutional focus hovered in the background and eventually asserted itself as we began to dig into the history of the school and community. On the one hand, Bay Street School's immediate history, the stories of Bay Street School, were much in our minds. We heard stories of it as a school with "racial problems," with "declining standards," a place to "send kids who were too troubled." We heard stories of the principal, new to the school, in which he was featured as innovative and community oriented. The school, with its newly appointed principal, was ideal for the purposes of our research grant. It was history, at least immediate history, that let us know this was the case. Later, we found narrative threads for these stories of school that reached back into the previous century, close to the time of Canadian Confederation. Since its opening in 1877, commentaries on Bay Street School have referred to its immigrant population mix. As we stepped into the principal's office to begin our fieldwork, we knew we were stepping into institutional narratives, but it was only later that we fully sensed the continuity and sweep of this history.

Perhaps a note is in order on how that sense developed. Had we been "inners" and "outers," in and out of the field in what Ray Rist (1980) called (in his title) "blitzkrieg ethnography," this history would never have surfaced except perhaps as interesting anecdotal material needed to dress up research texts. It was being in the field, day after day, year after year, that brought forth a compelling sense of the long-term landscape narratives at work. This too is one of the things that narrative inquirers do in the field: they settle in, live and work alongside participants, and come to experience not only what can be seen and talked about directly but also the things not said and not done that shape the narrative structure of their observations and their talking.

BEING IN THE MIDST IS
DIFFERENT FOR EVERYONE

Twenty years later, JoAnn Phillion, introduced in Chapter Three, wrote, as she entered Bay Street School to begin her doctoral studies fieldwork:

> This first visit I feel so apprehensive about the school and my participant. I remember that a social worker told me that Alexandra Park is a dangerous area. Getting off the subway Mick and I walk down a street littered with pieces of paper and other debris. The stores in this part of Chinatown haven't opened yet. People are sleeping over a grate in piles of clothes, mountains of plastic bags beside them. In the freezing late-November air, several people, coughing and wheezing, hold their hands out for change. As we walk along I see people sweeping the streets, pushing paper, fruit peels, and cigarette butts into the gutter. Children with backpacks, holding their mothers' hands, are on their way to school. We walk by the Day Care Centre. A small Black child is holding hands with an Asian child as they play a game together.
>
> Bay Street School is nestled in one of the most multicultural neighborhoods I have ever experienced. We walk down one of the major streets near the school. Both sides have a large number of stores and businesses, art galleries and curio shops reflective of the complexity and diversity of Toronto. There are signs in Vietnamese, Chinese, Korean, Portuguese, English and more. There are advertisements for restaurants from almost every culture I have heard of and ones that I have not. There is a lively, exhilarating atmosphere.
>
> All this makes me very nostalgic for the culture of the 60s which seems to be preserved, in small part, in this neighborhood. What residue of hippie culture do I cherish to this day? I think of myself as really open, accepting of differences, willing to listen to all sides, hear all perspectives. I think this will serve me in good stead as I engage in this research.
>
> Mick is reminiscing about the way the school looked in the years that he and Jean were doing research here. He mentions that the parking lot has been relocated; the large, broad walkway where we are walk-

ing took its place. He points to the community centre where the students went for their swimming lessons. I am aware of a sense of history and continuity: This is Bay Street School where Mick and Jean have spent years of their lives and have done much of their writing. I have a sense of belonging to something that is more than simply my project.

I am nervous and apprehensive about being in a school that means so much to Mick and Jean. Maybe I should have chosen a site that had no particular attachment for them. [1999, p. 55]

JoAnn's account of her moments of entry into her field of inquiry show again how much one is already in the midst when one arrives. She feels the force (perhaps *weight* is a better term to characterize the passages here) of the long-term inquiry that she is now on the edges of joining. For us, Bay Street's history crept slowly, and for a time unnoticed, into our own awareness. JoAnn does not have the luxury of holding at a distance, perhaps not even noticing, the ongoing narratives at work. With one of us walking beside her, commenting on parking lots, people, and places as they had changed, a version of the narrative history preceded her into her meeting with the principal. Moreover, JoAnn had read our work on Bay Street School, and had spoken to both of us about it long before the morning described above. She too had apprehensions, of a different sort than Geertz and different again than ours. No doubt, in some complicated way she wondered if she could sustain the fieldwork and write research texts that would eventually contribute to the Bay Street School narrative. A strong sense of narrative history brings with it narrative apprehensions brought on by the need to mark a place in that narrative in the future.

But JoAnn's personal narrative was neither Jean's nor Michael's. She was born in an urban setting, chose certain forms of alternative living, taught abroad, and became interested in multiculturalism. She is someone whose personal and academic life is built around matters of equity and equality. Her observations on the neighborhood as she walked along the street are observations born of this narrative. She felt these strongly and was meeting the principal that morning more for reasons of that narrative interest than for Bay Street School stories. In many ways, any number of school settings would have worked. Her apprehensions are partly a matter of recognizing a narrative history of which she is a part and wondering if that might not somehow or other swamp her main interest. At the same time, there is tension because she senses that being part of, and contributing to, that narrative history can strengthen her inquiries. The depth and context made possible by the Bay Street narrative would add a dimension and would take her a lifetime to achieve in other ways.

Our reflections on JoAnn's narrative highlights the importance of acknowledging the centrality of the researcher's own experience—the researcher's own livings, tellings, retellings, and relivings. One of the starting points for narrative inquiry is the researcher's own narrative of experience, the researcher's autobiography. This task of composing our own narratives of experience is central to narrative inquiry. We refer to this as composing narrative beginnings as a researcher begins his or her inquiries. For example, in our introduction to this book, we each told something of our narrative beginnings that framed our early work on teacher knowledge. As we compose our narrative beginnings, we also work within the three-dimensional space, telling stories of our past that frame our present standpoints, moving back and forth from the personal to the social, and situating it all in place. We see a glimmer of these narrative beginnings in JoAnn's field texts, as she tried to gain experience of her experience by constructing a narrative of that experience. These narrative beginnings of our own livings, tellings, retellings, and relivings help us deal with questions of who we are in the field and who we are in the texts that we write on our experience of the field experience.

Recall the question from Chapter Four: What do narrative inquirers do? They make themselves as aware as possible of the many, layered narratives at work in their inquiry space. They imagine narrative intersections, and they anticipate possible narrative threads emerging. There is apprehension in this process, as Geertz's entry to Sefrou, our entry, and later JoAnn's entry to Bay Street School show. But there is also hope and anticipation for the narrative inquiry future.

However cast—as a sense of being in the right place at the wrong time, as being in the midst of untold stories, as being in a prenarrative—there is for the narrative inquirer the inevitable sense of the merging of temporal flows, as researchers and participants meet in their inquiry field. The moment of arrival, as a careful reading of our own and later JoAnn's arrival at Bay Street School show, is filled not only with anticipation of what is to come but also with a sense of history. Narrative threads coalesce out of a past and emerge in the specific three-dimensional space we call our inquiry field.

LIVING, TELLING, RETELLING, AND RELIVING STORIES

Elsewhere (Connelly and Clandinin, 1990), we have written that as we begin work on a research project, we are beginning a new story. Thinking about an inquiry in narrative terms allows us to conceptualize the inquiry experience as a storied one on several levels. Following Dewey, our principal interest in experience is the growth and transformation in the life story that we as researchers and our participants author. Therefore, difficult as it may be to tell a story, the more difficult but important task is the retelling of stories that allow for growth and change. We imagine, therefore, that in the construction of narratives of experience, there is a reflexive relationship between living a life story, telling a life story, retelling a life story, and reliving a life story. As we emphasized in the preceding examples of our work at Bay Street School, we as researchers were already engaged in living and telling our stories—of ourselves, of the participants, and of our shared inquiries. As we began work with our participants at Bay Street, we began to tell and live new stories. Within the inquiry field, we lived out stories, told stories of those experiences, and modified them by retelling them and reliving them. The research participants at Bay Street School also lived, told, retold, and relived their stories.

WHAT DO WE DO NOW THAT WE ARE IN THE FIELD?

When researchers enter the field, they experience shifts and changes, constantly negotiating, constantly reevaluating, and maintaining flexibility and openness to an ever-changing landscape.

Negotiating Relationships

Shortly after our meeting with the principal and teachers, we found ourselves coming to Bay Street School for three days a week, Michael to work with Susan, a teacher-librarian, in the library, and Jean to work with Stephanie, a grade-one teacher, in her classroom. We "settled in for the long haul," working alongside our participants, making ourselves useful in whatever ways we could, and trying to maintain the momentum that brought us together. At first, the forces of collaboration are weak and the arrangements feel tenuous. Sometimes, this does not change throughout the inquiry, and one can feel on the edge almost as an uninvited guest throughout the fieldwork. For us, the early days felt a bit like it does when one is trying to start a car on a cold morning, and there is just enough power to turn the motor. Maybe it will catch and maybe it will not.

There have been times when the gap between a researcher's and a participant's narratives of experience have seemed to be too great. In his dissertation, Siaka Kroma (Kroma, 1983) wrote of beginning a narrative inquiry with one participant. They did not connect. To use our metaphor, the motor did not catch, and the participant and Siaka agreed not to work together.

For us, at Bay Street, the motor did catch. Throughout the inquiry, in our experience of being in the field, the researcher-participant relationship is a tenuous one, always in the midst of being negotiated. After Jean had been working in Stephanie's classroom for three months, the school year ended in June. Jean and Stephanie parted, agreeing that Jean would return in late August to help Stephanie set up her classroom for the beginning of school. When Jean arrived, Stephanie hesitantly told her that she had almost called to tell Jean not to come. She said that it was going to be hard to have Jean there for those early September days. After hours of conversation, Jean and Stephanie renegotiated their working relationship, and a sense of tentative ease returned. Though frequently not as dramatic as this instance was for Jean and Stephanie, the negotiation of a research relationship is ongoing throughout the inquiry.

Furthermore, though one may develop an intimate relationship with people and places on the landscape, there is always the recognition that the intermingling of narrative threads has loose ends off the landscape: we work in different places, have different purposes, and have different ways to account for ourselves as researchers and participants.

Good narrative working relationships carry with them a sad and wistful sense born of the possibility of temporariness. Jean experienced this when she moved to western Canada, and Michael a few years later when a research grant ended. JoAnn senses the sadness now as she writes her dissertation, not knowing where she will be a year from the time of writing, perhaps in another city or another country far from Bay Street School.

Negotiating Purposes

As we suggested above, one of the things narrative inquirers do is continually negotiate their relationships. Research lore would have it that negotiation of entry is a step completed at the beginning of an inquiry and over with once the researcher is ensconced in the field. This is not the way it is for narrative inquirers, as the example with Jean and Stephanie makes clear. In today's popular language, relationships need to be "worked at."

Part of the negotiation is explaining ourselves. We found ourselves continually explaining what we were trying to do. This was especially true for Michael as Susan continually asked if he was getting what he wanted and "was it okay." One soon discovers (if one pays close attention to these explainings) that one is never too clear on what one is up to. One of the important lessons to be learned for narrative inquirers from this is that they need to find many places, not only in the field, to explain to others what they are doing. We encourage narrative inquirers to establish response communities, ongoing places where they can give accounts of their developing work over time. As the explaining takes place, clarification and shaping of purpose occurs.

One of the methodological principles we were taught in quantitative analysis courses was to specify hypotheses to be tested in research. It does not work like that in narrative inquiry. The purposes, and what one is exploring and finds puzzling, change as the research progresses. This happens from day to day and week to week, and it happens over the long haul as narratives are retold, puzzles shift, and purposes change. Our NIE grant that took us to Bay Street School was framed in terms of the implementation of a race relations policy. However, as we worked at Bay Street School, our puzzle shifted as we became interested in the intersection of the board of education's race relations policy with its inner-city and language policies. An illustration of what happens over the long haul is our current project of returning to Bay Street School with a new set of school reform eyes and of thinking through different narratives than the ones embedded in our writing on the school.

What becomes apparent from the above examples is that not only does explaining ourselves to others help us get clear but also working with participants shapes what is interesting and possible under the field circumstances. Jean began her work with Stephanie thinking in terms of images as an expression of teachers' personal practical knowledge. She did not anticipate at the outset that she would sense the rhythms and cycles at work in Stephanie's life and teaching and that these would be important to thinking through dimensions of personal practical knowledge. As Jean and Stephanie worked together in Stephanie's classroom, Jean sensed the rhythms of life being lived out in the classroom. Being with Stephanie long enough to sense the rhythms, and being open to engaging in conversation with her as they mutually explained themselves, are part of what made the difference.

Over the course of the research, Stephanie developed a new sense of herself; she retold her story. In part, this had to do with the retold story of school that the reform-oriented principal, Phil, was working toward; and partly it had to do with the collaborative retelling of Stephanie's teaching found in Jean's narrative accounts, accounts that Stephanie read and commented on.

Negotiating Transitions

Perhaps the most dramatic transitions are the beginnings and endings of narrative inquiries. Above, we described negotiating the beginnings. But as we move from field to field texts to research texts, we need to negotiate many transitions in the midst of our narrative inquiries. JoAnn, currently in her Bay Street School work, is struggling over how many days to spend in the school and how to negotiate this with her participant as she makes the transition from field texts to research texts.

Though highly variable from person to person and place to place, narrative inquiries do end, at least in a formal sense. Reports are written, dissertations written, people move, funding stops. Negotiating this final transition is also part of what a narrative inquirer does in the field relationship. It is critical to the trust and integrity of the work that researchers do not simply walk away when "their time has come." Of course, when intimacy has been established, this kind of rupture is difficult to imagine; the researcher pulls away reluctantly.

It is not only field participants who run the risk of feelings of abandonment. During Phil's last year at Bay Street School, Michael worked with Phil and the staff to prepare a report on the school's Integrated Learning Centre and to produce three booklets for staff on school philosophy and computer use in the school. The materials were drafted over the summer and delivered to the school in the fall. Michael pretty much lost touch with the school that fall but does know that the booklets received little attention. This caused Michael some discomfort. But in retrospect, a new story of school was already being lived as a new principal came in. There was no working relationship between Michael and the new principal and no reason to think the booklets would be used. Indeed, they might well have run counter to new narrative threads.

Negotiating a Way to Be Useful

During the early going, when the motor is perhaps turning slowly, finding a place in the place is important. One can be "there" and feel like one does not quite belong. One of the hobbies of the critics of narrative inquiry often seems to be making the claim of co-optation of voice. The argument may run either that voices are heard, stolen, and published as the researcher's own or that the researcher's voice drowns out the participants' voices, so that when participants do appear to speak it is, after all, nothing more than the researcher's voice code. These are, of course, important matters to which narrative inquirers need to attend.

But the experience of being in the field sometimes feels quite the opposite. Sometimes—when the inquiry tends more to sensitive observation than to the intermingling of narratives and coparticipation—the narrative inquirer may feel silenced and voiceless on matters about which he or she feels passionate. A few years ago, Hedy Bach, a master's student, and Jean were engaged in a series of monthly conversations with eleven- and twelve-year-old girls. Jean met each girl for about forty-five to sixty minutes of conversation, just the two of them, each month. Frequently, one of the girls told a story of home or school that resonated with one of Jean's. Jean wanted to burst in with stories of her own experience of herself as a teacher, as a mother, as a girl. And yet she held back, partly because she felt her inquiry task was to faithfully record what her participants said. Although she realized in the writing of the research text that her voice could be present, in the field she felt silenced and voiceless.

There are variations on this theme of narrative inquirers' feeling silenced. Karen Whelan and Janice Huber are two teacher-researchers engaged in a narrative inquiry with a group of administrators. They frequently commented that at first they stayed silent, feeling they could not engage fully in the conversations because they understood so little of the administrators' narratives of experience. Now, as they write their research texts, they see the gradual mingling of voices, theirs and the participants, as a kind of border crossing, where there is an intermingling of narratives of experience.

Vicki Fenton joined Bay Street School in fall 1997 for her dissertation studies. Vicki's early field notes give a sense of her feeling that there is much to learn about the school, community, and classroom landscape. In one of her notes, she writes, "The school still feels like a maze to me and my mind is on information overload" (field notes, September 18, 1997). Everything, it seems to her, needs sorting out. And who is she in this maze? Following an introduction to another teacher by Vicki's participant, Vicki wrote in the margin of her field notes, "I am left with an uncomfortable feeling of being part of people's stories but not really writing any of it myself (field notes, September 23, 1997). Later, in a project meeting, Vicki reported to the group that she felt good on one of her visits to the school the past week because her participant asked her to work with a group of children. Vicki said that she had been feeling uncomfortable and useless, as she sat on a chair while her participant taught the classes. Michael recalls his experiences with Susan as being somewhat like Vicki's. He always felt, somehow, a bit of a visitor.

Getting a Feel for It

The sense of not belonging is related to Vicki's maze and information overload. In the extremes of hypothesis-testing inquiry, researchers lay out experimental plots, create their own inquiry fields, and manipulate variables according to the working hypotheses. The researcher is in charge. Various degrees of being in charge are at work in many forms of inquiry, quantitative and qualitative. But in narrative inquiry, the researcher tends to be at the other end of the continuum from the controlled-plot hypothesis tester. Here, the researcher enters a landscape and joins an ongoing professional life. One thing that narrative inquirers do is quickly learn that even if they are familiar with the kind of landscape—perhaps even members of that landscape, as teachers on sabbatical doing a thesis might be—there is a great deal of *taken-for-grantedness* at work in the moment-by-moment relationships and happenings on the landscape. Imagine for a moment that one was unfamiliar with schools. How strange the bells, the bursting forth at recess, the troops of students heading for the library or gym, the hanging around the principal's office, and the interrupting announcements that everyone stops for, must all seem. But for someone who knows the particular life in that school, none of this is surprising. These happenings are built into the very fabric of daily school life. The outsider is always asking, What is that? in reference to a name that might be a community center, a teacher, or a board policy for all the researcher knows, and Who is that? when a chuckle is elicited as one teacher talks to another and mentions a happening a year ago. There really is a sense, as Geertz said, of arriving too late because everything people notice and talk about has already happened and is in their doings and conversations. In Vicki's September 18 field notes, she wrote: "Feeling completely lost, I lose the names of the streets. I will have to ask her about that later. My mind is on information overload. There is so much to see and hear and to remember."

In order to join the narrative, to become part of the landscape, the researcher needs to be there long enough and to be a sensitive reader of and questioner of situations in an effort to grasp the huge number of events and stories, the many twisting and turning narrative threads that pulse through every moment and show up in what appears to the new and inexperienced eyes of the researcher as mysterious code. Intimacy, of the sort we feel toward Bay Street School, is partially tied to our having gained some measure of connection to the taken-for-grantedness in daily life. One might even say that intimacy for a narrative inquirer is being able to take with participants at least some of the same things for granted.

LIVING LIFE ON THE LANDSCAPE

Narrative has become so identified with stories, and stories have such a particular unique sense about them—often treated as things to be picked up, listened to, told, and generally rolled around as one might roll marbles around—that narrative inquiry has, for some, become associated with story recording and telling. One of the criticisms of narrative has taken this notion a step further and, in holding that story is the unit of analysis in narrative inquiry, argues that narrative inquiry is essentially a linguistic form of inquiry. Narrative inquirers, according to this critique, record stories. If I am an inquiry-oriented nursing educator, then I might listen for intern stories of life on the ward. Tape recorders are important in this version of narrative inquiry because the stories are the target; we need to get them right; and if linguistic analysis can tell us about story construction, then getting the words right by using the tape recorder is important.

But the stories of the narrative inquirers described above show that narrative inquiry is much more than "look for and hear story." Narrative inquiry in the field is a form of living, a way of life. Of course, there have been well-known, well-publicized narrative inquiries where researcher-driven interviews supported by tape recorders have been the method. These may be appropriate for their purpose but should not be mistaken for the whole of narrative inquiry. Most important, they should not be mistaken for what narrative inquirers do when they are in for the long haul and when they are working toward intimacy of relationship. Narrative inquiry, from this point of view, is one of trying to make sense of life as lived. To begin with, it is trying to figure out the taken-for-grantedness. And when that taken-for-grantedness begins also to be taken for granted by the researcher, then the researcher can begin to participate in and see things that worked in, for example, the hospital ward, the classroom, the organization.

One may observe a teacher in a classroom and count the number of student utterances and the number of teacher utterances or any sophisticated version of kinds of utterances one might be interested in. But the narrative inquirer hardly knows what to make of this without knowing the narrative threads at work. Those narrative threads are complex and difficult to disentangle.

Consider again the rhythms and cycles in Jean's work with Stephanie. Without an understanding of the way Stephanie experienced the entire year, with its seasons and holidays, one could make very little meaning out of the daily events. Of course, any number of for-the-moment and on-the-spot studies might well be done and published: Stephanie's use of scientific-biological terms in a study done in September and October, religious-symbolic language used in December and the month preceding Easter, and so forth. But it is the rhythm of the entire year that helped make meaning of Jean's work with Stephanie and allowed Jean to write of images of home and the curriculum as a vehicle for celebrating cultural difference among children. Narrative inquirers also know that the taken-for-grantedness is never exhausted and that mystery is always just behind the latest taken-for-granted sense making. Stephanie is partially who she is as a teacher because of where she is in her career, her religious life, and her private life. These and other narrative threads important to making meaning are always one step behind where one is now knowledgeably working.

What this means for the narrative inquirer is that stories, at least specific stories one can catch hold of like nuggets, though not unimportant, can play a relatively minor role as the narrative inquirer writes field notes about life in its broadest sense on the landscape. The narrative inquirer may note stories but more often records actions, doings, and happenings, all of which are narrative expressions. This is the stuff of narrative inquiry for the researcher in for the long haul and concerned with intimacy.

CHAPTER SIX

From Field to Field Texts
Being in a Place of Stories

T he phrase *experiencing the experience* is a reminder that for us narrative inquiry is aimed at understanding and *making meaning* of experience. This is the baseline "why" for social science inquiry. Why use narrative inquiry? Because narrative inquiry is a way, the best way we believe, to think about experience.

INTRODUCTION

This chapter presents some of the challenges that narrative inquirers encounter in the field. How does one deal with distance and closeness, for instance? For us, the careful composing of field texts helps meet many of the challenges. Field texts aid the inquirer to move back and forth between full involvement with participants and distance from them. We explore how field texts assist memory to fill in the richness, nuance, and intricacy of the lived stories and the landscape. We discuss the place of field texts in dealing with relativism and in assisting the researcher to view both the personal and the social. Finally, the chapter discusses the complexity (and depth) brought on by composing field texts in a three-dimensional inquiry space.

When narrative inquirers are in the field, they are never there as disembodied recorders of someone else's experience. They too are having an experience, the experience of the inquiry that entails the experience they set out to explore. If one is inquiring into life in a hospital ward, one is becoming part of life on the ward and is therefore becoming part of the experience being studied. The narrative researcher's experience is always a dual one, always the inquirer experiencing the experience and also being a part of the experience itself. In Chapter Four, we illustrated something of this in Michael's story with Ming Fang He and Long Him. As he engaged in his inquiry with Ming Fang, Michael was taken back in time to his childhood and recognized something of his own experiential history. The study of identity formation in Ming Fang's life was experienced by Michael as part of his own life. As we noted earlier, we are in the parade we presume to study.

FALLING IN LOVE, SLIPPING TO COOL OBSERVATION

There are tensions and dilemmas in studying the parade of which we are a part. Some worry that if inquirers do not become fully involved in the experience studied, they can never truly understand the lives explored. Others feel that by becoming fully involved, objectivity will be lost. To become fully involved implies that the researcher takes the same things for granted, adopts the same standpoints, and has the same practical intentions as participants. This would suggest that the researcher will simply play out the narrative threads at work—a conformist, conserving research agenda say some critics.

These tensions of how to experience the experience as a narrative inquirer are always present. Various solutions are offered, for example, the one by Leon Edel ([1959] 1984, p. 29), who writes that a biographer should never fall in love with his or her subject. He makes this prescription in an attempt to advocate for distance, for maintaining objectivity.

Inevitably, narrative inquirers experience this tension, for narrative inquiry is relational. They must become fully involved, must "fall in love" with their participants, yet they must also step back and see their own stories in the inquiry, the stories of the participants, as well as the larger landscape on which they all live.

This tension of moving back and forth between full involvement and distance is, as with relationships in everyday life, the responsibility of neither the inquirer alone nor the participant alone. Whatever distance happens to be at work at any one point in time is co-constructed by inquirer and participants. These distances are elastic, sometimes close, other times more distant. Jean's story of how Stephanie hesitated at letting Jean into her class in September after having agreed to this in June gives a sense of how relationships pulse over time, of how negotiable among parties relationships actually are, and of how distance is mutually constructed.

These tensions around relational distance are always present in narrative inquiry. How we deal with the tensions is of more importance than merely naming them. Take for example the fear of losing objectivity. Moving into close relationships with participants is necessary work in narrative inquiry. Why not fall in love with one's participant? The reason that we believe that this intimacy and the ensuing possible loss of objectivity (as some would call it) is not so serious after all is the presence of field texts and what attention to them entails. If a narrative inquirer stops writing field texts, if falling in love with one's participants or one's field leads one to forget to construct field texts or to feel as if the making of all kinds of field texts is devious, surveillant, or faithless to participants, then perhaps a narrative inquirer might be said to have crossed the line and become too involved, too much in love. Under these circumstances, Edel's caution might seem judicious. But so long as researchers are diligently, day by day, constructing field texts, they will be able to "slip in and out" of the experience being studied, slip in and out of intimacy. Being in the field allows intimacy. Composing and reading field texts allows one to slip out of intimacy for a time. This movement back and forth between falling in love and cool observation is possible through field texts.

Those who write on the practical importance of reflective practice, such as Donald Schön (1983), write about a way for someone both to lead a life and to reflect on it, thereby combining living with self-criticism and growth. It is like this with the experience of being in the field, the composing of field texts, and then the reflection on those field texts. The inquirer scribbles in a notebook, dictates into a Dictaphone, or types onto a screen a flood of descriptively oriented field experience observations. These are a mixture of you and me, the participant and researcher—notes on what you did, notes on what I did with you, notes on what was around us, notes on where we were, notes on feelings, notes on current events, notes on remembrances of past times.

These records, descriptively made to record events, happenings, attitudes, and feelings, freeze specific moments in the narrative inquiry space. One, or three, or ten years later, we might remember, with a touch of nostalgic glow, the camaraderie of a field trip with our participant teacher and students to a park to plant trees. These feelings about the field trip may be born out of narrative reconstructions driven by our having fallen in love with the field. Our field texts of that day, unchanged by the passing years, uninfluenced by intervening experiences and memories, may show a more complex, perhaps even different, picture of the day's events. The texts may show that some children misbehaved, one was hurt and threw the supervisors into a minor panic, and so on. Field notes, photographs, students' written work, teachers' planning notes are all field texts that help us step out into cool observation of events remembered within a loving glow.

REMEMBERING AN OUTLINE, SLIPPING INTO DETAIL

Memory, as Annie Dillard (1988) remarked, tends to smooth out the details, leaving a kind of schematic landscape outline. Field texts help fill in the richness, nuance, and complexity of the landscape, returning the reflecting researcher to a richer, more complex, and puzzling landscape than memory alone is likely to construct.

An episode in the science fiction television series *Star Trek: Voyager* dramatically makes this point about the place of field texts in narrative inquiry. The episode opens in an alien species museum, seven hundred years since the spaceship Voyager passed through the star system and seven hundred years into the future from the television viewers' perspective. A history lesson led by an alien scientist is under way, in which the subjugated role of his species to another is explained by Voyager's intervention seven hundred years earlier. Voyager's crew is portrayed as a team of brutal space warriors who, in return for the dominant species giving Voyager the coordinates of a wormhole that would return them to earth, commit genocide on the now-subjugated race, a descendant of whom conducts the history lesson.

Everything is familiar to the viewer. Physical appearances are perfect—the ship, its interior layout, its crew, their appearance, and their technology. The topography of the landscape is just right. Yet everything is wrong. No one acts in character: the captain, known to the viewing audience as a caring leader, is portrayed as brutally authoritarian;

crew members, known as concerned and cooperative, are vicious and competitive; alien civilizations, protected by a Voyager code of non-interference, are manipulated ruthlessly for Voyager ends; and the ship's holographic doctor, strictly governed by the Hippocratic oath, is diabolical in concocting biological weapons.

An artifact is found on the alien planet, which turns out to be, in part, a copy of the program for Voyager's holographic doctor. When the hologram is activated, the Voyager doctor is astounded at the historical lesson led by the alien scientist. Though seven hundred years of experience have intervened for the scientist and his defeated culture, the doctor, like a field text, is unchanged, his program deactivated for seven hundred years. He is, as are we viewers, dumbfounded by the historical reconstruction that is so right and yet so wrong to the doctor and the viewers with no memory of intervening experience. As the doctor recounts the seven-hundred-year-old events, including some characters, some physical surroundings, and some events, he portrays the Voyager crew "in character," yielding a different interpretation of the events that led to the current racist social division in the alien world.

In addition to the hologram program, the artifact contained specific data—field texts of the actual events seven hundred years ago—which, when decoded, demonstrate to the doctor and the viewing audience's satisfaction the accuracy of the doctor's rendition of events. The disbelieving alien scientist slowly comes to understand how a particular set of events, interpreted via a racial ideology crucial to the identity of his subjugated species, led to their entirely convincing but erroneous view of history.

The *Star Trek: Voyager* story helps make the point about the importance of using field texts to fill in broad historical outlines constructed through memory. Yet, there is a sense in the *Star Trek: Voyager* story that there is a truth, a correct version. In narrative inquiry, our field texts are always interpretive, always composed by an individual at a certain moment in time. As researchers, we may take a photograph as a field text, but that photograph is one telling, one shot, one image.

We vividly see this now as we read and reread field texts from research in Bay Street School some fifteen years ago. Michael constructed field notes of school events. Jean attended the same events and also made notes. We kept both, recognizing that the notes were not identical. Different details were noted, different words highlighted. Who we were as researchers, what our relationships were to participants, and how we lived within the three-dimensional space made a difference in the field notes we composed.

Now, as we reread these field notes, we are reminded again that there is no one true version of events that happened fifteen years ago, contrary to the implication in the *Star Trek: Voyager* story. We tell each other stories of past events and then "slip" back to field notes to fill in details. In our current research project, we are rereading these fifteen-year-old field notes, not in search of a truth or one true version or to correct each other's story of what happened then and how we got to where we are now, but rather to understand the story of the school from within a new research agenda in which we construct a narrative understanding or theory of school change and reform.

In small, often unnoticeable ways, all of us, researchers and others, are like the alien species. We retell our stories, remake the past. This is inevitable. Moreover, it is good. To do so is the essence of growth and, for Dewey, is an element in the criteria for judging the value of experience. Dewey's reconstruction of experience (for us the retelling and reliving of stories) is good in that it defines growth. Enhancing personal and social growth is one of the purposes of narrative inquiry. Yet, there is always the danger that in retelling our stories, we construct, as did the alien species, a less-than-adequate, even unhealthy, story and find ourselves in what Dewey called a *miseducative experience.* Honoring our field texts can help us escape these miseducative ends.

NARRATIVE TRUTH AND NARRATIVE RELATIVISM

The tension for narrative inquirers in adopting this value stance is the relativism implied, the notion that all have their own interpretation of events and each is equally valid. Taken to this point, narrative inquiry loses its narrative quality because the tension between experience and the meaning we make of it is lost. A disconnected sense of meaning replaces grounded narrative meaning. From a narrative inquiry point of view (as in the *Star Trek: Voyager* episode), there are, based on the evidence, the field texts, both better and poorer interpretations of that history.

The *Star Trek: Voyager* episode dramatized the relativism issue. The doctor wished to deactivate himself when he learned that public awareness of his version of history was creating violent societal disruptions. He thought that the alien species was best served by its version of history even though he "knew" that version to be wrong. His intention to deactivate himself implied a relativistic view of truth. In a Hollywood ending worthy of the 1950s, the alien scientist, now firmly committed to the doctor's version of history, convinces the doctor to stay the course. Both species rethink the origins of their inequitable relationship. Racial harmony is established, the society finds a new sense of purpose, and the doctor sets out to follow Voyager home. Though narrative inquirers, who are used to dealing with subtleties of meaning, doubtful narrative explanations, and ambiguous endings, might be offended at the Hollywood quality of this script, its moral message for narrative inquiry is clear and apt. Mere relativism will not do. Field texts need to be kept and continually referenced by narrative inquirers.

TURNING INWARD, WATCHING OUTWARD

Another tension as we move from field to field text is embedded in the task of composing field texts that are interpretive records of what we experience in the existential world even as we compose field texts of our inner experiences, feelings, doubts, uncertainties, reactions, remembered stories, and so on. In Chapter Four, we have one illustration of this, as Jean tells her story of her grade-four experience as a remembered story in a response to Karen's story recorded in a transcript of an inquiry group meeting.

In the following example, Vicki Fenton's (September 18, 1997) dual field texts (field notes that record the existential, outward events; journal notes that record her inner responses) are illustrative.

My mind is on information overload. There is so much to see and hear and try to remember. I imagine this is so because this type of community is different from my

We continue west along Smith Street. There are many small businesses on the opposite side of the street with signs in many languages. The businesses give way to homes, some with gardens, others with interesting, unique characteristics. There is a mural of cartoon characters painted on the fence and a 3–4 foot model of the Canadian National Tower atop one balcony or rooftop. These homes on the north side of the street, then, give way to Toronto Hospital.

own. I have the	On the south side of the street we pass an outdoor
feeling of it being	swimming pool and ice rink sandwiched between
quite dense and	the school to the east and the community centre
much to absorb.	on the west.

These September 18, 1997, field texts were made of a walking tour of Bay Street School's immediate neighborhood, a walking tour conducted by a school-community worker. Fenton's field notes are descriptions of place. But her column on the left is a kind of journal entry in which she makes observations on her inner experiences. Her journal comments on how she is experiencing the experience directly as "information overload" and gives a tentative idea of why this is happening to her as she contrasts the places around Bay Street School with the places she knows best. These journal-style reflections on her experience of the experience help maintain a sense of moving in and out of the experience. As we noted earlier, practitioners in any field maintain an educative sense of critique and growth about their experience by being reflective on it. This is what Fenton is doing in these dual field texts—her field notes turned outward and her journal reflections turned inward.

Both Jean's and Vicki Fenton's field texts show how field texts slide back and forth between records of the experience under study and records of oneself as researcher experiencing the experience. We wish to make a further point that occurs when one becomes more intimately involved with the experience studied; for example, in Jean's work with Stephanie and JoAnn Phillion's work with Pam. The point we wish to make is a version of what some, from a different inquiry point of view, have called the "problem of the influence of the observer on the observed." After having worked with a participant or in a classroom for the long haul, it can perhaps be seen more clearly that we are shaping the parade of events as we study the parade. As researchers, we watch ourselves shape the events under study, the classroom events, the relationships with children, and so forth. Annie Davies's field note of October 17, 1994, recorded in Chapter Seven, is illustrative. In the field note, Davies describes a classroom setting with two teachers, Tom and Liz. Part of the field notes describe Davies's involvement with the children in the classroom and their responses to Liz's instructions. As researcher, Davies is studying not only Liz and the children but also herself as she works in the classroom with them.

In summary, what we want to emphasize is that in the dual field texts that we create—the field notes of the existential conditions and the journal entries of the internal conditions—there is also the possibility of yet another dualism. As field notes of an existential situation are written, we may, in situations of intimacy, such as in Davies's study, find ourselves as part of that situation. Narrative inquirers who have established intimate relationships over the long haul study situations and come face-to-face with themselves.

We have emphasized the dual quality of the researcher's notes on themselves—their notes on themselves as part of the field experience being studied and their notes on themselves experiencing that experience, that is, reflecting upon it. It is also the case though that the researcher needs to be alert to a duality for participants. Just as a narrative inquirer has joined a field experience, so too have field participants joined an inquiry. Composing field texts means being alert to what one's participants do and say as part of their ongoing experience, and it means keeping records on how they are experiencing the experience of being in the inquiry. They too have feelings and thoughts about the inquiry.

We see something of this in Davies's inquiry with a group of team teachers. Davies makes field texts of participating teachers' feelings and thoughts on what they are coming to understand from their participation. At one point in a conversation with Davies, Tom, a member of the participating team teachers, says, "I think what I'm figuring out with this research is that there are many stories. The school is full of stories, and what you're capturing is still only going to be part of it. It'll be part of what Liz, Carol, Jane, and I have done together this year. It'll be reduced to 250 sheets of paper and some ink and still won't be the whole story" (conversation with Annie Davies, July 7, 1995) (Davies, 1996, p. 246).

Carol, another of the participating teachers in another conversation with Davies, says, "Talking to you actually helps me with my own growth because when I speak out loud, I'm actually giving this topic thought. I can see where I'd like to move more to the collaborative . . . and I can improve there" (conversation with Annie Davies, June 12, 1995) (Davies, 1996, p. 248).

These two examples make clear that the participants in the inquiry are influenced by their participation in the inquiry, by their experience of being in the research experience.

These reflections—this experience of the experience by the participants—turn up in research texts just as the researchers' experiencing of the experience turns up in research texts. We pick this up in Chapter Nine, where we are concerned with research texts and where we show that participants as well as researchers come to new understandings as part of what happens in a narrative inquiry.

THE AMBIGUITY OF WORKING IN A THREE-DIMENSIONAL INQUIRY SPACE

In Chapter Four, we introduced the idea of a three-dimensional narrative inquiry space. Even as we introduced this idea, we realized that the idea of such a space may put unnatural and constraining boundaries on inquiry. For us, doing narrative inquiry is a form of living. Living, in its most general sense, is unbounded. The structures, seen and unseen, that do constrain our lives when noticed can always be imagined to be otherwise, to be more open, to have alternative possibilities. This very notion is embedded in the idea of retelling stories and reliving lives. Our narrative inquiry intention is to capture as much as possible this openness of experience.

But there is a potential paradox if the inquiry space is viewed as being boxlike rather than infinitely open, as more current notions of space suggest. Our hope is that on balance the idea of a three-dimensional space will open up imaginative possibilities for inquirers, possibilities that might not as easily have been seen without the idea.

The inquiry space, and the ambiguity implied, remind us to be aware of where we and our participants are placed at any particular moment—temporally, spatially, and in terms of the personal and the social. Our awareness carries over to our field texts, where a text is always dated and placed and situated on a personal-social continuum. For example, Fenton's note above is primarily about place in the here and now as she sees it. Her journal note on the experience of the experience is a blend of the personal and the social. She records something highly personal and in the next sentence reflects on it from a very different point on the personal-social continuum. She thinks of her personal state of mind as connected to the contrast between the milieu she observes and the milieu she knows.

Living within the ambiguity of the three-dimensional inquiry space becomes most complex when we add in the temporal. One's experience becomes tinged with time, making it sometimes difficult to sort out where exactly one is located in time. The history of Bay Street School that slowly seeped into our inquirers' consciousness, something we described earlier, took us on a journey into the well-kept board of education archives. There we found letters, journals, news-paper clippings—a history in the making—of Bay Street School.

When one feels the temporal flow, the history, and grounds it in names and dates and events, one can never enter the place in quite the same way. Two friends entering a house together, one having been born and raised there and the other coming to the house for the first time, will experience exactly the same events of walking up the steps, opening the door, and going into the kitchen in entirely different ways. Their experience of the experience is not the same.

Bay Street School is not the same, is not experienced in the same way, once its temporal flow has infused the inquiry. Phillion, no doubt in part because of our history with Bay Street School, came in touch with the school's temporal flow comparatively early in her research. Here is a short passage she wrote as she began drafting her disserta-tion. Phillion read the diary of Bay Street School's first principal, ap-pointed in 1877. After reading the diary, she carefully wove the time periods together, moving from 1877 as the principal prepares to open the school to 1997 when she was a researcher in the school. She writes:

> Bay Street School was modern in every way. It had a heating system, running water, washrooms in the basement, cloakrooms, blackboards, and individual desks. As the principal thought of the heating system, his mind drifted from his planned speech for the school opening to supervising the delivery of fifty-six cords of wood. He had been told that the heating system was the best available, so he was perplexed that over the last few days the school had been so cold. They would have to use the little wood heaters to keep the classrooms warm after all. The students would be sent home if the classrooms were below 40 or 45 degrees. He did not want that to happen, particularly on the first day. More than that, he was worried about the sharp tongue of the head of the female department housed on the second floor. She would surely complain if her room was too cold. Little did he know how often he would have to face her wrath.
>
> It was over one hundred and twenty years later. In the winter the heaters sputtered and popped, then hissed loudly. My participant and I loved the sound as it was indicative that warmth would soon follow. Last year the heating system was replaced at great expense. The prin-cipal announced in a staff meeting that this would eliminate problems with cold temperatures. Immediately a vocal female member of the staff spoke about the heat in the summer. I wondered if the first prin-cipal was having a chuckle over this.

I also wondered if the washrooms were the same ones as the girls used so long ago! They appear to be ancient enough to be an artifact from 1877. [Phillion, 1999, pp. 81–82]

In the above comment, Phillion stays rooted in one place, Bay Street School, as she jumps back and forth temporally over a 120-year span. When she reads the archive records, she no doubt has the school, as she has experienced it in the here and now, in her mind. When she attends a present-day Bay Street School staff meeting and listens to the exchanges over the new heating system, she hears them with the first principal's archived journal records in her mind.

Field texts are like this. Narrative inquirers need to be sensitive to the temporal shifts that take place in all sorts of ways at any point in time. Phillion says that a conversation with her Caribbean-born teacher participant will often change place and time in a matter of seconds—a discussion of a child in the classroom, a reference to his pre-immigrant home, an interpretation offered from a Caribbean-education perspective, and a reference to teaching some years ago in another inner-city school.

Trying to keep all of this in mind may seem like a forbidding task for a narrative inquirer. The inquirer needs to be aware of the details of place, of the nuanced warps in time, and of the complex shifts between personal and social observations and their relations. And they need to do this for themselves and their participants and to be aware of the mutuality of the interaction. We might reverse a well-known motto here and say it is easier done than said. A sensitive inquirer will spontaneously, almost without forethought, live these shifts in place and time and along the personal and the social. Lively conversations for instance just happen. But capturing the nuances of this living in field texts is complex and filled with ambiguity.

For narrative inquirers, keeping the three-dimensional space in mind is helpful. For instance, if one has forgotten to note the details of place (easily and often done), thinking about the three-dimensional inquiry space helps one notice the "where." The complexity brought on by composing field texts in this three-dimensional space is illustrated as we work through Davies's field texts in Chapter Seven.

Composing Field Texts

W e focused on being in the field in both Chapters Five and Six. We were concerned with our experience of entering the field in Chapter Five and with our experience of being in the field in Chapter Six. In Chapter Seven, our purpose is to describe the kinds of records, normally called data, that for us are better thought of as field texts. We call them field texts because they are created, neither found nor discovered, by participants and researchers in order to represent aspects of field experience.

INTRODUCTION

In this chapter, we explore ways in which our researcher relationship to ongoing participant stories—the stories being lived and told— shapes the nature of field texts as well as the kinds of field texts that may be composed. As we do this, we are mindful of working within the three-dimensional narrative inquiry space.

To illustrate the various kinds of field texts the narrative inquirer can use, we look at a variety of field texts employed and interwoven by one researcher. We explore the use of teacher stories; autobiographical writing; journal writing; field notes; letters; conversation; research interviews; family stories; documents; photographs, memory boxes, and other personal-family-social artifacts; and life experience— all of which can make valuable field texts. We conclude the chapter with a discussion of the importance of careful positioning of field texts to the final integrity of the work.

COMPOSING FIELD TEXTS IS AN INTERPRETIVE PROCESS

Because field texts are our way of talking about what passes for data in narrative inquiry and because data tend to carry with them the idea of objective representation of research experience, it is important to note how imbued field texts are with interpretation. As we move into our inquiry fields, we are already telling ourselves and others stories of our research purposes. Our special interest in the situation is (as we showed in our sections on negotiation in Chapter Five) repeatedly and continually stated and negotiated with participants. Therefore, the way we enter the inquiry field influences what we attend to. We deliberately select some aspects that turn up in field texts. Other aspects, less consciously and deliberately selected, also show up in field texts. To understand what narrative inquirers do as they write field texts, it is important to be aware not only that selectivity takes place but also that foregrounding one or another aspect may make other aspects less visible or even invisible. Field texts, in an important sense, also say much about what is not said and not noticed.

This is perhaps seen most easily in the keeping of field notes. For example, when a narrative inquirer moves into a bustling classroom, school, hospital, or other institution, there is much going on. Many varied aspects of place, persons, things, events, and histories, small and large, are in evidence. A researcher is, even with the best of intentions of getting everything down, unable to do so. We see something similar as one engages in document collection and selectively chooses which documents to collect. Sometimes, for example, we might selectively choose only policy documents and choose not to collect teaching documents.

Although we sometimes choose with conscious awareness, at other times we choose without being aware that we are making choices. At Bay Street School, we asked school secretaries to set up a school mailbox for us and to put all materials that went into regular staff mailboxes into our researchers' mailbox. We made that choice consciously. Later, we realized that some documents were circulated in other ways than by being put in mailboxes. After the fact, we learned that our document collection process was a selective one.

This general point applies to the whole range of field texts one might create. Consider a structured interview, perhaps the least common form of interview used in narrative inquiry because of its nonrelational quality. As researchers, we select the moment to turn the tape on, we select the questions to be asked, and so on. But more important to our point that all field texts are inevitably interpretive texts, we pick up on some participant responses by responding in certain ways—for example, by smiling, by asking a question that seems related at the moment, or by asking for clarification. Because of our body responses, the participant in the interview may respond with more detail or may change the response. Equally, as we engage in the interview, there is only a certain amount of time. When a researcher encourages response and discussion on one point, still other points are left uncovered or less well developed. The field text is shaped by the selective interest or disinterest of researcher or participant (or both). What may appear as an objective tape recording of a structured interview is already an interpretive and contextualized text: it is interpretive because it is shaped by the interpretive processes of researcher and participant and their relationship, and it is contextualized because of the particular circumstances of the interview's origins and setting.

WRITING FIELD TEXTS EXPRESSES
THE RELATIONSHIP OF RESEARCHER
TO PARTICIPANT

Central to the creation of field texts is the relationship of researcher to participant. Although we noted above that all field texts are selective reconstructions of field experience and thereby embody an interpretive process, we want to add to this the importance of the relationship. Researcher relationships to ongoing participant stories shape the nature of field texts and establish the epistemological status of them. We assume that a relationship embeds meaning in the field text and imposes form on the research text ultimately developed. What is told, as well as the meaning of what is told, is shaped by the relationship. The field texts created may be more or less collaboratively constructed, may be more or less interpretive, and may be more or less researcher influenced. It depends. Researchers need to be attentive to this and need to write journal entries that portray the relational circumstances of the situation represented in the field text.

FIELD TEXTS IN A THREE-DIMENSIONAL INQUIRY SPACE

Before turning to a detailed presentation of field texts in one study, we want to remind readers of the complexity of the task and of the kinds of things they need to be aware of as they experience the experience and compose their field texts. In Chapter Six, we wrote about field texts as necessary in order to allow inquirers to move between intimacy with field participants and a reflective stance: field texts need to be routinely and rigorously kept. We also wrote about field texts as necessary to fill in the spaces created by memory accounts of events: field texts need to be richly detailed. We addressed the issue of narrative relativism by illustrating the value stance of field texts in the retelling of stories and the possibility that retelling might lead to change: field texts allow for growth and change rather than fixing relations between fact and idea. We made the point that a researcher needs to be attentive to composing field texts on the existential conditions as well as on the individual's internal responses: field notes and other field texts need to be complemented by still other field texts, such as journal entries on research responses. We addressed the issue of the ambiguity of working within an open and boundless three-dimensional inquiry space: in making field texts, researchers need to be aware of where they and their participants are placed at any particular moment—temporally, spatially, and in terms of the personal and the social.

As we turned to the presentation of field texts, we realized that presenting a list of kinds of field texts creates the impression that texts are isolated, clearly definable records constructed in the course of an inquiry. In order to present field texts in a way more consistent with what narrative inquirers do, we give a sense of the range and interplay of field texts within one complete study. Annie Davies's doctoral dissertation research, "Team Teaching Relationships" (1996), is the study used.

INTERWOVEN FIELD TEXTS

We begin with a brief overview of Davies's work and then move through her inquiry, giving examples of various field texts she composed. As we do this, we show how they interweave, one with another.

Davies is an experienced elementary school teacher in western Canada who has taught for a number of years, sometimes working alone with children in a classroom and sometimes working with one or more team partners. As she began her doctoral research, it was a puzzle about how teachers negotiated team teaching relationships that fascinated her. Questions about how the storied professional knowledge landscape interconnected with individual teachers' narratives of experience intrigued her. She inquired into the experiences of teachers who found themselves working together because of a board of education mandate. How do they share space that was, until the mandate—according to professional knowledge landscape research—a safe space for living secret stories of teaching? What happens when secret classroom teaching stories become public on the out-of-classroom place on the landscape?

She began her narrative inquiry with an autobiographically oriented study of her own schooling experiences in Britain and followed them forward to her early teaching experiences in Canada, where at first she taught as a subject matter specialist in physical education. Some years later, she began work in team teaching situations. In this first phase of her study, she undertook a narrative inquiry into her own narratives of experience.

Davies linked her study of her narrative beginnings to her account of that first team teaching experience. As she completed her account, she realized that she wanted to hear the stories of her team partners from some twelve years earlier. How did they tell their stories of that team teaching experience? This began a second phase of her narrative inquiry. She sought out former team teaching partners and asked each of them, through memory accounts, to tell their stories of that time together. As Davies wove these multiple accounts together into a richly textured account of narratives told through memory relationships, she realized she wanted to further engage with a group of teachers who were currently team teaching.

Davies felt that the professional knowledge landscape was changing, and she wanted both to study the changing landscape in which team teaching was embedded and to join with a group of team teachers as a phase in her narrative inquiry. She wanted, in this third phase of the inquiry, to engage in ongoing relationships with four team teachers and to study their classroom practice. Further, she wanted to engage with each teacher in order to construct narrative accounts that linked their pasts to their current practices to their possible futures. Of course, these phases are not a map for others to follow. Each study has its own rhythms and sequences, and each narrative inquirer needs to work them out for her or his own inquiry.

Davies worked within the three-dimensional narrative inquiry space. There are layers of complexity within each of the dimensions. Temporally, she begins with her past, her childhood experiences of growing up in Britain. She slides forward to her early team teaching experiences in Canada and then moves to a present-day participant observation study with a group of team teachers.

There is a temporal sweep in the overall three-phase structure of the study—childhood, first team teaching experiences, and current participant observation research. Furthermore, within each phase she moves backward and forward temporally for each participant as that individual looks at his or her childhood experiences and moves forward to present-day experiences. In phase one, her autobiography has a temporal sweep. In phase two, her inquiry with participants in the first team teaching experience is a study of memory relationships over time. In phase three, her participant observation study is done over a three-year period and, furthermore, engages participants in autobiographically reflective discussions that take them, individually, across time.

She pays attention to place. She moves from one country to another and to different schools in a board of education district. At the same time as she attends to time and place, she pays attention to the personal-social dimension. She studies individual teachers' narratives of experience and situates the personal in a shifting professional knowledge landscape in education. In the following, we present different kinds of field texts—teacher stories, autobiographical writing, research journals, oral histories, family stories, field notes, conversations, researcher letters to participants, participant letters, stories of families, and documents. These are the field texts used by Davies. Following presentation of her field texts, we present additional kinds of field texts from other studies.

TEACHER STORIES AS FIELD TEXT

Situating herself in time and place in the first month of her doctoral studies in Edmonton, Davies slips quickly, temporally, backward in time to remembered stories of growing up in Britain. Writing these stories served in part to situate her in the midst of stories that she is living and telling as she begins the inquiry. Davies wrote several stories of herself in the form of field texts about her experiences as a child. Her first story was entitled *A New School* (1996, pp. 1–3):

> home from work . . .
> his back to the fireplace
> my father stands . . . serious
> I'm not asked to recite a nursery rhyme
> today he seems not to notice me —
> my mother brings tea
> they talk —
> his spoon stirring in sugar
>
> "Bill's son can read
> he's just six
> he can do things Robert can't
> Robert is nearly seven —
> he's a long way behind —
> we must find a better school"
>
> already my father knows of a school —
> I hear new words
> fees, nuns . . .
> what are those?
>
> and a journey by train
> for both of us
>
> "Oh good," I think to myself
> I love trains
>
> I have my last turn
> on the nursery school rocking-horse —
> I won't miss him

his tail is half gone
I say goodbye . . .
chattering about shopping
for my uniform
even though I don't know
what a uniform might be

in grey blazers
with royal blue trim
Robert and I stand proudly —
mom gives our shoes
one last shine with a duster
she adjusts my hair ribbon
checks for clean faces . . .
my father says,
"Look after your sister"
Robert nods

we cross the canal bridge
to get to the station . . .
and even though I'm five
Robert holds my hand
giving a little tug
when I slow down
I won't look for barges on school days —
mom gives him a smile of approval
we both smile back
loving our adventure

at the station
we buy tickets
Liverpool to Blundellsands — return
the ticket collector punches them . . .
on the platform we see big girls
in the very same blazer
mom chats with them
I see them nodding
they will look after us
on the train ride home
then mom will meet us

our train stops
at many stations
mom says their names
we repeat them . . .
when the big girls stand up
we know our stop
"This won't be hard," mom says
and the big girls say,
"Don't worry, we'll take care of them"

more walking
we see a sign
mom reads aloud
"Ursuline Convent School"
it seems like the castle
in my fairy tale book
special yet mysterious
I know I will like my school

Written in poetic form, this story is one of three composed by
Davies early in her inquiry. As Davies tries to find her place within the
inquiry space, she places herself within her first experiences of school.
Beginning as a student again in her doctoral work sends her back to
her childhood learning experiences in another place, as she begins the
struggle of crafting her inquiry.

One of the first things that narrative inquirers do is what we see
Davies doing; that is, positioning herself "in the midst." Writing stories of one's own experience is one way to do this. As she writes this
first storied poem, it reminds her of other beginnings in school, and
her second story is about beginning full-time teaching. The significance of these stories of beginnings relates to Davies's interest in teachers' experiences of team teaching and is instrumental to the way she
eventually frames her research puzzle. For Davies, the link is that her
first full-time teaching job on returning to classroom teaching after
years of parenting and part-time work was in a team teaching situation. The bulk of Davies's subsequent field texts, then, are in and
around her own and other teachers' experiences of team teaching.

Of course, stories are not necessarily presented in poetic form. In
fact, they are more likely to appear as prose. As we read ahead to other
field texts, many stories are embedded, either in sketched-out form or

as full-blown stories. In Davies's work, they appear in autobiographical writing, in oral history interviews, in daily field notes based on classroom participation, and in conversations.

AUTOBIOGRAPHICAL WRITING AS FIELD TEXT

These stories are sometimes autobiographical, as Davies's storied poem is. The storied poem is simultaneously an example of a story as field text and of autobiographical writing as field text. For Davies, autobiographical writing in the form of her storied poem gets her going in the midst.

Autobiographical writing is a way to write about the whole context of a life. In Davies's storied poem, her autobiographical writing gives one rendition of her early life and sets the context for her telling of her later school life. The story is of a very small slice of time and of a very particular event, a trip one morning to school. But it is more than an isolated, decontextualized note, as a journal entry might be. We learn about her family life, something about her religious life, about parental attitudes toward education, something of the community in which the family lives, something of the class system in Britain at the time, and so forth. The poem is full of autobiographical details that illuminate the context of her life.

Molloy (1991) notes that autobiography is always a "re-presentation, that is, a retelling, because the life to which it supposedly refers is already a kind of narrative construct. Life is always, necessarily, a tale" (p. 5). As narrative inquirers, we recognize that any piece of autobiographical writing is "a particular reconstruction of an individual's narrative, and there could be other reconstructions" (Connelly and Clandinin, 1988, p. 39).

There can always be a rich array of possible field texts as we write autobiographically. As we look across the range of possible kinds of field texts, we see that many of them have an autobiographical quality.

There is a fine line between autobiographical writing used as field texts and autobiographical writing used as research texts. Autobiography and memoir are recognized forms of research texts. We return to them in our chapter on research texts, Chapter Nine. For now, however, we want only to point out that autobiographical writing can be used in different ways. Inquirers need to be thoughtful of its uses within their inquiry. In this chapter, we discuss Davies's autobiographical field texts, which were used to write a research text that was not primarily autobiographical. Davies's dissertation—her research text—is not an autobiography. The same autobiographical field texts could, of course, have been used by Davies to write an autobiographical research text.

JOURNAL WRITING AS FIELD TEXT

Often, autobiographical writing of the sort with which Davies begins is closely related to journal writing. Davies wrote journals for many years, most frequently connected with her work as a teacher researcher. She wrote a journal that documented her classroom practice on a regular basis. For a time, she was part of a teacher research group in which members of the group shared their journals with an understanding that they would respond in one another's journals. In Davies's case, we imagine that the journals written for herself as a reflection on her practice were not intended as a research field text. However, we imagine there might have been a shift in her thinking about her journal as a kind of field text as she joined the teacher-research group. We imagine that these journals might have taken on a different tone, and perhaps she might have recorded different things in different ways.

This reminds us of the extent to which field texts are always interpretive, and it also raises the question of audience for field texts. Mallon (1984) makes a wonderful comment in which he reflects on the influence of self as audience on the kind of journal kept, as he argues that a personal journal always has a sense of audience. He writes: "I can recall a few times when during the day I've decided not to do something (usually something small and mean) because I realized that if I did it I would have to mention it to the diary that night. This may be the result of a Catholic upbringing—during which confession was a deterrent to sin, not just an antidote—or it may just be an excuse I occasionally give to myself to be better than I am" (p. xiv).

Contrary to the sense that research data are audience free, in narrative inquiry, audience is always a presence and interpretively shapes the field texts constructed.

Journals are a powerful way for individuals to give accounts of their experience. As May Sarton (1982) notes, "Journals are a way of finding out where I really am. . . . They have to do with encounters with people who come here, who talk to me, or friends whom I see, or the garden. They sort of make me feel that the fabric of my life has a meaning" (p. 25).

Journals are a method of creating field texts. Because, for Davies, they were such a part of her teacher-researcher life, she turned to them as a way of creating field texts in her research. In the following research journal entry, Davies writes about her first day at her research site in the third phase of her work:

> . . . my need for a setting where I feel comfortable, my need to be in relationship with the teachers in my study and to be with teachers who believe in team teaching. I said that I wanted to be at Riverview School and I knew that Tom and Liz were teaming. I wondered if they would be interested in a research relationship.
>
> I visited the school on Monday October 3. I'd gone there at recess to ask the staff to participate in a survey for one of my university classes. I received a great welcome and was delighted. Tom was eager to hear how things were going for me and I thought I would just casually explore the possibility of working with him and with Liz. He was very excited at the prospect and straight away insisted that I come to the classroom at 10:45—the time when he would begin his day with Liz. He told me how thrilled he was with his teaching and with the team teaching experience. . . .
>
> Once inside the classroom . . . I felt an immediate sense of being at home. . . . Tom and Liz seemed genuinely pleased to have me there. . . . Their teaching reminded me of a conversation between friends. They smiled a lot as they interacted with each other and with the children. They were having fun in a relaxed learning environment. [journal entry, October 16, 1994] [1996, pp. 58–60]

Davies's research journal is an interesting blend of detailed field notes on her visit to the school interwoven with journal reflections on how she felt about the experience. She records the existential conditions of what she is doing, situating them in a place, at a certain time, with detail of particular events noted. She then turns inward to give an account of her feelings, of being delighted, and of metaphorically "being at home." In this research journal entry, we see her weaving together what Vicki Fenton in Chapter Six separated into a dual field text, with field notes that recorded the existential outward events and journal notes that recorded her inner responses.

Journals may, and often do, take on an intimately reflective puzzling quality, perhaps less a way to give accounts of experience, as noted for Sarton, and more a way to puzzle out experience. JoAnn

Phillion, an inveterate journal writer throughout her fieldwork, refers to her journals as "spaces for struggle." Davies too wrote many journals with this puzzling-out quality. In Davies's case, these journals were not, for the most part, worked into her research texts. They were nonetheless important field text resources for her ongoing inquiry and for the construction of her research texts.

The novice narrative inquirer might find the making of journal entries a time-consuming distraction with a feeling that they are not adding up to much. We have heeded Emily Carr's admonition when she writes that her journals seem to be "made up of scraps of nothing" (1966, p. v). She likens her journal entries to the small English candies called Hundreds and Thousands, which are "so small that separately they are not worth eating" (p. v). However, she writes, "It was these tiny things that, collectively, taught me how to live. Too insignificant to have been considered individually, but like the Hundreds and Thousands lapped up and sticking to our moist tongues, the little scraps and nothingnesses of my life have made a definite pattern" (p. v). Researchers such as Davies have found these patterns emerging as they write their research texts. What may have appeared to be insignificant nothingnesses at the time they were composed as field texts may take on a pattern as they are interwoven with other field texts in the construction of research texts.

FIELD NOTES AS FIELD TEXT

In most of our narrative inquiry work, field notes are the most important way we have of recording the ongoing bits of nothingnesses that fill our days. These ongoing, daily notes, full of the details and moments of our inquiry lives in the field, are the text out of which we can tell stories of our story of experience. In Chapter Six, we wrote about field notes as one of the most important kinds of field texts that allow us both to fall in love with our field and to slip into cool observation, as well as to provide the detail that fills in our memory outline. Field notes combined with journals written of our field experience provide a reflective balance.

In the following illustration of a field note as field text, we excerpt a piece from one of Davies's field notes, as she works in the first-grade classroom of Tom and Liz, two participating team teachers:

Tom reviews what they've done so far using one child's notebook. With Jessica's book Tom shows the children that she is going page by page "always on the next page."

Liz and Tom's voice trade off in easy conversation as the science concept is explained. Tom writes a title on the board, *Fall Changes to Winter.* He relates this to the heavy snowfall of that weekend. Liz takes over. She creates a vocabulary list which the class reads: frost, snow, slush, water, air is cold, trees have no leaves. While Liz works on vocabulary, Tom goes to talk to Cameron one on one. The work he needs to do with Cameron does not disrupt the classroom. Cameron is being helped towards more appropriate behavior.

Returning to the front of the group, Tom explains how to record personal observations on a double page of their science notebook.

I roam around chatting with kids, helping them to make a start and trying to learn names. Erik is drawing a tree. He also shows underground water going to its roots. Erik draws from his knowing [*sic*] as Liz suggests. Danny tells me, "That's what they do to grow." Standing up, he adds "I'm going to copy my tree from outside." I'm impressed that he has picked up on Liz's comment that "scientists look." Taking his book and pencil with him, Danny walks to the window. [field note, October 17, 1994] [1996, pp. 100–101]

Although field notes may be written by researchers or by participants, these notes were made by Davies as researcher. She notes the activities of both Tom and Liz and the children they interact with and of herself and the children she interacts with. Field notes may be written in more or less detail with more or less interpretive content. In these field notes, Davies is trying to record as much detail as she can even as she participates in the classroom.

Researchers need to be conscious of the kinds of field notes created, particularly about the relationships they have as researchers with participants. In Chapter Six, we emphasized the role of field notes in influencing the kind of relationship established between researcher and participant, but it is also the case that the relationship established influences the kinds of field notes made. As emphasized earlier, it makes a great deal of difference if we distance ourselves from events in order to record notes or if we actively participate in events as a partner. Similarly, it makes a difference as we create field notes if we see ourselves as recorders of events "over there" or if we see ourselves as characters in the events. In this case, Davies clearly sees herself as participating in events as a partner and as a character in the events.

In our opinion, researchers are often more reluctant than necessary to use field notes. They worry that field notes will be insufficient to capture field experience adequately. When this happens, tape recorders and videotape tend to be overused, with severe transcription penalties later as field notes are made on the basis of the transcripts. In any event, it is the fear that somehow experience will be lost that drives researchers to try to record or tape all of experience. What we fail to acknowledge clearly enough is that all field texts are constructed representations of experience.

Photographs taken by participants or researchers are, in our view, a kind of field note. In narrative inquiry, researchers are now often turning to the use of photographs. For example, in a study with young girls, Jean gave the girls cameras and asked them to record, using photographs, aspects of their experiences in and out of school. These photographs were developed and were the topic of research conversations in which the girls talked about what they were trying to capture in the photographs. DeCarion (1998) and Bach (1997) both made extensive use of photographs, taken by themselves and taken by their participants, as a kind of field note.

LETTERS AS FIELD TEXT

Letters are written to someone else with the expectation of a response. In letters, we try to give an account of ourselves, make meaning of our experiences, and attempt to establish and maintain relationships among ourselves, our experience, and the experience of others. In narrative inquiry, letters as field texts may be used among participants, among research collaborators, or among researchers and participants. In each case, one of the merits of letters is the equality established, the give-and-take of conversation. In the following letter as field text, Davies (letter, November 12, 1994) (1996, p. 112) writes a weekly letter to Tom and Liz, her two participating teachers:

Dear Tom and Liz,
    As I watched Aaron I wished his mom could see her son's behavior in relation to his peers. School is such a different experience for a young child. I thought too, of the many conversations I've had with teachers about "on the edge behavior"—the way youngsters position

themselves in a group. I noticed Jenny, always so close—never on the edge. Why do some children write an on the edge script for themselves? Aaron didn't have a partner for the paired art activity. This wasn't a surprise. When frustrated he did silly things, like dumping his tub out to look for scissors. When successful, with support, he was capable of a perfect job. With an adult all to himself he was fine. As one of 23 or 48 he experiences difficulty and perhaps this is the part the mom can't know. With his mom beside him at the kitchen table, Aaron's work would be terrific. I'll keep an eye out for him now. By the way Liz, I thought your note home to his mom . . . gave him ownership of the conversation he needs to have. . . . You made a space for conversation that isn't the parent and teacher solving Aaron's problem, in his absence.

See you next week,
Annie

The most notable quality of the letter is its conversational, personal tone. This differed dramatically from Davies's field notes, illustrated earlier. There was little sense of audience and no evident expectation of response. The notes had a kind of "now this, then that, and then . . ." sense about them. In the letter, Davies attempts to look across the daily "nothingnesses" as she searches for patterns, which at this stage in her inquiry, are patterns of puzzles, things she wonders about. We see this in how she tries to figure out how two children, Aaron and Jenny, make sense of who they are in the classroom. She remarks on the difference that working one-on-one with Aaron makes compared with working as part of a large team teaching group. She gives feedback to Liz on what she sees Liz's letter to Aaron's mom doing in terms of their ongoing work.

Letters as field texts may also be authored by participants. In the following field text letter, Liz, as participant, writes to Davies (letter, November 5, 1994) (1996, p. 174) in order to make meaning of the team-planning meetings. This field text, authored by a participant to a researcher, becomes another kind of field text.

Dear Annie:
I find these meetings quite frustrating and am very grateful that Tom is there to ease the strain. I have learned over the years that it is important to say what you believe and listen to others give their

philosophy. I try hard to listen and be supportive of the teaching strategies of others and I will continue to work on this. That is one of my goals for this year. Carol has her own way and that is best for her but, because my way is different, I plan to stick up for what I believe in, when it is important, and not sweat the small stuff.

Love,
Liz

In the letter, Liz tries to make sense of her experience in writing. There is, again, the expectation of response and conversation.

Davies (1996, p. 176), commenting on her use of letters as field texts, writes:

The thing about letters is the fact that you can get in touch with your own thoughts and feelings, in your own time and space. It allows, I believe, for a deeper level of reflection on the part of the writers (in this case Liz). Liz felt compelled to write in response to my letter to her. Letter writing offers privacy of thought and clarity. Thinking back on this now I realize how much I know about letter writing from my experience of writing to my parents each week and from reading about other letter writers such as Virginia Woolf and the Bloomsbury Group. Letter writing for me isn't the choice of a methodology, as it were, from a list of possibilities, but it is a more complex response to the context that is particular to how I have been shaped and my desire to be in relationship with my participants. For me, letter writing has to fit . . . has to make sense. There is an authenticity to it. Letter writing honours the time and space of the other. Time for Liz was a premium. Letter writing could fit into her life on her terms. She felt it connected us.

CONVERSATION AS FIELD TEXT

As we noted above, letters as field text, illustrated by Davies's letter to Liz and Liz's letter to Davies, take on the quality of a conversation, albeit a written one. However, conversation is more often a way of composing a field text in face-to-face encounters between pairs or among groups of individuals. In the following excerpt from her research text, we see Davies (conversation, November 9, 1994) (1996, pp. 110–111) as researcher posing a question, and Liz and Tom engaging in conversation about their classroom practice:

I first heard about Aaron, a child in Liz's responsibility group, one lunch hour. Liz was late joining Tom and me for our taped lunch-time conversation in the classroom. She had received a call from an upset parent explaining that her son did not like school. When Liz finally joined us, I asked what she was planning to do about the situation:

LIZ: I'm going to talk to Aaron this afternoon, one on one, to find out why he's so unhappy about school and hates it. He doesn't want to come back.

TOM: Maybe something happened today on the way home, that we don't know about?

LIZ: Remember, yesterday, the lunch room supervisor took away his big bag. . . . I have a feeling that's his soft toy for sharing. He's had it since he was two.

TOM: He was hitting people with it. Does his mom know about his behavior?

LIZ: I told her—she knows.

TOM: That contributes to a child not liking school.

LIZ: We'll work it out. He's a very bright boy.

As Davies makes clear, this was a taped lunchtime conversation, which was later transcribed. Conversations and interviews are clearly two of the interactions during which a researcher may wish to use a tape recorder. It is possible, of course, to imagine a reconstruction of field notes or a reconstruction of daily events. But it would be difficult to capture the interpersonal-exchange dynamics. In addition, the tape recorder frees the researcher to participate in the conversation.

As is clear in the above segment, conversations are marked by equality among participants and by flexibility to allow participants to establish forms and topics appropriate to their group inquiry. We see this as Liz and Tom explore troubling questions around a child's behavior. Conversation entails listening. The listener's response may constitute a probe into experience that takes the representation of experience far beyond what is possible in an interview. Indeed, there is probing in conversation, in-depth probing, but it is done in a situation of mutual trust, listening, and caring for the experience described by the other.

RESEARCH INTERVIEW AS FIELD TEXT

A widely used method of creating field texts is interview (Mishler, 1986), which may be turned into written field texts through a variety of means. Whole tapes can be transcribed; field notes can be made as one listens and relistens to the tape recordings; or partial transcriptions can be made for segments of the taped interview, depending on the researcher's interests.

The way an interviewer acts, questions, and responds in an interview shapes the relationship and therefore the ways participants respond and give accounts of their experience. The conditions under which the interview takes place also shape the interview; for example, the place, the time of day, and the degree of formality established. Imagine, for example, the differences that might develop between an interview of a senior administrator conducted in a central downtown head office compared with the same person interviewed in her home. Further, imagine the differences if the senior administrator were interviewed in a school where a particular policy was applied or even in the home of a child coming under the jurisdiction of a policy.

The point about the way an interviewer acts, questions, and responds is graphically illustrated by Anderson and Jack's (1991) commentary on an interview study, in which they write, "Interviewers had either ignored these more subjective dimensions of women's lives or had accepted comments at face value when a pause, a word, or an expression might have invited the narrator to continue" (p. 12).

Research interviews normally have an inequality about them. The direction of the interview, along with its specific questions, are governed by the interviewer. However, researchers who establish intimate participatory relationships with participants find it difficult, if not impossible, to conduct such interviews with participants. Even when they begin with the intention of conducting an interview, the interview often turns into a form of conversation.

There is also the possibility that research interviews may be controlled by participants. They may ask to be interviewed on a particular topic, so they have an opportunity to give an account of themselves around that topic. However, whether the topic is chosen by participants or by researcher, the kinds of questions asked and the ways they are structured provide a frame within which participants shape their accounts of their experience. Minister (1991) says that "topic selection determined by interviewer questions, one person talking at a time, the narrator 'taking the floor' with referential language that keeps within the boundaries of selected topics" (p. 35) makes a difference to the content of field texts.

Oral history interviews are one of the most common interview formats in narrative inquiry. There are various strategies for obtaining an oral history, ranging from using a structured set of questions in which the researchers' intentions are uppermost (Thompson, 1978) to asking participants to tell their own stories in their own way (Anderson and Jack, 1991), in which case the participants' intentions are uppermost. In commenting on their own work, Anderson and Jack (1991) write that shifting attention "from information gathering where the focus is on the right questions, to interaction, where the focus is on the process" (p. 23), illustrates the dynamic potential of collaboratively constructed oral history field texts. In the latter case, we might imagine researcher and participant as engaging in oral history conversation, during which each brings forward oral history material.

Davies conducted oral history interviews with each of her participants over the course of her study. The following is an excerpt from a transcription made from the oral history interview with Tom. The oral history interviews conducted by Davies tended to be closer to using a structured set of questions than to asking participants to tell their own stories in their own way.

TOM: I was fourth of five. I barely remember my older sister living at home because she went off to nursing training when I was still in elementary school and my next sister went off to nursing school as well. So when I was really young we had . . . family camping trips and Christmas with the house full of people. We lived in a very small house in northwest Calgary.

ANNIE: So you were born in Calgary?

TOM: Yes in 1952 . . . my mother always said our house was too small and she hated it because she was a stay-at-home mom. . . . My brother . . . was three years older. . . . He, being the first boy, had to sort of break in the parents in terms of boy things. He always felt like I had it easy and I always felt like my little brother had it the easiest. I'm still quite close to my second sister. We talk to each other quite often on the phone . . . but I'm not close at all with my oldest sister and I think it's simply because she never lived at home . . . that I can remember. I remember our camping trips, when we had the whole family, but sometimes you don't know if you remember it or just know it from photographs. [1996, pp. 68–69]

Oral history interviews are autobiographical and contain stories, something clearly seen in this extract of a transcript made from Davies's and Tom's oral history interview.

Frequently, we involve participants in creating what we call *annals and chronicles* as a way to create a framework on which to construct their oral histories. Through the process of composing annals and chronicles, participants begin to recollect their experiences and to construct the outlines of a personal narrative. Annals and chronicles may be thought of as the rudimentary shaping and narrating of personal and social histories. We use the notion of annals and chronicles routinely in formal instructional settings where students are engaged in the construction of personal narrative histories. We think of *annals* as a list of dates of memories, events, stories, and the like. Students or participants construct time lines beginning, for example, at birth; at some distant, important period or date in the past history of the person's family; or at some more recent date, as a kind of beginning benchmark. We think of *chronicles* as the sequence of events in and around a particular topic or narrative thread of interest, for example, the teenage years or the traveling years. Sometimes, the time line— and the annals and chronicles constructed in and around the time line—are especially useful in constructing oral histories and in writing narratives. At other times or for other people, they may be less significant.

This sense that certain kinds of field texts may be more or less important to different people at different times tends to apply to all field texts described in this chapter. Sometimes, photographs are seen to be extremely important, sometimes field notes, sometimes annals, and so on. Ultimately, it is the interweaving of the field texts and the crafting of a meaningful research text that are the final arbiters of the relative significance attached to any particular kind of field text. These matters are discussed in more detail in Chapter Nine.

FAMILY STORIES AND STORIES OF FAMILIES AS FIELD TEXT

By family stories, we mean those stories that are handed down across generations about family members and family events. We often tell them when we are trying to give an account of ourselves and when people, frequently parents, are establishing values. We see something of this in how a music teacher established a legacy for Tom to live up to:

> I went off to a regular high school program and took Music 10 which was taught by the music director of my church. He knew my mom and dad intimately. He had both my sisters in music and so the first day of class when he's doing the roll call, he comes to my name and he looks up and says, "You're not?" And I said, "Yes I am." "Well I'm sure you'll be one of the best singers in here. . . ." There was this legacy that I had to live up to. He knew my family. [1996, p. 71]

We see this as a family story handed down that shapes Tom's identity.

An example of a story of family is seen in the oral history interview transcript in which Tom tells a story of his family in which his mother stories herself as a "stay-at-home mom," living in a house that was "too small."

The experience of family stories has existential and internal conditions, as Stone (1988) notes: "The family's first concern is itself, but its second realm of concern is its relation to the world. Family stories about the world are usually teaching stories, telling members still at home the ways of the world according to the experiences its elders have had. . . . Family stories seem to persist in importance even when people think of themselves individually, without regard to their familial roles. The particular human chain we're part of is central to our individual identity" (p. 7).

DOCUMENTS AS FIELD TEXT

There are a range of documents in any inquiry field. As researchers, we need to decide which of these documents are relevant to the narrative inquiry. As noted earlier in this chapter, we selectively decided to choose policy documents and not teaching documents as relevant to our Bay Street inquiry. With that frame in mind, we also reviewed and collected archival material filed in board of education offices and elsewhere.

Davies collected policy documents in the school related to team teaching, recent and archived board of education documents related to team teaching, and related contextual documents around the particular team of teachers with whom she worked. Some of the documents collected and analyzed by Davies were parent reports to the school council, media stories, historical board of education evaluation reports, school and board of education policy documents, board of education memoranda, and other communications. We have already noted that in our earlier work in Bay Street School, we set out to collect every document that teachers received by having the school secretaries create a mailbox for us but learned, after the fact, that teachers also received materials in other ways.

Perhaps one of the most important points for us to make is to note how easily, in our experience, it is to forget or ignore the existence and relevance of documents. The researcher who establishes intimate participant relations can become so focused on the relationship that the flow of documents that help contextualize the work goes unnoticed.

PHOTOGRAPHS, MEMORY BOXES, AND OTHER PERSONAL-FAMILY-SOCIAL ARTIFACTS AS FIELD TEXT

Many of us collect a variety of materials as we compose our lives. We do this as researchers and our participants do it. We may collect and save photographs of people remarkable to our lives in some way, of special events, of places. Each photograph marks a special memory in our time, a memory around which we construct stories. Other things find their way into something called *memory boxes.* These are collections of items that trigger memories of important times, people, and events. All of these items can be triggers to our memories, to recollecting the "little fragments that have no beginning and no end" (O'Brien, 1991, p. 39) and around which we tell and retell stories. It is these artifacts, collected in our lives, that provide a rich source of memories. Viewing these documents in the context of a narrative inquiry constitutes something that might be called an archaeology of memory and meaning.

Archives and museums have a similar role to play in narrative inquiry concerned with exploring social narratives. For example, during Canada's centennial year in 1967, communities across the country established small museums, in which artifacts from various community members were collected. These small museums became a kind of memory box, a collection that expressed the social narrative of their community. At the same time that these museums were created, many local communities formed writing committees that were devoted to collecting family histories and family stories that were later compiled into locally distributed books. These too are a rich source of field texts for the construction of social narratives.

LIFE EXPERIENCE AS A SOURCE OF FIELD TEXTS

Narrative inquiry has the compelling, sometimes confounding, quality of merging overall life experiences with specific research experience, realms of experience often separated in inquiry. It is almost a maxim in many forms of research to bound the phenomena and maintain distance from them. Narrative inquiry always has purpose, though purpose may shift, and always has focus, though focus may blur and move. Narrative inquiry boundaries expand and contract, and wherever they are at any point in time, they are permeable, not osmotically permeable with things tending to move only one way but interactively permeable. Researchers' personal, private, and professional lives flow across the boundaries into the research site; likewise, though often not with the same intensity, participants' lives flow the other way.

The consequence of this fluidity for making field texts is that there is a virtually endless list of life experiences that might be and frequently are turned into field texts of value to the inquiry. Even to speak in categories is to produce a very long list, for example, dance, theater, music, film, art, and literature. Students coming to narrative inquiry often report with a kind of happy amazement that they see story everywhere and that what they see connects to their narratives— riding the subway, listening to radio, watching television, shepherding a ball team. Our theory courses in narrative inquiry require students to write reading logs on course and other readings. One element of the log is to connect the reading to their developing inquiry. Phillion says that she writes field notes on film, an art form that happens to be one of her life interests.

Perhaps it is important to note that, as with the reading logs noted above, field texts on life experiences that are not directly connected with the research field and its inquiry need to be linked to the inquiry. One needs to puzzle through why it is that one felt the need to make a field text (a field note, a photograph, a poem, a story, and so forth). When making field texts following a film viewing, for example, the researcher needs to explore possible meanings of the experience for aspects of the inquiry; for instance, for the researcher, for participants, for children, or for the field as a whole.

WHAT IS IMPORTANT FOR INQUIRERS TO KNOW ABOUT FIELD TEXTS?

What becomes clear as we work our way through the different kinds of field texts used by Davies in her study is that they are not clearly differentiated one from another. Stories slip into autobiographical writing, autobiographical writing fades into journals, and so forth. Furthermore, as we worked our way through each section in Davies's work, we wanted to make clear that the possibilities for other kinds of field texts and for different nuances of what story or journal or field note meant were virtually endless.

As we puzzled over this disarray, we felt that our original plans for this chapter kept going astray. We began by thinking it important to provide a list of kinds of field texts along with examples of what was meant—journal, an example; metaphor, an example; family story, an example; and so forth. We realized the limitations of this because studies are wholes and stand on their own, and the field texts used in any particular study are interwoven throughout the whole study. We thought that by presenting a single, complex study such as Davies's, we would give a sense of this field text interweaving, and by adding other examples later, we would flesh out the field text typology with which we originally thought to begin.

However, as we worked through this plan, we realized the plan would not reveal the things that we thought most important in our teaching of how to be a narrative inquirer, in our advising of the many master's and doctoral students who write narrative inquiries, and in our own work ongoing for many years. We do not advise with a list of kinds of field texts in hand, nor do we set out to do our research with a predetermined notion of what kinds of field texts will be important. Rather, we encourage other narrative inquirers, and ourselves, to be open about the imaginative possibilities for composing field texts. It is true that in our own work we almost always set out to write field notes. But we also tape-record conversations and make many other kinds of field texts. Furthermore, as our students come to their work and ask, "Is it all right to keep a running record as a field note?" we say, "That will be fine, but you will also have to find some way of keeping a record of your inner responses." When students ask if they need to make a map of the classroom where they are working, we talk to them about an array of imaginative possibilities for describing place, such as taking photographs or using children's descriptions. When a student asks if a field note can be written as a story rather than in the form that we, Michael and Jean, use in our own work, we say, "Fine, provided the experiential detail is captured." When a student says that a character in a theater performance reminds her of the dilemmas facing her participant, we say, "Write about it."

As we think again about what is important for narrative inquirers to know about field texts, we return to our notion of working within the three-dimensional narrative inquiry space. In previous chapters, we discussed what narrative inquirers do in terms of their positioning within that space. Now, as we think about the field texts that we create as inquirers, it is similarly important to position our field texts within that space. Their position is not identical with ours. For example, suppose we take Davies's storied poem, *A New School*. In placing the poem along the temporal dimension, we see that to begin with, the poem refers to a time in her childhood. But when was the poem written? Was it something written by Davies as a child? Was it something written at the time she began her dissertation? Or was it something written by her at some other time in the inquiry process, or even, was it written by someone else, such as Davies's mother? If so, did her mother write it then or later? Positioning the poem along the dimension of place leads us to ask questions such as, Was it written in England or Canada? There are added layers of complexity as the field text, the poem, is positioned along the personal-social dimension. Was the poem a kind of fictional construction designed to convey a sentiment or feeling after viewing family photographs? Was it based on a memory, an image remembered? Did Davies construct it alone? Or was it written with someone else? Was it a fictional construction, so Davies could convey the social situation at the time of her childhood? Was it written at the time of her becoming aware of the class system in Britain? Or was it constructed to represent a kind of social-cultural difference between her experiences in Canada and those in Britain? As these questions make clear, the positioning of field texts within the three-dimensional space is complex as one locates field texts along the three dimensions.

It is important for narrative inquirers to address these questions of how their field texts are positioned, because their position has consequences for the epistemological status of the texts and, ultimately, of the research texts that draw from them. For example, as narrative inquirers construct accounts of their childhood, they often give them the status of an objective fact. However, paying attention to the complexity generated by thinking of them in terms of the three-dimensional space makes clear the extent to which the texts are contextual reconstructions of events. Without this careful positioning of our field texts, and our explicit acknowledgment of how they are positioned, the research texts ultimately constructed from them are endlessly open to unanswerable questions and criticisms about knowledge claims being made and meanings generated.

CHAPTER EIGHT

From Field Texts to Research Texts

Making Meaning of Experience

Them ove from field texts to research texts is another difficult and complex transition. Beginning narrative inquirers tell us that this is one of the hardest transitions they make. In our own inquiries, we too know the difficulties as we work through the many aspects and dimensions in making this transition.

INTRODUCTION

As inquirers come to this difficult transition (a transition in the midst of their inquiries), matters that were thought through early in the inquiry, and that perhaps have lain dormant as inquirers have been working in the field and composing field texts, reemerge. The topics of justification, phenomena, method, analysis-interpretation, the place of theoretical literature, positioning, and the kind of text intended and composed rise again to the foreground of the inquiry, all of which we examine in this chapter. In order to bring these topics forward for ourselves and for those with whom we work, we keep before us a set of these topics that need to be considered and woven into the development of research texts. The topics come in and out of focus as our work progresses. Each topic has its place as we move from field to field texts to research texts and each, though perhaps buried and out of sight during fieldwork, comes strongly to the fore as we imagine our research texts taking their place in the world.

We could have discussed these topics earlier in the book, perhaps in Chapter Four, where we first ask the question, What do narrative inquirers do? We chose, however, to situate our discussion here because we were concerned that a reader not see these topics as a series of questions and issues to be raised, worked through, and answered once and for all. We wanted to take readers through some of our inquiries to give a sense that narrative inquiry is a process of learning to think narratively, to attend to lives as lived narratively, and to position inquiries within a metaphorical three-dimensional space.

These topics are ones that guide our inquiries from beginning to end and beyond as we present our work in public research texts. In this chapter, we work through these topics as we consider how they are lived out in the transition from field texts to research texts. But readers will want to imagine themselves addressing these topics as they frame research proposals, as they negotiate their work in the field, as they compose multiple field texts, and as they prepare public research texts, whether in the form of lectures, papers, books, or dissertations.

WHAT DO NARRATIVE INQUIRERS DO?

We first raised this question in Chapter Four. In this chapter, we focus the question to ask, What do narrative inquirers do as we make a transition from field texts to research texts? What do we do as we begin to think about writing up our work, presenting at conferences, writing for journals, presenting in classes, and writing theses and books? As we make this transition, we ask questions of meaning, social significance, and purpose.

These questions are important as the inquiry begins; for example, as proposals are developed, entrance to the field is negotiated, and working relationships with participants are developed. As our work progresses and as we fall in love with our participants, the field, and then our field texts, we may tend to lose sight of questions of significance, meaning, and purpose. But as we make the transition from field texts to research texts, questions (such as Who cares? and So what?) reemerge. How do we know that our inquiry interest is anything more than personal or anything more than trivial? How do we know that anyone will be interested? Will our inquiry make a difference?

In some general sense, the questions of meaning, significance, and purpose are questions of who, why, what, how, context, and form. For whom will we write? Who are the characters in the study? Why are we writing? What are we trying to convey? What personal, practical, and theoretical contexts give meaning to the inquiry and to its outcomes? What forms could our final research texts take?

A place for us to begin our discussion is with the topic of justification, a topic always close to the surface, even during fieldwork when one is frequently called on to justify the inquiry.

JUSTIFICATION (WHY?)

Narrative inquiries are always strongly autobiographical. Our research interests come out of our own narratives of experience and shape our narrative inquiry plotlines. For us, it was our teaching backgrounds and our strong interest in the experience of teachers and children that led us to the study of teacher knowledge and eventually to our framing of teacher knowledge studies in terms of narrative knowledge.

As we began this line of work many years ago, we fell into what Schwab (1960) called *fluid inquiry*, a way of thinking in which an inquiry is not clearly governed by theories, methodological tactics, and strategies. There are numerous false starts and dead ends. As we sought a way to justify our own work, we kept trying to find points of contact with others. We had a file of journal rejections that came about, in part, because reviewers and editors did not see the social significance of the work and tended to see it as only personal. They often labeled the work idiosyncratic and narcissistic.

One of our projects allowed us to sponsor a two-year invited seminar series, which culminated in a personal knowledge symposium over a several-day period. Mark Johnson, whose place in our thinking is noted in Chapter One, attended. Though at the time we did not see it quite as clearly as we present it here, we were trying to find a way of communicating with people, of finding points of contact between our interests and theirs. In short, we were jolted into trying to link our personal sense of justification with a public, social sense of significance. Our own interests and ways of thinking were not enough. We needed to have the work connect with larger questions of social significance.

Over the years, we learned to keep the topics of both personal and social justification before us. Even as we write this, we realize that we may not, for any given inquiry, think these matters through to the satisfaction of others, but we do know their importance, and we try to continually address both. For narrative inquirers, it is crucial to be able to articulate a relationship between one's personal interests and sense of significance and larger social concerns expressed in the works and lives of others.

While writing this section, we slid over the fact that it is not so easy to establish a personal sense of justification. To read the literature, one might imagine that expressing personal interests comes easily as a simple expression of the obvious. On the contrary, most of us are astonishingly unclear about what our inquiry interests are and how to justify them in personal terms. When asked why we are interested in a topic and why we have chosen to frame it in the way we have, we are often unable to answer clearly. Because of this difficulty (often unrecognized and often hidden), in our classes and in our work with beginning narrative inquirers, we frequently ask people to write a series of stories around their phenomena of interest. Jean encouraged Hedy Bach (1997) to write stories of her own girlhood experiences as she began her narrative inquiry with young girls. As Bach wrote her stories and received response from others, she began to weave a personal sense of justification around her own experience of what is evaded in the curricula of young girls.

Although we encourage the justification of inquiry interest in personal terms, the norms in inquiry have it that people should only justify their inquiry in social terms. There tends to be a rule to the effect that research texts should be written almost as if there were no personal inquirer, no "I" in the process. Injecting that "I" is not easy.

In our own narrative inquiries around teachers' experiences in school, at first we found it easier to leave our researcher "I's" out of our written texts. Initially, we found it easier to continue third-person accounts of teachers such as Stephanie because reviewers, editors, and granting agencies found our personal "I" accounts problematic. Indeed, writing "I" created an opening for being called narcissistic, though we felt we had finally triumphed and developed some written sense of why something was of personal significance.

We need to be prepared to write "I" as we make the transition from field texts to research texts. As we write "I," we need to convey a sense of social significance. We need to make sure that when we say "I," we know that "I" is connecting with "they." We say more about this in Chapter Nine, where we deal with issues of voice, signature, and audience.

Another question of justification that reemerges as we make the transition from field texts to research texts concerns the question of why we selected narrative inquiry for our inquiry. Why not an ethnography? A grounded theory study? Why narrative inquiry? What do we imagine that we can learn about our phenomenon by engaging in narrative inquiry that will be special or unique? How will a narrative inquiry fit with, enlarge, or shift the social and theoretical conversations around our phenomenon of interest? We need to be prepared to give an account of what we learn about our phenomenon that is special, something that could not be known through other theories or methods.

We frequently faced this question in our early work as narrative inquirers. For example, in Jean's doctoral defense, one of her committee members asked why she had engaged in living with Stephanie in her classroom. Why had Jean not just asked a series of interview questions to learn of her images. What had Jean learned from engaging in narrative inquiry with Stephanie that she would not have learned in an interview study? Although we are asked this question less often now, we feel it is important to ask this question of all of our inquiries. What *does* narrative inquiry help us learn about our phenomenon that other theories or methods do not?

Joy Ruth Mickelson (1995) undertook a narrative inquiry into the experiences of four mothers whose sons were labeled *behavior disordered*. Mickelson worked for many years as a school psychologist and social worker. In her work, she was required to assess children using various psychological and sociological measures and to arrange appropriate educational placements for the children. The social discourse in the area was one of assessing children to determine deficits and subsequently determining appropriate educational placements for remediation or treatment. The theoretical discourse was, for the most part, drawn from psychology and education and was based on learning and development theories. There is a great deal of research in the area of diagnosis, assessment, and treatment of youngsters seen as behaviorally troubled. However, mothers' experiences were largely silent, and it was within this silence that Mickelson positioned her narrative inquiry. Her narrative inquiry intention was to hear stories of the mothers' experiences. Through hearing their stories, she was able to raise questions about the ways a deficit model shaped the responses of teachers, administrators, parents, and psychologists in working with the children. A narrative inquiry allowed her to create a research text that illuminated the experiences not only of and for the mothers but also of how the discourse of the social and theoretical contexts shaped the mothers' relationships with their children.

What Mickelson learned from engaging in narrative inquiry with the mothers could not have been learned in other ways. This consideration is an important one not only as one begins to frame an inquiry proposal but also as one makes the transition from field texts to research texts. We need to continually ask questions about the way narrative inquiry illuminates the social and theoretical contexts in which we position our inquiries.

To return to the question at Jean's doctoral defense, engaging in narrative inquiry with Stephanie allowed Jean to understand how teacher knowledge is narratively composed, embodied in a person, and expressed in practice. Had Jean engaged in an interview study, this conceptualization of teacher knowledge would not have been possible.

PHENOMENA (WHAT?)

Narrative inquiries are always composed around a particular wonder, a research puzzle. This is usually called the research problem or research question. However, this language and wording tend to misrepresent what we believe is at work with narrative inquirers. Problems carry with them qualities of clear definability and the expectation of solutions, but narrative inquiry carries more of a sense of a search, a "re-search," a searching again. Narrative inquiry carries more of a sense of continual reformulation of an inquiry than it does a sense of problem definition and solution. As we think about the phenomena in a narrative inquiry, we think about responding to the questions: What is your narrative inquiry about? or What is the experience of interest to you as a narrative inquirer?

In our own studies of Bay Street School, our early work focused on trying to understand how a teacher's knowledge was constructed as the teacher experienced policy implementation settings in school. This statement more or less summarizes our 1980 project proposal to the NIE. At one level, in any funded project, there is a statement of public purpose that the agency is supporting. But our experience of being in the field led to a kaleidoscope of research puzzles, each with a slightly different take on the phenomena: how the organization of time in schools influenced teachers' experiential knowledge, how shifting policy contexts shaped teacher experience, how the positioning of teachers on their educational landscape shaped their experiences of who they were and formed their identities, and so forth.

At one level, it would seem that to identify a phenomenon of interest is clear and straightforward. Indeed, as graduate students work their way from course to course in their doctoral programs, they laugh as they avoid the questions of naming their research problems. Jean remembers trying to shrink into corners of elevators as well-meaning faculty asked her what her study was about, with the seeming view that she would be able to name her phenomenon as the elevator moved from the main floor to the tenth floor where she could gratefully escape. Jean realizes now, as she engages in narrative inquiry, that being able to say what phenomenon a narrative inquiry is about is not an easily answered question. It is not one that is answered with finality at the beginning of an inquiry or in the research proposal. As an inquirer reads and rereads field texts on the way to composing research texts, the phenomenon, the *what* of the inquiry, is among the topics that press in on the inquirer. These explorations of naming the inquiry phenomenon are necessary. Jean remembers trying to name her phenomenon with a focus on both experience and knowledge and being given responses that indicated she should study teachers' personal constructs, the implementation process, or do an ethnography of a classroom. She remembers being confused and uncertain, yet she needed to address what her inquiry was about as she composed her research text.

A more recent example occurred with JoAnn Phillion, who became reasonably clear on her phenomenon at the time of her proposal hearing. Tongue in cheek, she named herself Ms. Multicultural after what she initially named as her phenomenon. In the course of her fieldwork in a bustling classroom situated in a busy school, the phenomenon got away from her. The complexity of the field experience swamped her sharply defined research phenomenon. As inquirers, we tend to define our phenomenon as if life stood still and did not get in our way. But life does not stand still; it is always getting in the way, always making what may appear static and not changing into a shifting, moving, interacting complexity. As Phillion writes her research text, she needs to once again figure out what she is studying. Having been swamped in the complexity of the field, she now realizes that it will not be the same phenomenon that figured so clearly in the proposal.

Recognizing that the phenomena in narrative inquiry are a kind of shifting ground, we make spaces for beginning narrative inquirers to name their inquiry phenomena at many points in their inquiry journeys. They say what they are studying in courses that lead up to their candidacy-proposal hearings, in their proposals, in works-in-progress seminars as they compose interim research texts, in the many iterations of dissertations and theses, and in brown-bag public seminars leading up to final defenses. In a sense, these situations compel inquirers to say something that they are not quite ready to say. We see these situations as uncertain plateaus in naming the phenomena.

As we listened to Ming Fang He and Annie Davies over a number of years as they worked on their inquiries, we saw their struggles to gain first one and then another plateau. Though Davies stated her phenomena as teachers' team teaching experiences, as expressions of their knowledge, and He stated hers as the experience of women teachers moving between China and Canada in their final research texts, these were statements of naming their phenomena that were not possible for them to make until their inquiries were completed.

We want to emphasize that the shifting ground of the inquiry phenomenon, illustrated in He's and Davies's work, is not a question of their inexperience. We too undergo the same uncertain moves from plateau to plateau in trying to name our own phenomenon.

Phenomena also shift depending on how we frame their contexts and our researcher positions within the contexts. For example, as we positioned the phenomenon of teacher knowledge within classroom practice, some features were highlighted. As we repositioned the phenomenon of teacher knowledge within both in-classroom and out-of-classroom practices, other features were foregrounded, while still others slid into the background. As we positioned ourselves as researchers on the out-of-classroom place, we understood teacher knowledge as expressed in teacher practices in different ways than when we positioned ourselves within the classroom place. Our phenomena at Bay Street School also shifted along the personal-social dimension. Our earlier inquiry focused on the teachers' personal construction of knowledge, and our recent inquiries focused on the educational landscape on which teachers work. In effect, the complexity of the three-dimensional inquiry space is the basis for the shifting ground.

As beginning inquirers try to name their phenomena, they sometimes confuse questions of phenomena with questions of method. In our work at Bay Street School, it would have been possible for us to name our phenomena as Stephanie and Phil, two participants, or perhaps as the race relations policy and the language policy, two key board of education policies at work in the school. Davies could have confused her teacher participants with the experience of team teaching, and He could have confused her experience of shifting identities with her three women teacher participants.

METHOD (HOW?)

There are three sets of considerations within questions of method in narrative inquiry—theoretical considerations; practical, field text–oriented considerations; and interpretive-analytic considerations, as we move from field texts to research texts. In this section, we try to share our thinking about these considerations with a particular focus on the move from field texts to research texts.

Theoretical Considerations

As we have tried to make clear throughout the book, theoretically, the main issue is for inquirers to sort out a narrative view of experience. This issue first appears when beginning narrative inquirers, fresh from studying other forms of qualitative inquiry, want to find a space amid the other methods for narrative inquiry. We know something of this desire for sorting and classifying methods because before we began to think of our research as narrative inquiry, we sought out other methods as possibilities for studying experience. There were a number of what seemed to be similar theoretical approaches; for example, *phenomenology, ethnography, ethnomethodology,* and *grounded theory.*

When we began our study of teacher experience, we began by looking through the various qualitative methods that were gaining some credence on our campus in the late 1970s and early 1980s. For example, we explored grounded theory methods, such as those that Glaser and Strauss wrote about. We became entranced by their ideas of theoretical memos and themes and categories as a way to read interview transcripts. We also spent time studying, through various kinds of communities, phenomenology, ethnography, and other methods. We played with the ideas of imaging events, using methods made popular by phenomenologists; and we played with ideas of school maps as a way to understand contexts, ideas used by the ethnographers. As we did this, we had to fight against an urge to lose ourselves in the wonders and complexities of the various methods. There was a kind of seductiveness to method that we found compelling, a seductiveness that threatened to wrap us into the ideas and concepts that drove the method. It was difficult to keep before us our research puzzles about experience when the methods seemed so interesting in their own right.

Our own journey through the various possible methods gives us a sense that although it may be interesting, we do not think it is very helpful to begin with a search in which we sort and place theoretical methods beside one another. Beginning narrative inquirers frequently worry their way through definitions and procedures of different methodological theories, trying to define narrative inquiry and to distinguish it from each of the others, trying to find a niche for narrative inquiry amid the array of theoretical qualitative methodological frames presented to them, but we do not encourage this approach

Although this may be worthwhile for an understanding of the broad range of methodologies, it is of no great significance for narrative inquiry because, as we discuss in Chapter Three, the place of theory in narrative inquiry differs from the place of theory in formalistic inquiries. In Chapter Three, we pointed out that formalists begin inquiry in theory, whereas narrative inquirers tend to begin with experience as lived and told in stories. Here we wish to point out that for narrative inquiry, it is more productive to begin with explorations of the phenomena of experience rather than in comparative analysis of various theoretical methodological frames.

As work proceeds, narrative inquirers will discover that aspects of their work have features that some call ethnographic, and other aspects have features that some call phenomenological, and so forth. As one makes the transition from field texts to research texts, these theoretical considerations again come to the fore as inquirers position their research texts theoretically. In our work, we keep in the foreground of our writing a narrative view of experience, with the participants' and researchers' narratives of experience situated and lived out on storied landscapes as our theoretical methodological frame.

As we make the transition from field texts to research texts, we try to interweave our researcher experience of the experience under study with narrative ways of going about and inquiring into that phenomenon. As we pursued our work at Bay Street School, we focused on trying to understand teachers' experiences narratively, which meant thinking about their experiences in terms of the three-dimensional inquiry space; that is, along temporal dimensions, personal-social dimensions, and within place. In our book, *Shaping a Professional Identity: Stories of Educational Practice* (Connelly and Clandinin, 1999), based on a series of studies, we give a sense of understanding teachers' experience through what we term *stories to live by.*

Practical Field Text–Oriented Considerations

The practical strategies for creating field texts is the topic of Chapter Seven. Whereas we discussed the issues of composing field texts in detail in Chapter Seven, here we bring forward issues that surface in particular ways as we make the transition from field texts to research texts.

In Chapter Five, we discussed negotiations in which narrative inquirers engage participants in the field—negotiating relationships, negotiating purposes, negotiating ways to be useful, and negotiating transitions. As we begin to make the move from field texts to research texts, these negotiations reemerge. The transition from field texts to research texts can be difficult, but it is important. As inquirers, we need to move away from the close contact, the daily conversations, the frequent meetings and working alongside one other to begin to focus more directly on reading and rereading field texts and on beginning to compose research texts. This does not imply that the close relationships with participants have ended but rather that the relationships shift from the intensity of living stories with participants to retelling stories through research texts.

Jean remembers how difficult it was to leave her regular three-day-per-week time with Stephanie in her classroom as Jean began to write research texts. In order to facilitate the transition, she tried at first to go less frequently, perhaps one day per week. However, although that seemed to make sense to Jean as researcher, it interfered with the rhythms of classroom life, as children asked where she was on her formerly regular days and why she only came sometimes. This experience helped Jean see that she needed to carefully negotiate an exit from being in the field in the same way that she had earlier negotiated entrance. She needed to find a way that was useful to life in the classroom, a way that fit into ongoing daily life. She needed to negotiate a new way of being in relationship with the participants in the field, a way that would allow her to fulfill her purposes of composing a research text, a way of sustaining the relationships, and a way of still being useful in the field.

We see the same thing in work such as the conversation group narrative inquiries being undertaken by Janice Huber (1999) and Karen Whelan (1999). In their inquiry, they met with a group of teachers and another group of administrators over a two-year period. However, as they began to compose research texts, their meetings with their conversation groups became far less frequent. One of their difficulties was negotiating a way that would sustain the relationships in order to negotiate research texts with their participants and that would also allow them concentrated time for writing research texts. These are matters that need to be considered as we move from field texts to research texts.

This is all made more complex when we realize that we may have fallen in love not only with our participants but also with our field texts. Sometimes, our field texts are so compelling that we want to stop and let them speak for themselves. As we tried to make clear as we worked our way through Davies's field texts, field texts consist of inviting, captivating letters, conversations, storied poems, and other compelling material. But as researchers we cannot stop there, for our inquiry task is to discover and construct meaning in those texts. Field texts need to be reconstructed as research texts.

Interpretive-Analytic Considerations

This brings us to the third set of considerations, that is, considerations of analysis and interpretation. As we move from field texts to research texts, our field texts are the texts of which we ask questions of meaning and social significance. What are the meanings of Davies's storied poem, of Tom's oral history transcript, of the daily field notes? Why does it make a difference to figure out the possible meanings? These are the general questions that drive the transition from field texts to research texts as analytical and interpretive matters come to the fore. These questions are made more complex as we ask them in the midst of trying to negotiate a new way of being in relation with our participants, and as we fight against our desire to let field texts speak for themselves.

For a narrative inquiry of reasonable scope, the constructed field texts may appear overwhelming. There are computer files, binders, file folders, photograph collections, and other organizing tools. As the quantity of field texts becomes unmanageable, we have occasionally turned to computer programs. In our own work, we have begun to use Non-numerical Unstructured Data Indexing Searching and Theorizing (NUDIST). However, this is not a program that works without some adaptation, for it seems designed for more microlevel studies, such as a limited set of interview transcripts, transcripts of focus group meetings, and the like. We have not found these computerized programs particularly useful in inquiries with massive amounts of field texts of different kinds composed over a span of years.

Before coming to the question of what to do with all the field texts, we need to know what there is. At one level, this is an archival task. We need to make sure that we read and reread all of the field texts and in some way sort them, so we know what field texts we have. This involves careful coding of journal entries, field notes, documents, and all the rest, with notation of dates, contexts for the composition of the field texts, characters involved, perhaps topics dealt with, and so forth.

For us, these considerations of what there is—that is, archival considerations—return us to issues of positioning our field texts within the three-dimensional narrative inquiry space, something we addressed in Chapter Six. When we consider questions of positioning the field texts within the inquiry space, we open up questions of analysis. But the question of analysis goes far beyond this difficult positioning task. Although in some people's minds, narrative inquiry is merely a process of telling and writing down a story with perhaps some reflective comment by researchers and participants, the process of moving from field texts to research texts is far more complex. A narrative inquirer spends many hours reading and rereading field texts in order to construct a chronicled or summarized account of what is contained within different sets of field texts. Although the initial analysis deals with matters such as character, place, scene, plot, tension, end point, narrator, context, and tone, these matters become increasingly complex as an inquirer pursues this relentless rereading. With narrative analytic terms in mind, narrative inquirers begin to *narratively code* their field texts. For example, names of the characters that appear in field texts, places where actions and events occurred, story lines that interweave and interconnect, gaps or silences that become apparent, tensions that emerge, and continuities and discontinuities that appear are all possible codes. As narrative researchers engage in this work, they begin to hold different field texts in relation to other field texts.

However, it is responses to the questions of meaning and social significance that ultimately shape field texts into research texts. These are the questions that shape the analysis and interpretation parts of our work. In general, field texts are not constructed with reflective intent. Rather, they are close to experience, tend to be descriptive, and are shaped around particular events. Field texts have a recording quality to them, whether auditory or visual. Research texts are at a distance from field texts and grow out of the repeated asking of questions concerning meaning and significance. Like Carr's (1966) example of Hundreds and Thousands, an inquirer composing a research text looks for the patterns, narrative threads, tensions, and themes either within or across an individual's experience and in the social setting. For example, in the research text that Davies eventually composed, she looked for ways to give an account of each individual's story of the year of team teaching, including an account of her own story. These were richly detailed accounts of experiences that drew the field texts forward to retell individuals' stories. But she also composed a research text that illustrated how the social narrative of professionalism shaped the professional knowledge landscape and gave form to teachers' cover stories. In her research text, she was able to write about penetrating cover stories because of the relationships she had created and into which spaces the teachers told and lived their stories.

It would be tempting to view this overall process of analysis and interpretation in the move from field texts to research texts as a series of steps. However, this is not how narrative inquiries are lived out. Negotiation occurs from beginning to end. Plotlines are continually revised as consultation takes place over written materials, and as further field texts are composed to develop points of importance in the revised story.

The move from field texts to research texts is layered in complexity in still other ways. There is no smooth transition, no one gathering of the field texts, sorting them through, and analyzing them. Field texts have a vast and rich research potential. We return to them again and again, bringing our own restoried lives as inquirers, bringing new research puzzles, and re-searching the texts. For example, at first our research intentions with the field texts composed at Bay Street School were to understand how a teacher's knowledge was held in the form of images. We returned to the field texts a few years later as we tried to understand the shaping of a teacher's knowledge expressed in practice as the intersection of a school's temporal cycles and a teacher's embodied rhythms of practice. We are currently engaged in rereading the archived field texts of Bay Street School, this time with an inquiry intention to understand school change over time. This time we are not alone in rereading these field texts. Other inquirers work with us, reading and rereading the field texts, texts that seem to have taken on a life of their own. These new inquirers, unfamiliar with the themes, times, and characters portrayed in the field texts, bring their own lives, their own stories, to the field texts. Whether we read the field texts alone or with new readers, the search for patterns, narrative threads, tensions, and themes that shape field texts into research texts is created by the writers' experiences as they read and reread field texts and lay them alongside one another in different ways, as they bring stories of their past experiences forward and lay them alongside field texts, and as they read the field texts in the context of other research and theoretical works.

As we learned to be narrative inquirers, we realized there is no one bringing together of the field texts into research texts. We find ourselves frequently engaged in writing a variety of different kinds of *interim texts,* texts situated in the spaces between field texts and final, published research texts. In our work, we have experimented with many ways of writing interim texts, most of them designed to be shared and negotiated with participants.

These interim texts take on different forms and vary according to the circumstances surrounding the life of the inquiry and particularly the research and scholarly life of the inquirer. Sometimes, these interim texts are built into the inquiry process—that is, they are built into the negotiations that bring the researcher to the field. For instance, in Jean's dissertation studies, she deliberately built in a series of accounts she called "interpretive accounts," accounts designed to negotiate preliminary interpretations with Stephanie. Davies built in a similar process, though hers were written more relationally in the form of letters. They differ in another way in that, whereas Jean intended her interpretive accounts to be part of the final research text, Davies had no such intention. Her interim texts were intended to facilitate ongoing conversation with participants as she was writing her field notes. One way of looking at these two interim texts is that in Davies's work, the texts tended to be closer to her field texts; in Jean's work, the texts were closer to her research texts.

Both Jean's and Davies's interim texts, as described above, are part and parcel of the ongoing research defined by the inquiry. It often happens that a researcher's academic life outside the particular inquiry may also bring about the writing of interim texts. These initiatives may come from practical or more theoretical sources. Phillion's first set of interim texts came about because of an academic conference talk she was giving. The materials appeared in the form of a spoken paper negotiated with her participant prior to delivery. The timing of the conference came in the midst of the time when Phillion was in the field. Although she had composed and collected some field texts, she intended to be in the field for a much longer time. For her, those interim texts drew only from early field texts. We have learned, however, that the writing of interim research texts often occurs as soon as field texts begin to be composed.

Interim texts are written at different times in the inquiry process and for different purposes, and they also take different forms. In addition to letters, interpretive accounts, and paper presentations, we have experimented with writing storied accounts of particular events that developed around an idea or concern. Three instances of storied accounts from our own work are what we call the discipline bench story, used in a book chapter; the story of the principal of Bay Street School's personal philosophy, which appeared in a paper; and a storied account of the school's curriculum resource center, which was never published. We used the latter account to puzzle out the theory-practice relationship being lived out in the developing resource program at the school. We were particularly nervous about bringing this account to the two resource teachers. However, when we negotiated the accounts with them, they resonated with how we portrayed them in these accounts; and through reflection on our own anxiety and concern, we learned more about the process of moving from field texts to research texts. In this case, however, the document was not used in any further way in the creation of research texts. Sometimes, perhaps quite often, interim texts serve their function in the transition from field texts to research texts without ever appearing in research texts.

Our own anxiety and concern about sharing interim texts with the two resource teachers, one of our first experiences of this, taught us much about the transition from field texts to research texts. As one begins to work on analysis and interpretation, this transition is filled with uncertainty. There is no clear path to follow that works in each inquiry. The circumstances surrounding each inquiry, the relationships established, the inquiry life of the researcher, and the appropriateness of different kinds of interim and final research texts mean that the inquiry is frequently filled with doubt. The doubt and uncertainty are lived out in endless false starts. As we begin to write interim and final research texts, we may try out one kind of research text and find it does not capture the meanings we have in mind, find it lifeless and lacking in the spirit we wish to portray, find that research participants do not feel the text captures their experience, or find the research text to be inappropriate to the intended audience. We try out other kinds and continually compose texts until we find ones that work for us and for our purposes. This inevitable experimentation with narrative form is discussed in more detail in Chapter Nine.

In addition to doubt, there is panic, or at the very least, considerable nervousness. We both remember the nervous anxiety we felt when we drove to Bay Street School to share that first interim text with the resource teachers. One of the poignant moments in narrative inquiry is always the moment when research texts are shared with participants. The concern is that the written research text will alter the working relationship between the researcher and the participant. The fear behind this concern ranges from a fear over losing a research site to a fear that a friendship between researcher and participants may be lost. A researcher in an intimate relationship with a participant does not want the research document to be hurtful to the participant. Even now with many years of experience as narrative inquirers, these concerns arise anew for us each time we share research texts with participants.

This set of considerations returns us, as narrative inquirers, to negotiating relationships with participants. This sense of continually moving back and forth between being in the field, field texts, and research texts is always present as we negotiate the inquiry.

THEORY AND LITERATURE

We have written briefly above about positioning field texts within the three-dimensional inquiry space as we move from field texts to research texts. This is one kind of positioning we consider. Another kind of positioning that comes to the fore as we make the move from field texts to research texts is the contextualizing of the work both socially and theoretically. When we think about our own work, we consider the positioning carefully, for we realize that different academic communities frequently read within a particular bordered set of discourse. For example, sometimes academic communities in education are bordered by subject matter areas, such as language education and science education. Sometimes borders fall around departmental areas, such as educational administration and educational psychology. Sometimes borders fall around issues, such as school reform and inclusive education. Whatever our sense of the bordered discourse, as narrative inquirers we need to be mindful of how we position our work.

We use a metaphor of conversation as we think of positioning our work socially and theoretically. We ask ourselves which conversation we want to participate in. For example, in our early narrative inquiries we positioned the Bay Street work within the large question of how theory and practice are related in school practice from a knowledge-use perspective. We wrote research texts with the intention of engaging in the conversation around epistemological and ontological issues of teacher knowledge. Later, we positioned our inquiries with the intention of engaging in the conversation around school reform.

Another consideration that becomes particularly relevant as one makes the transition from field texts to research texts is also one of positioning—that is, positioning the work relative to other streams of thought, research programs, and ideologies. Whereas this consideration is important when we frame research proposals, it fades to the background as we begin work in the field and as we compose field texts. It reemerges as we make the transition from field texts to research texts. We noted above that questions of social significance resurface as we begin to compose research texts. We ask questions about what scholarly conversations we want to engage in. This, of necessity, asks us to position our inquiries beside other inquiries.

For example, in our early work at Bay Street School, we became fascinated in our inquiries of trying to understand personal knowledge. We found a rich philosophical literature on personal knowledge in work by Polanyi (1958), Johnson (1987), and Code (1991).

After reading the philosophical literature, we turned to the burgeoning educational research literature, which used the personal to define teacher knowledge. We reviewed the literature to understand "what is personal in studies of the personal" and used that as a way to position our own understanding of teacher knowledge as personal practical knowledge amid the array of other streams of thought. This positioning of our inquiries is necessary if narrative inquiries are to contribute to questions of social significance.

KIND OF TEXT INTENDED

A last consideration we attend to as we make the transition from field texts to research texts is the consideration of the kind of research text we intend to write. Although we devote Chapter Nine to discussions of research texts, we wish to highlight some emerging issues. As we stated earlier in this chapter, we may write a variety of interim research texts in the process of composing public research texts. We noted that there may be innumerable false starts as we experiment with different forms. In Chapter Nine, we deal with the internal conditions of voice and signature and the existential conditions of inquiry purposes, narrative forms, and audience.

However, as we make the transition from field texts to research texts, we begin to understand that there are a range of possible forms of representing our research texts. We often begin with a kind of inquiry into our personal preferences. We suggest you do something similar. For example, do you like to read memoirs? Arguments? Photography Collections? Poetry? Reports? Dramas? Asking yourself these questions, looking through your bookshelves, studying your pattern of library borrowing are all ways to begin to formulate a response to questions of the kind of research text intended. Such an inquiry opens up a range of possibilities and frequently suggests innovative and compelling forms that might otherwise not be available.

As we ready ourselves to begin to compose research texts, we often read other researchers and writers we find particularly thoughtful. We read books on writing, such as Natalie Goldberg's *Writing Down the Bones* (1986) and *Wild Mind* (1990) and Annie Dillard's *Writing Life* (1987). These books open up our minds to new possibilities and help us address wonders about fictionalizing, representing multiple voices, and interweaving various genres, such as journal entries, transcribed talk, and photographs. We turn to these and other considerations of research texts in Chapter Nine.

Composing
Research Texts

H ere, we walk through the process of what we call the "back and forthing" of writing research texts for the narrative inquirer.

INTRODUCTION

In this chapter, we discuss how the beginning of the writing process brings the researcher back to the formalistic and reductionistic boundaries. We look at the tensions that living life at the boundaries creates and that must be negotiated as we compose research texts. We explore the place of memory in composing research texts and the task of dealing with uncertainty. In most instances, research purposes that were clear prior to entering the field have shifted and changed, leading the writer to feelings of doubt about the purposes of the research text. Several issues that must be considered carefully in the midst of this uncertainty are *voice, signature, narrative form,* and *audience.* We devote the last part of the chapter to an exploration of the complexities of choosing the best narrative form for one's research text. We tell of the journeys of two narrative inquirers as they worked through these choices.

EXPERIENCING TENSIONS
AS WRITING BEGINS

The moment of beginning to write a research text is a tension-filled time. There is, on the one hand, tension associated with leaving the field and wondering what to do with masses of field texts. There is, on the other hand, tension as we consider our audience and whether or not, or in what way, our texts might speak to our readers. There is tension as we turn inward to think about issues of voice and about whether we can capture and represent the shared stories of ourselves and our participants. There is tension as we turn outward to think about issues of audience and form. And there is tension as we consider how to represent the situatedness of the inquiry within place.

We know we cannot ignore the tensions that surround the narrative inquiry by choosing to focus on one or another of these dimensions. We cannot focus too heavily on the past; that is, on the field and the field texts, without consideration of the future; that is, the audience and the social and personal impact of the work. If we compose research texts without enough attention to the field and field texts, we run the risk of writing a text disconnected from the inquiry experience, a text that serves the interests and motivations of the inquirer but without obvious connections to participants' experiences. We cannot focus too heavily on issues of voice, trying only to capture our experience with participants without taking into account who we are writing for and what sense and meaning the inquiry might have for them. These tensions for a narrative inquirer composing a research text are the tensions we experience as we try to position our work in the three-dimensional narrative inquiry space.

As we begin this chapter, let us pause and look back at what we have written. What the writer of a narrative inquiry research text has is a diverse collection of storied field texts. Each field text is, to a degree, an individual and isolated text with its own narrative qualities. Some are more storied than others. In some field texts, the story quality is more implied than expressed. Because these field texts have been collected and positioned within the three-dimensional narrative inquiry space, the set as a whole has the potential to represent a more complete sense of the narrative of the inquiry field. The task now facing the narrative inquirer is to find a way to select and fit together these field texts into an overall narrative text. Following the notion of the three-dimensional narrative inquiry space, the writer tries to compose a text that at once looks backward and forward, looks inward and outward, and situates the experiences within place.

WRITING RESEARCH TEXTS AT THE BOUNDARIES

Before proceeding to a discussion of the tensions of writing research texts in a three-dimensional inquiry space, we return to the tensions of living life at the boundaries that were introduced in Chapters Two and Three. The tensions of thinking narratively at reductionistic and formalistic boundaries of thought—important and noticeable at the beginning stages of an inquiry—are mostly lost from sight while in the field. There, the inquiry proceeds on its own terms. It is in the construction of research texts and the associated dialogue, imagined and desired, with an audience that one's narrative terms rub up against the reductionistic and formalistic terms discussed in Chapters Two and Three. We pointed out in those chapters that these other sets of terms are part of everyone's intellectual world: they are not merely someone else's contending terms at the boundaries; they are terms that are part of us all.

Writing Research Texts at the Formalistic Boundary

Mary Shuster, writing a dissertation based on two years of work with second-generation immigrant Honduran women teachers, finds herself, as she was at the outset of her study, concerned with their social and economic status. Though her ongoing fieldwork was highly personalized with only three participants, she finds herself fighting the urge to select field texts that build a case for racist and sexist social attitudes endemic to the participants' society. She finds herself wanting to write a revelatory account of inimical hegemonic social structures.

In thesis discussions over this possible writing agenda, it seems that in order to write the formalistic text on social structures, a different kind of study would have been stronger. Furthermore, if she does pursue this text, she senses the extent to which her participants, whom she wishes to honor in the research text, would become secondary figures cast in a demonstrative role of social inequality. Shuster recognizes that her field texts show that the nuances in each person's life fragment the categories of race and gender. Race and gender work, in general, but not specifically for her participants. One participant, for instance, describes her family as one in which children are valued equally. Yet, the gender category implies that in a Honduran Catholic immigrant family, girls are oppressed. When participants are known intimately as people, not merely as categorical representatives, categories fragment. But Shuster has a problem because she wishes a better world for her participants and thinks that showing how society perpetuates racist and sexist attitudes will do some good for what she perceives as her participants' somewhat unhappy state, hence the urge to write *over* her participants and cast them as representative in a formalistic research text.

There is surely a great deal of tension in this because she wishes both to honor her participants and to critique social structures through backgrounding her participants' experiences by seeing them only as exemplars of formalistic categories. She needs to find a form to represent their storied lives in storied ways, not to represent storied lives as exemplars of formal categories.

Writing Research Texts at the Reductionistic Boundary

For others, many perhaps, the interplay between narrative and reductionistic terms creates tension in two and possibly more ways as they compose research texts. The first way involves memory and its place in narrative inquiry. For example, sometimes field texts so outweigh the researcher's ability to reasonably deal with them—there may be too many notes, and perhaps they are not well enough organized— that in the writing the inquirer resorts to memory of the field experience and composes, without reference to field texts, a statement of remembered events in support of one point or another in the research text. It may also be, as is often the case, that the researcher is using memory records; for instance, interviews with participants in which participants are recollecting their narrative histories. Another instance is the writing of autobiographical research texts out of memory unaided by field texts. In these three cases, memory tends to take on a factual, unnuanced quality. A participant may have said, for instance, that he remembers a childhood in a certain way but that he also knows from discussions with siblings and others that certain events in the childhood seemed to be understood and remembered in different ways by different family members. Without returning to the field texts,

the researcher may fall into an unnuanced rendition of this participant's childhood. What was a nuanced, interpretive rendition in the
field experience becomes an asserted fact, a thing, in the research text.
Thus, what was a narrative field text becomes reduced to positive fact
in the research text. This form of reductionism is common in autobiographical texts, in which writers may describe an earlier event or feeling as if it were exactly so. But memory is selective, shaped, and retold
in the continuum of one's experiences.

The story of Ivan Schmidt illustrates the second way there is tension at the reductionistic boundary as one composes a research text.
Schmidt, writing a dissertation on people's experiences of becoming
social workers, finds himself, at the end of several months of conversations with five social workers, concerned with how to write his research text. His ongoing fieldwork with the social workers was highly
personalized. He talked with them, heard their stories of growing up
with their families, of spending years in school, of working with families and children in various informal settings, of moving into one career, and then, feeling dissatisfied, moving into another. Together, they
told stories, looked at photograph albums of the participants' lives,
and shared participants' old letters and journals.

As he begins to think about his research text, he wants, on the one
hand, to create a richly textured research text that represents the complex narratives of experience that led the social workers to their stories to live by as social workers. But feeling the tension of saying
something generalizable, he wants, on the other hand, to write a research text that creates themes that cut across the five narratives of experience. However, he recognizes that if he wants to write generalizable
themes, another kind of study would have been more appropriate. If
he gives in to the latter tension and writes themes intended to be generalizable, he will lose the richness of the narratives of experience,
without acquiring the desired generalizability because he only has five
participants. If he gives in to the tension of writing the unique narratives that honor the experiences of his participants, he worries that his
research will be judged not good enough to meet the criteria for research established by those who work in more reductionistic ways.
There is, surely, tension here because he wishes both to honor the experiences of his participants and to create a generalizable theory about
social workers' decisions to become social workers.

Schmidt's tension represents a common invasion of reductionistic
terms in the writing of a narrative inquiry research text, an invasion

that becomes apparent when a writer wonders whether to write a research text with individual chapters devoted to minibiographies of participants or to look at common threads and elements across participants. It is not surprising to meet doctoral students who are working with three participants and who wonder if, by adopting a common set of analytic terms, they might be able to create themes for cross analysis of participants. The writers imagine themselves to be writing a generalizable document, in which the threads constitute generalizations and participants fade into support roles, much as they did in our example with Schmidt. This kind of reduction, a reduction downward to themes (rather than upward to overarching categories as in the formalistic) yields a different kind of text with a different role for participants.

WRITING, MEMORY, AND RESEARCH TEXTS

Above, we alluded to connections among memory, field texts, and research texts. One way of thinking of field texts is to view them as memory signposts. Reading a field text allows us to tap into a base of memories of field experience. To an extent this is true. But field texts are as much memory transformers as they are memory signposts. To begin with, the writing of field texts shapes the experience. Furthermore, as one reads and rereads them over time, they become less of a signpost to the field experience and become all that is left of it. The field text, and of course any intervening research texts that one might have written, are mostly what remains of field experience.

Now, as we return to our twenty-year-old field texts at Bay Street School, we try to remember and tell stories to each other of Bay Street field experience. Sometimes, we are successful in this memory work. We find ourselves embellishing the field texts with what we think are recollected memories triggered by the field texts. For the most part, the events themselves would not likely be brought forward, let alone remembered in any rich experiential sense, without the field text records. More often than not, however, the field texts are all that remain of specific situations and events. Dillard wrote: "If you prize your memories . . . don't write a memoir—the act of writing about an experience takes so much longer and is so much more intense than the experience itself that you're left only with what you have written, just as the snapshots of your vacation become more real than your vacation. You have cannibalized your remembered truth and replaced it with a new one." (Zinsser, 1987, p. 27).

When there is a huge volume of field texts, which is not uncommon in a narrative inquiry, considerations of ways of handling field texts are important. Sometimes, computer files and coding systems are used. Memory plays a role regardless of whether computers are used in the process or not. Provided the total volume of field texts is not overwhelmingly huge, it is possible that the role of memory for those who code using computers and those who code without computers might be similar in their construction of their dissertation research texts. However, if field texts are used for subsequent studies years later, as in our return to the Bay Street field texts, matters are dramatically different, mostly because of the role of memory. For field texts not entered into computer files and coded and categorized in computers, pencil notes fade, contextualizing and relevance notes are lost, and connections among codes pass away unremembered. But computerized records remain. Without computerized files, there is a sense that the research text may be all, or mostly all, that is left of memory. Without computerized files, it would be difficult to imagine a construction of alternative research texts in the future. But with computerized records, memory is lodged not only in the constructed research texts but also in the computerized field texts.

In our view, there is nothing wrong with a noncomputerized approach to ways of organizing field texts that stand up just long and strongly enough to link field experience to field texts to the writing of a single main research text. However, we do urge those with an eye to the future, grounded firmly in the past, to use the best technology at their disposal to record and organize their field texts. Though we have only recently begun using NUDIST, we have since the beginnings of electronic word processing used word processing software programs such as Microsoft Word.

WRITING RESEARCH TEXTS IN THE MIDST OF UNCERTAINTY

In Chapter Five and in the opening of this chapter, we described narrative inquirers as being in the midst of a three-dimensional narrative inquiry space, always located somewhere along the dimensions of time, place, the personal, and the social. Furthermore, we see ourselves as in the mind-set of a nested set of stories—ours and theirs. We and our participants are together in the midst. This same sense of being in the midst characterizes what narrative inquirers do when they write their research texts. However, being in the midst as one writes research texts may, and almost always does, feel different from being in the midst in the field. Inevitably perhaps, the writers are less confident of what they are doing and what they want to say than they were when they entered the field, and most certainly, they are less secure and at ease with themselves than they were as the field experience, if successful, unfolded.

In Chapters Three and Eight, we discussed the place of theory in narrative inquiry. We stated that theory plays a somewhat ambiguous and confounding role in the place of practice, the site of inquiry. Things that are seen clearly from a distance and prior to fieldwork as understandable or researchable or interpretable in theoretical terms lose their precision when the daily life of field experience is encountered. Shuster, in the study noted above, not only wanted to interpret her participants in terms of race and gender but also began her inquiry thinking in those terms. It seemed quite clear to her—given the gender dynamics as she understood them in Honduras and Canada, and given cultural attitudes in Canada—that her participants would represent the theoretical categories. But the field experience destroyed those easy understandings. There is an irony in this for narrative inquirers because they tend to be less sure of themselves, less clear of what it is they have to say, *after* investing themselves intensely over time in their research than they were prior to doing their research. If research experience is supposed to yield clarity, most do not feel it when they come to writing research texts.

Part of the writer's uncertainty comes from knowing, and caring for, specific participants. Abstract theoretical categories might be uppermost prior to the research, but participants, and one's relationship to them, are key by the time the research text is to be written. The researcher learns that people are never only (nor even a close approximation to) any particular set of isolated theoretical notions, categories, or terms. They are people in all their complexity. They are people living storied lives on storied landscapes.

Part of the narrative inquirer's doubts come from understanding that they need to write about people, places, and things as *becoming* rather than *being*. Their task is not so much to say that people, places, and things are this way or that way but that they have a narrative history and are moving forward. The narrative research text is fundamentally a temporal text—about what has been, what is now, and what is becoming. The writer must find ways to write a text that is "in place," not abstracted but placed. And place, too, needs to be seen as becoming. As JoAnn Phillion writes about her life with Pam in Bay Street School, she writes about Bay Street School as a place with a history, a place that is, and a place that is leaning toward the future. Pam, in place, is in temporal transition—a complex event that is determined by the past and is determining, in exceedingly unclear ways, the future.

Still another confounding matter leading to writer uncertainty is the relation of person and place to context now, in the past, and in the future. It is not enough to write about Bay Street School in place temporally. Phillion needs to place Bay Street School in its context, which also has a narrative history—the community and how it developed, Canada and its history, and policies of immigration and refugee protection. Both Pam and Phillion are in relationship, and they are in each other's context. Furthermore, each of them is in her own context. All of these intersecting contexts make a difference to understanding the work. For example, part of Pam's context (as is Phillion's) is Bay Street School's context. Pam too has a life independent of Bay Street School, a life with a history relevant to her teaching. Phillion, a developing scholar, has still another context with its own history and future. How do narrative inquirers such as Phillion, working in the midst of composing research texts, create plotlines that emerge from the tensions of people, places, and things in relationship, in context, and in becoming?

No wonder then that the writing of research texts is so confounding. Writers need to hold in mind, and put on paper, so many disparate but intimately connected matters in the three-dimensional inquiry space. Writers know that it is not enough to name the various parts. Naming does not make for scholarship. All of these parts need to be held in mind as writers struggle with issues of meaning and significance. This is all made more complex as they search for ways to convey the stories, lived and told, with participants. Matters such as voice, signature, narrative form, and especially audience must be attended to. We now turn to a brief treatment of these matters.

Voice

In its broadest sense, voice may be thought of as belonging to participants, researcher, and other participants and other researchers for whom a text speaks. There is a rich, developing literature on voice. In narrative inquiry, there is a relationship between researchers and participants, and issues of voice arise for both. One of the researcher's dilemmas in the composing of research texts is captured by the analogy of living on an edge, trying to maintain one's balance, as one struggles to express one's own voice in the midst of an inquiry designed to tell of the participants' storied experiences and to represent their voices, all the while attempting to create a research text that will speak to, and reflect upon, the audience's voices. Voice, and dilemmas created by the consideration of it, are always sorted out by the exercise of judgment. The researcher is always speaking partially naked and is genuinely open to legitimate criticism from participants and from audience. Some researchers are silenced by the invitation to criticism contained in the expression of voice.

There are other considerations around voice. One key consideration is the multiplicity of voices, both for participants and for researchers. We need not to see our participants as univocal, not tied to one theoretical structure or mode of behavior that would leave them with the appearance of being unidimensional. We, and our participants, live and tell many stories. We are all characters with multiple plotlines who speak from within these multiple plotlines. As we try to capture this multiplicity, we need to consider the voices heard and the voices not heard. Or, to look at voice in another way, we may include the voice of a participant in such a way that the context of the research text obscures or silences important parts of that participant's voice. As researchers, we too struggle to speak our research texts in our multiple voices. Our silences, both those we choose and those of which we are unaware, are also considerations of voice in our research texts.

Signature

Voice and signature are closely connected in the writing that transforms field texts into research texts. When a veil of silence is lifted and a writer knows he or she has something to say and feels the power of voice, that writer still must find a way of saying what he or she wishes to speak. It is, says Geertz (1988), difficult for a writer to sort out how to be in the text. "Getting themselves into their texts (that is, representationally into their texts)," he says, "may be as difficult for ethnographers as getting themselves into the culture (that is, imaginatively into the culture). For some, it may even be more difficult" (p. 17). For Geertz, there are multiple ways of being there in the field as well as multiple ways of being there in the text. Being there in the special way that marks each of us as writers constitutes our research signature. The dilemma is the dilemma of how lively our signature should be: too vivid a signature runs the risk of obscuring the field and its participants; too subtle a signature runs the risk of the deception that the research text speaks from the point of view of the participant.

The risks of an overly vivid signature are well known in the literature and come under the heading of the abuses of subjectivity. The risks of too flimsy a signature are not as well thought through, and it is here that narrative inquirers need to pay close attention to their writing. The signature can be too thin because other texts and other theories, rather than the writer, sign the work. Equally, the signature can be too thin because the researcher imagines that the participants and their field texts author the work. Both ways of thinning the signature need to be guarded against. In gaining a voice, and a signature for it, researchers put their own stamp on the work. The text that follows from the signature has rhythm, cadence, and expression, which mark the signature and make the work readily identifiable as the work of a certain author or set of collaborators. This expression of the signature is called *discourse* by Geertz. The signature and its expression in discourse create an author identity.

Signature is commonly thought of as attached to the researcher but may as well be thought to refer to participants. When narrative inquirers return to participants with text, their question is not so much, Have I got it right? Is this what you said? Is this what you do? Rather, it is something much more global and human: Is this you? Do you see yourself here? Is this the character you want to be when this is read by others? These are more questions of identity than they are questions of whether or not one has correctly reported what a participant has said or done. Does Pam emerge as a person in Phillion's writing? Do we, and she, recognize her way of being in the multicultural classroom? Does this give a tone and feel for how she knows the world of teaching and learning diversity? For now, as a kind of placeholder in our own thought, we use the term *participant signature* to capture what we have in mind, but a different, more enriched term might be more appropriate to our understanding. We imagine a term that recognizes the influence of participants on the signature of the text, a term that recognizes that the signature may be negotiated among researcher and participants. (The sections on voice and signature are adapted from Clandinin and Connelly, 1994.)

Audience

Audience, alive in the researcher's imagination at the outset of inquiry, mostly forgotten during fieldwork, now looms large. It is a necessary condition to be fulfilled by narrative research texts. The pleasure of a good relationship with a sense of shared meaning and significance between researcher and participant is important but insufficient for the writing of narrative inquiry texts. A sense of an audience peering over the writer's shoulder needs to pervade the writing and the written text. It is excusable to misjudge an audience and write a text that is not read as meaningful by others. But it is inexcusable not to have a sense of audience and a sense of what it is about one's research text that might be valuable for them.

Admitting audience, however, creates still another tension and another balancing act as writers construct their research texts. Writers may feel mildly faithless to their participants as they write about their fieldwork for an audience. Sticky matters arise over shared moments, intimacies, secrets, and the desire to find a place for them in the research text. A writer's struggle to respect working relationships and to make a place for participant voice and signature tends to be in tension with the notion of audience.

Tensions Among Voice, Signature, and Audience

Establishing voice and signature pulls us inward to the inquiry and to the field and its participants. As pointed out in Chapter Eight, our first audience is almost always our participants. After that, audience is almost always in imagination and outside the inquiry. As with all the other tensions of writing narrative inquiry research texts, the adoption of the extremes yields inadequate research texts. A cold, depersonalized, unsigned, voiceless document addressed in full to an audience has at times in social science research, even now, been seen as good or ideal. The construction of such research texts takes a form in which the researcher is "the researcher" and not "I," and the participants are "the subjects" and not "Pam." But the other extreme is equally inappropriate to a narrative inquiry text. A text in which "I" and "we" and "Pam" and others are written in such a way as to establish a fraternal intimacy, causing the reader to feel mildly embarrassed to intrude, does not constitute a good narrative research text. Unfortunately, this caricature of narrative inquiry research texts has tended to be popularized by critics. Charges of solipsism are commonly attributed to narrative work. Sometimes, when empathetic feelings overpower the writing, the charge is fair.

The writer of the research text continually balances signature and voice with audience. Sometimes, perhaps in some passages, chapters, or even whole texts, audience may loom largest. In others, signature and voice and the construction of intimate texts may loom largest. Always, both sides of this writer's tension need to be addressed and consciously written into the research text.

Another tension that comes into play as one begins to write a research text is a tension associated with choosing a narrative form. In Chapter Eight, we suggested that narrative inquirers should consider a range of possibilities that they like in research texts. The question to the writers is, What do you like to read? This is a question that we frequently ask ourselves as we begin to compose our research texts. We almost always ask thesis and dissertation students to explore the question. However, this makes it seem as if one makes the choice purely on the basis of personal taste. This is not the case. There is always a tension between voice, signature, and audience. Furthermore, there is a tension between the personal—that is, what seems to fit with the experiences of the inquirer and the participants—and the social—that is, what seems to fit into the ongoing conversation that surrounds the matters addressed in the inquiry.

In work undertaken by Janice Huber, Karen Whelan, and Wendy Sweetland (in progress), we see one example of how they negotiate the complex tensions of composing a research text. Huber and Whelan are doctoral students undertaking a narrative inquiry with a group of teacher participants. They selected a paper format for their dissertations, a format that allows each of them to write five articles based on their field studies for publication. Sweetland is one of the teacher participants. By including Sweetland as both participant and coauthor, they begin the complex tension of addressing issues of voice and signature. Sweetland's voice will be part of the research text. Huber and Whelan will not speak for her. The text will be coauthored. They agreed to write individual sections, respond to one another's pieces, and include some of these responses. They each write their own stories, drawing on their autobiographical experiences; the field texts made as part of the fieldwork; and the responses to one another's writing. The complexities of negotiating a coauthored text that draws on common field texts illustrate some of the tensions around voice. But this is only part of the tension. Each of the sections that they author has been imprinted with their own signature. Each piece bears the unique stamp of the inquirer who wrote it. How do they weave these unique pieces into one text that has an overall signature, a signature that adequately speaks for the collective authors?

Again, this is only part of the tension. They must still consider issues of audience. What journal are they writing for? What is acceptable in the scholarly discourse of that journal? Of that academic community? It is in the midst of negotiating these tensions that issues of narrative form emerge.

NARRATIVE FORM

"I want to get started on my dissertation writing," said Bev Brewer as she opened a thesis meeting discussion. "I think I have written something that is in a dissertation style. I am wondering if I am on the right track. Can we discuss it from that point of view?" Bev is in the midst of a dissertation study on adult education in community colleges. The text she brought to the meeting, fifteen or so pages in length, was a description of a series of meetings with a research participant. "It was," she said, "an introduction to her participant." She also said that she hoped to use the description for three possible purposes—a conference talk, a publishable paper, and a dissertation section.

Michael read the text. Subsequently, he and Bev found themselves in the midst of a conversation on narrative form. Their discussion rambled for the appointed hour. Viewing the text as potential conference material, they talked about Bev's allocated speaking time, whether or not she wanted a paper to distribute to the audience, and whether the paper was intended to be a text from which to read or whether she hoped it would be a larger document intended for journal publication, in which case the paper and talk would be different texts. They talked about how specific journals tend to have specific formats and of how useful it might be to have one or another journal in mind as the talk was prepared. They talked about what kinds of and how many ideas, points, and theses could reasonably be addressed in a ten-minute talk or a twenty-five-page paper. They tried to imagine differences between a text for speaking and one for a journal.

They also talked about the writing of these interim texts as possibly fitting into the final research text, the dissertation. Would they fit at the beginning, somewhere in the middle, or even at the end? Could they imagine how the conference paper, an interim text if it were to be that, could at the same time be a dissertation segment? What might later need to be done to reshape an interim text for a final research text, the dissertation? What might a conference paper need to contain that a dissertation segment would not?

Both of them were really in the midst of the tensions of composing research texts. Without a firm idea of the immediate purposes and audience for the text—talk, talk-paper, dissertation, talk-paper-dissertation—they had little idea of where to begin. They needed to work through those tensions.

Their difficulties ran deeper. Suppose it was decided to use the writing before them primarily for the dissertation? Where would it fit? Given the nature of the discussions contained in the text, it might have been possible to use the text to introduce the dissertation—its central puzzle, the quality of its phenomena, and the kind of inquiry to be pursued. It might have fit somewhere in a methodology section, where the material would have been used both to introduce participants and to present something of the conversational methodology used in the fieldwork. It could have been used as a key story far into the thesis as critiques of the adult education literature and practices were being argued. On the other hand, if they imagined the writing to be used as the basis for Bev's possible interim texts, conference talk, and paper publication, they had to know something more about what it was that Bev wanted to say at the conference and in the paper. Just as the writing might have fit into any part of her dissertation, depending on how she thought of it, the writing might have been shaped to make any number of specific points for her upcoming conference presentation and possible paper.

How should they think about this? How should they proceed? In its simplest sense, they had to look ahead and imagine their end before they got there.

Bev and Michael discussed Aristotle, and she left the meeting thinking in terms of form and matter, ends and means. Aristotle says formal and material causes, combined by efficient causes, yield final causes: an architectural plan combined by an architect and builders with building materials yields a building; an idea for a painting combined by a painter with art materials yields a painting; and an idea of a dissertation combined by a researcher with field texts yields a dissertation text. This is, of course, an oversimplified view of what is at stake.

Bev and Michael also talked about John Dewey's notion of ends-in-view as practical work proceeds, the idea being that one never does, or makes, things blindly, but rather holds in mind an end-in-view to help shape the doing, or the making, which in turn itself shapes the end-in-view.

Narrative form is something like Aristotle's formal cause or Dewey's end-in-view. Narrative inquiry writers, without overspecifying and limiting themselves, need to imagine a shape for the final dissertation text. Sometimes, it may be possible to imagine something specific, such as a document that has the marks of a good fictional literary text with well-developed characters, plot, and scene. At other times, one may only vaguely have in mind one kind of text or another. It may be possible for someone to imagine potential chapters, or it may only be possible to think in terms of parts—a first part that more or less does this, a second part that does that, and a third part that does something else. Bev had been reading, for journal review, two books in adult education that she thought helped create new ways of thinking about adult education and that were somewhat along the lines of the work she was doing. She thought she might be able to hold these up as a kind of idea, a preliminary notion of narrative form, with which she might imagine possible dissertation sections, perhaps even chapters.

These considerations are at the heart of questions on narrative form. Of course, they become more refined as we work through composing our research texts. Yet, they are never fully clear until the final research text is complete. As the writing of texts progresses, form changes and grows. There is an organic notion at work, a kind of developmental genetics of form. The writing itself makes a difference to the actual form of the final text. There is a kind of growth or development from rudimentary notions of form, of the sort that Bev and Michael were grappling with in their conversation, to the form that is finally realized in the written text.

As inquiry conversations often are, their discussion was discursive, fragmented, filled with halting moments. The search for form, even the floundering in confusion before even realizing that one is reaching for form, is part of what narrative inquirers do.

In Chapter One, we wrote that we are in the midst of an upheaval of thought about the possible ways to construct research texts, texts that are, in Geertz's words, "unsatisfactory, lumbering, shaky, and badly formed: a grand contraption" (1995, p. 20). Marcus and Fischer (1986) call this time (in their title) an "experimental moment." There is a willingness to experiment with narrative form. Literary (Bakhtin, 1981), visual (Chatman, 1990), poetic (Rose, 1990), dramatic (Turner, 1980), and other modes of expression are evident. These and other forms have recently been set out by Eisner (1991) and are discussed in Denzin and Lincoln (1994). Denzin and Lincoln describe our time as a "fifth moment" (p. 11) in qualitative research and sketch out their predictions for a sixth moment.

The excitement in this fluidity might lead a reader to think that anything goes, and to an extent it does, provided it works and is convincing for the audience. Barone and Eisner (1997), urging experiments in form, write, "The implications of exploring and exploiting new forms of representation for the conduct and display of educational research are profound" (p. 92). In graduate courses and in playful academic conferences, there are experiments with a range of what are often called arts-based forms of inquiry as devices for structuring research texts. A bulletin board poster in one of our institutions announces "a series of collages exploring artful research." However, Edel's notion that garments fit the biographical subject suggests that not any form will do for any particular inquiry.

In writing narrative research texts, we must be mindful of balancing the tensions of writing within the three-dimensional narrative inquiry space, of writing in ways that narratively capture the field experiences, and of balancing these with audience. Although there are imaginative possibilities in constructing research text forms, writers are constrained by the particularities of their three-dimensional narrative inquiry space.

Before turning more directly to issues of form for narrative inquiry research texts, we want to remind readers that narrative inquiry research texts are indeed "grand contraptions" built on multiple, fluid foundations and formed into ambiguous shapes that may ring more, or less, crisp and clear as one thing from one vantage point and another from another vantage point.

Writers and readers of narrative inquiry research texts need to muster a certain tolerance for the unease that may accompany ambiguity and the abandonment of what Dewey called *The Quest for Certainty* (1929). We struggled with how we might convey the complexities entailed in considerations of form as we understand them. Though we found many structures in the literature—for example, Bruner's (1990) paradigmatic and narrative knowing; Chatman's (1990) three text types (narrative, description, and argument); and Wolcott's (1994) ways of transforming qualitative data (description, analysis, and interpretation)—none reflected our experience of what is involved in shaping narrative inquiry texts. We found ourselves searching for a metaphor to help convey our meaning. We likened narrative form to *a soup*.

This metaphor is a useful place for us to begin our explorations of narrative form. Imagine for a moment a rich steamy soup filled with various chunks and pieces of vegetables, rice, and noodles, spiced with herbs, salt, and pepper. Imagine another soup of slightly different ingredients, different amounts, different-sized chunks, spiced in other ways. As we began to play with the metaphor of a soup, we realized that like the soups there could be different ingredients in our narrative pots. Parts of our research text can be composed of rich descriptions of people, places, and things; other parts can be composed of carefully constructed arguments that argue for a certain understanding of the relations among people, places, and things; and still others can be richly textured narratives of the people situated in place, time, scene, and plot. For us, all of these can be narrative texts. Working with Chatman's three text types, all of the types—argument, description, and narrative—are there. However, depending on the field experience being represented and depending on the inquirer, they are there in differing proportions. We cannot, for example, call a text narrative inquiry if it leaves out description and narrative and gives only argument. Nor can we call a text narrative inquiry if it is pure narrative without description and argument.

The soup metaphor opens up another necessarily troubling feature of narrative texts. Sometimes, the container in which the soup is put is clearly laid out. For example, the shape of the container may seem clear. Perhaps we are writing a dissertation in a department or university where a form is specified. Or perhaps we are writing a narrative text for a journal that requires the text to be twenty-five pages or less. The container establishes the form for us, and we work within that form to write our narrative inquiry text. Part of the opening story of this section, about Bev and Michael's discussions, dealt with the uncertainties and the importance of identifying the container.

Another way of thinking about the container is to think of the field experience and of how this experience shapes form. In the work of Carol Dietrich, "Narrative of a Nurse-Educator: The Interconnected Beginnings of a Daughter, a Teacher, a Friend, Family—A Personal Source of Practical Knowledge" (1992), it is clear that she was working on a memoir. There are certain literary forms that constrain or shape memoir writing in some ways. In other cases, such as that of Joy

Ruth Mickelson, "Our Sons Are Labeled Behavior Disordered: Here Are Our Stories" (1995), the kind of container is less clear. In her study of mothers of boys labeled "behavior disordered," her work with the mothers required an interactive and responsive representational format, and considering the requirements of her work, she used letters sent to the mothers as her narrative research text format.

Our metaphorical soup became a way for us to imagine the complexity of form of narrative inquiry research texts. Although we began with ideas such as Chatman's (1990) categorical idea of text types in the service of one another, we realized that category systems such as Chatman's do not work well with composing narrative research texts. To the extent that we are right in thinking that the tensions associated with composing narrative inquiry texts at the boundary are in each of us, we imagine there is no such thing as a pristine text, one that is relentlessly and exclusively narrative from beginning to end. All writers, each time they write, work through the tensions and compose a text that can always be otherwise, always be improved, a text that is inevitably only a step, a kind of placeholder, from which still other inquiries with still more field texts may be imagined and pursued. We make sense of this as we work our way through two dissertations, both well-done narrative inquiry research texts. We deal first with Ming Fang He's (1998) "Professional Knowledge Landscapes: Three Chinese Women Teachers' Enculturation and Acculturation Processes in China and Canada" and then with Chuck Rose's (1997) "Stories of Teacher Practice: Exploring Professional Knowledge Landscapes."

Narrative Form in He's Dissertation

He wrote a narrative dissertation drawing on fieldwork with three participants, Shiao, Wei, and herself. Her field texts consisted primarily of stories and accounts of life in China and in Canada brought forth through recorded conversations among the three women. The thesis opens with a Prologue, in which she begins with a story set within a three-dimensional narrative inquiry space. This story looks backward to the past for her and her two participants and forward to the puzzle of who they are and who they are becoming in their new land. She looks inward to her personal reasons for doing this study and outward to the social significance of the work. She paints landscapes of China and Canada and the in-between places where she imagines herself to reside. In her five Prologue pages, she writes what Welty (1979) might call "ingots of time" and "ingots of plot" (p. 164). These ingots are both story containers and conveyors of stories, expressions that "speak of life-in-the-movement" (Welty, p. 164) with a beginning and an end. The Prologue gives over to Chapter One, "The Story of How We Began Our Search for Our Landscapes." Even from the title, a reader can see how structure has been introduced into the text by the ingots of the Prologue. We understand that participants are in transition, that there is a search, that it is put in the form of a story, and that we are placed somewhere near what He has named, for purposes of the narrative, the beginning. This chapter begins with a story of a dinner party, and remembrances of life in China emerge in the form of a conversation among the three women.

The dissertation is divided into chapters that narrate the three women's lives. An early chapter narrates their childhoods prior to the cultural revolution, still another recounts their immigrant Canadian lives, and yet another the academic life during postgraduate studies. The thesis is written in metaphorical language and has pauses and gaps in the three story lines that entice a reader into wondering how the recounted lives will end. The three women are portrayed as living "in between" cultural landscapes; their lives filled, as their stories conclude in the dissertation, with unsettled tensions and new identity puzzles. The dissertation concludes with a more conventional chapter of "learnings from the study."

In Chapter One, He uses stories told through conversations to begin to fill in the ingots of plot that she introduced in the Prologue. She also includes descriptions of how her work is positioned in the literatures of *acculturation* and *enculturation*. She briefly sketches out the argument for the thesis when she writes, "This study will provide an opportunity for gaining greater insights into the explorations of the interface among different cultures and ethnic groups" (pp. 20–21).

In Chapter Two, "Searching for a Path to Narrativize the Landscape: Methodology and Theoretical Backgrounds," she crafts a personal journey, told in chronological order, of her attempt to locate and make sense of literature related to the inquiry as she understood it. Partway through the chapter, He introduces readers to the story of meeting her participants and takes us into the midst of their collaborative inquiry field. Here also, she begins to narrate ethical issues embedded in the shared stories she and her participants tell.

Chapter Three, "Narrativizing the Landscapes in Which We Were Brought Up: The Tales from Me, Shiao and Wei," tells the Chinese school stories for each of the three participants. These biographical narratives are filled with detailed descriptions of school and social life in China. Many of the details are presented in the form of specific stories at particular points in time. In a brief paragraph at the end of Chapter Three, she tells us which part of her overall argument is explored and revealed through these narratives. She finds her assumption—that the three women had a Chinese first culture—is in question.

Chapter Four, "Conflicting Stories of Teaching In-Between Cultural Landscapes," follows the same format as Chapter Three; that is, individual biographical narratives with rich descriptive detail, and specific stories conveying much of the detail. This chapter contains a prelude that foregrounds the cultural context in broad brush strokes, in which the stories take place. Context is implied throughout, but occasionally, as in this prelude, it is explicitly recounted. In the interlude that concludes Chapter Four, He returns again to an explanation of how the stories are connected with her developing argument around the question of identity.

Chapter Five, "Strangers' Stories in an Exile Landscape," describes the participants' lives in Canada, but now the dissertation format has changed. It is again conversational, drawing on her field texts. He pulls out stories and interweaves them with interpretation. She is, much more so than in earlier chapters, constructing an argument—balancing interpretive and argumentative passages with narrative ones.

In Chapter Six, "Stories of Learning to Do Educational Research in a Foreign Landscape," He links the idea of learning to do research with the stories of her transformations begun in childhood. There is a narrative continuity established between Chapter Six and the earlier chapters. Once again, this is constructed mainly as a journey based on stories that connect fragments of conversation. In places, using a split-text format, she continues to construct her overall argument in parallel with the stories and conversation fragments.

In Chapter Seven, "Stories of Learning to Be a Fluid Narrative Inquirer and Scholar in a Foreign Landscape," He continues the journey begun in the previous chapter. Once again, she uses conversation fragments interwoven with argument sections, personal reactions, and split-page text. She ends this chapter by using a journey metaphor to link the stories of all three women as told in the various chapters throughout the dissertation. She adopts the notion of boundaries to account for the different parts of the journey marked out by the chapters. This final section summarizes her argument on identity formation as new landscapes are experienced.

In He's last chapter, "Crafting Identities Through Cultural, Educational and Linguistic Changes: Identities on Parade," she does something quite different from what she does in any other part of the dissertation. As she summarizes what she calls her thesis findings, it is almost as if the container form of the dissertation has taken over and shapes what she puts into the metaphorical soup. The tension between the two forms shows up in the language, in which she uses the notion of a parade to hold onto the idea of a journey but presents the bulk of the writing in terms of generalizations and insights, which she labels "findings."

In the first few pages of the Epilogue, "A Life Long Inquiry Forever Flowing Between China and Canada," He returns to a more narrative storied format. She then describes how the three women's stories are pointing into the future, and she describes the changing landscapes in Canada and China.

Narrative Form in Rose's Dissertation

Rose wrote a narrative inquiry dissertation drawing on field texts with three participants, Sara, Clark, and himself. His field texts consisted of field notes of school and classroom participation, participant journal entries, conversations, and personal stories told from memory.

Chapter One, "Introduction," is autobiographical and introduces his research puzzle and main terms. He carefully situates the study within the three-dimensional narrative inquiry space, looking backward to a childhood in schools situated not far from where his teaching and principaling stories are lived out. He begins with a story from the recent past when he returned to a school as principal after a sabbatical leave; then he turns backward in time to autobiographical stories of being a child in school, of being a teacher in school, and of beginning school principaling. He slides forward in time and ends the chapter by using the opening story of how teachers responded differently to a student wearing a hat in his most recent school as a metaphor for setting up the field as he sees it and for building his argument. He draws a sharp contrast between teachers who were tolerant of students choosing to wear hats and those who were not and the dilemma he felt as a principal over what to do with the boy who had been wearing a hat. The conflicting stories around this particular incident return again and again as he tries to understand the landscape where he worked as a principal. He returns to the hat story throughout the thesis. He looks inward to his personal reasons for doing this work and outward to the social significance of his work.

The dissertation is divided into chapters that at first glance appear like those we are accustomed to seeing in dissertations—"Introduction," "Literature Review," and "Methodology." However, Chapters Four, Five, and Six take us into a series of letters that tell the stories of Rose's experiences with Clark and Sara, his two participants. All three of them are portrayed as shaping and being shaped on the professional knowledge landscapes. The dissertation concludes with Rose retelling his own stories of his life as a principal.

In Chapter Two, "Review of the Literature," Rose writes a descriptive analysis of the fields of teacher knowledge and teacher education. He concludes the chapter by linking the literature review to the hat story and to his field of inquiry by introducing one of his participants, Clark. He tells us that the literature offers him a conceptualization "which seems to fit and a language of practice that is relevant" (1990, p. 49). As he writes this chapter, Rose positions his study within the scholarly conversation of teacher education, a conversation framed by considerations of teacher knowledge.

In Chapter Three, "Methodology," he carefully structures an argument in support of his choice of narrative inquiry as his method. Although the chapter primarily follows the format of the literature review chapter (that is, by describing and building an argument), there are two narrative sections in which Rose introduces his participants and describes his negotiation of entry to the field.

In Chapter Four, "Narrative I," Rose presents a narrative of Clark's early childhood experiences, school experiences, and teaching experiences. The narrative tends to be presented chronologically. However, the chronology is divided into labeled sections with titles that refer to theoretical interpretations connected to his argument. For instance, one section, which chronicles Clark's first teaching experience, is titled, "Beginning Teaching: One More Professional Knowledge Context." The entire chapter is presented in the form of a letter addressed to Clark. The letter is composed of stories, conversation fragments, and field notes, all of which are interspersed with interpretive comments. The letters are not quite what we normally think of as letters. Rose refers to them as "mutual constructions" (p. 208), indicating that the narratives are collaboratively constructed accounts between him and his two participants.

Chapter Five, "Narrative II," is a second letter to Clark, using the same format and similar field texts. This second letter indicates in its closing paragraph that the letter is intended as an interpretation of Clark's practice. Rose writes the final section around what he sees as a series of "problems and dilemmas" (p. 140) and invites Clark to respond. In this, we gain a sense that the relationship between Rose and Clark will be an ongoing one.

In Chapter Six, "Narrative III," Rose writes a letter to his second participant, Sara. Chapters Four, Five, and Six all start with a salutation, for instance, "Dear Sara." He begins the letter with a chronological account of their work together and then outlines a number of threads, such as "Community as Family: Welcome, Acceptance, Caring" (p. 150). Each thread is developed using both narrative and description to illustrate the thread. He weaves terms such as professional knowledge landscape, in-classroom place, and out-of-classroom place into the threads. He ends the letter and the chapter by inviting Sara to respond.

In Chapter Seven, "Shaping in the Contexts of Teaching," Rose frames one of the major components of his argument, which is that context shapes teacher knowledge. The chapter brings forward stories told in Chapters Four, Five, and Six as exemplars of various points and subarguments he wishes to make. The chapter is richly filled with references to and reminders of the stories so vividly presented in the letters of the three previous chapters. The pages are filled with people, events, and summaries of their stories, not with theoretical literature. Still, it is an argument that Rose is up to. The reader walks away with a strong sense that Clark and Sara have, indeed, been shaped by the contexts in which they began their teaching.

In Chapter Eight, "Daunting Possibility," Rose, in a sense, does everything. The chapter is a careful blend that brings us back to Rose's puzzles and dilemmas as a principal. He wonders about his work with Clark and Sara and what he might be like as a principal in the future. He does this without literature references but with reference to abstract narrative categories, such as cover stories and landscapes, which he uses to help imagine the lives lived out in the previous chapters. Because Rose narrates an overall argument about teacher knowledge woven together with theoretical terms and linked to the characters and events of the dissertation, this chapter has a reflective tone. He ends the chapter by returning to both the personal and the social significance of the work, reminding us as readers that narrative inquiries need to do both.

SEARCHING FOR NARRATIVE FORM

The story of the conversation with which we began this section on narrative form has within it the heart of what we do, and what we ask those with whom we work to do, as narrative inquirers on the way to composing research texts. In the following section, we outline ways of working that we find helpful in composing research texts.

Reading Other Narrative Dissertations and Books

Whether we read the dissertations of He (1998) or Rose (1997) or the narrative inquiry texts of Vivian Paley (1989, 1990), we read, and we encourage beginning narrative inquirers to read, the works of others. We encourage this for two reasons. One of them is to try to imagine taking our field texts and our puzzles and fitting them within the form that another inquirer has created. This imaginative process of reading another narrative inquiry text as a prelude to composing our own text is a way to open ourselves up to possibility, a way to break out of the bordered space created by the plotlines of formalistic and reductionistic inquiries that we have learned to live within. As we read others' research texts, we see the possibilities for pushing at the boundaries between these and narrative ways of thinking.

Another, and perhaps more important, reason is to imaginatively reconstruct the inquiry process of another as a prelude to living out our own inquiry process. Reading and imaginatively reconstructing the inquiry experience of another allows us to see possibilities. In our own work with beginning narrative inquirers, we often ask them to think about a completed dissertation from the inside, as if it were their own inquiry. We ask them to put themselves in the inquiry situation of the writer of the dissertation and to try to imagine the process, the dilemmas, the boundaries, the choices over field texts, and so on.

In a course that each of us teaches at our respective institutions, a major course assignment is for students to choose a dissertation of interest to them and to present that dissertation in class. We ask them not so much to present the problem and its findings, but rather to reconstruct the inquiry process. We ask them to read the proposal and to make links between the proposal and the completed dissertation. We ask them, whenever possible, to speak with the dissertation writer and to ask the person to give an account of the experience from the writer's point of view and to talk about academic life since completing the dissertation. In this way, we try both to reconstruct the experience of the inquiry and to put it into the context of the writer's overall academic life journey. Our overall purpose in doing this is not to reach for strategies, though specific things may emerge that would be helpful, but rather to help novice inquirers imagine themselves living out a narrative inquiry.

Looking for Metaphor

Over the years of working with narrative inquirers, we have noticed that people often use a metaphor, or several metaphors, to help them think about their work. Various research texts have been written using metaphors—for example, narrative portrait (Bowers, 1993), visual narrative (Bach, 1997), river delta (Hedges, 1994), journey (He, 1998), and others, which have used metaphors such as collage, web, quilt, pilgrimage, and chronicle. Edel ([1959] 1984) writes of chronicles, portraits, and novels as possible text forms. Mallon (1984) writes of chroniclers, pilgrims, travelers, creators, apologists, confessors, and prisoners. These authors, and others, suggest possible metaphors that may be helpful to the writer of narrative research texts.

Writers deliberately setting out to use metaphor need to do so with some caution. We are convinced that metaphors may have a kind of liberating effect for a writer searching for form, but there are also risks. Lakoff and Johnson (1980) point out that metaphors break down at some point in their application. Sometimes, a narrative inquirer can select a metaphor and hold too firmly to it, with the result that the research text develops a feel as if the field texts were being squeezed into an artificial form. When this happens, less, rather than more, meaning is the result. Nevertheless, as long as one is aware of the possible dangers, metaphors may be helpful in the creation of narrative form.

Noticing Reading Preferences

Paying close attention to the kinds of texts we read is also part of the process of creating a narrative form that fits with our particular narrative inquiry. Both Michael and Jean read extensively. Jean recalls all of the moments when, looking up at her bookshelves, she has said, "I know I have that book. I finished reading it only a short time ago." It was in reflecting on moments such as these that she realized that many of these "lost" books were on her home bookshelves. In realizing this, she understood that she could no longer draw a line between her personal and professional reading materials. When one engages in narrative inquiry, fiction such as Ann Marie MacDonald's *Fall on Your Knees* (1996), which experiments with different literary genres, such as journal entries, dialogue, and letters, becomes both pleasurable reading and material that informs issues of narrative form. Jean no longer knows when she reads May Sarton's journals if this is for personal or professional reasons. Is Robert Coles's *Call of Stories* (1989) important reading for narrative inquiry or for personal insight?

Jean's confusion over where she keeps her books is the outward sign of how blurred the distinction between personal and professional is for her and for other narrative inquirers. This blurring of personal and professional becomes even more difficult as we compose reading lists for individuals and suggest possible readings for others. Being awake to all of our reading preferences is something we encourage narrative inquirers to do as they engage in the process of composing narrative inquiry research texts. We encourage them to notice across what may have once been firm distinctions between personal and professional, fact and fiction, and so on.

Not only extensive reading of many kinds of texts but also noticing the kinds of texts read is part of what helps us, as narrative inquirers, experiment with new possible narrative forms. Alvarez speaks of the importance of reading each morning as part of her writing rhythm:

> I consider this early-morning reading time a combination of pleasure-reading time, when I read the works and authors I most love, and finger-exercise reading time, when I am tuning my own voice to the music of the English language as played by its best writers. That is why I avoid spending my early-morning reading time on magazines and fast-read books and how-to books and newspapers, all of which I enjoy, but all of which use language to provide information, titillation, help, gossip, and in many cases in our consumer culture, to sell something. That's not the chorus I want to hear. [Alvarez, 1998, p. 286]

We resonated with Alvarez's sense of possibility for the place of reading others' texts and attending to the kinds of texts we read, as a prelude, and an accompaniment, to composing our own.

Experimenting with Form

Occasionally, students appear in Jean's doorway who have come to narrative inquiry in the midst of their inquiry. Frequently, another researcher, student, or faculty member will send a student with a request that Jean help write up the student's inquiry in a narrative form. This presents a challenge for several reasons, but for our purposes here, the most central reason is that narrative inquiry, for us, is not an add-on. We do not begin to do narrative inquiry at the final stages of an inquiry as if we can convert any kind of study into a narrative inquiry. This is not to say that stories cannot be composed from non-narrative field texts, but for us, such research texts composed after the fact of the inquiry are not narrative inquiry texts.

Questions of form for a narrative inquirer are with us from the outset of an inquiry. Even as we tell our own researcher stories prior to entering into the midst of the field stories, there is a tentative sense of plot. As we engage with research participants and live and tell stories with them, the plotlines under composition are restoried, that is, they are relived and retold. All of these tellings and livings prefigure the narrative forms of our research texts.

As researchers, as we begin to move away from the intensive fieldwork with participants and begin to read, reread, and code our field texts, and as we continue to read the texts of narrative inquirers and others, we may see other possibilities for retelling. These new possibilities provide still other ways of imagining narrative form. We encourage novice narrative inquirers to see themselves as engaged in an ongoing inquiry experiment with narrative form. Huber, Whelan, and Sweetland, whose work is addressed earlier in this chapter, engaged with composing many versions of narrative texts prior to selecting the one they eventually created. They would begin one, compose part of a text, try it out on themselves and on other inquirers, and then, full of questions about whether it was working for their purposes, their field texts, and themselves, they would try something else. Issues of audience, voice, and signature were woven together with issues of form as they engaged in the research for forms that would work. When they came to Jean for conversations about their emerging texts, she found herself responding not so much with comments about preestablished and accepted forms but with response that raised questions situated within the three-dimensional narrative inquiry space.

Response plays a central part in this process of experimentation with form. We encourage beginning narrative inquirers to form into works-in-progress groups, groups in which ongoing work is shared and response from several individuals is given. We talk about these response groups as sustained conversations in which narrative inquirers have an opportunity to share their research texts over several weeks or months as they are composed. Although Alvarez does not speak of the importance of a sustained community of responders also engaged in writing, she highlights what we have learned about reading our work aloud. "Actually, I've found that even if a listener doesn't respond in a negative way, the process of reading my work to someone else does tear apart that beauteous coating of self-love in which my own creation comes enveloped. I start to hear what I've written as it would sound to somebody else. This is not a bad thing if we want to be writers who write not just for ourselves and a few indulgent friends." (Alvarez, 1998, p 289).

In our experience, material is read, response is given, revisions are undertaken, and then texts are shared again. These sustained works in progress are most successful when everyone is engaged in an inquiry task. As each inquirer struggles with issues of composing research texts, they understand in some complex ways the difficulties of composing these texts. These groups support the ongoing experimentation with form.

For example, one of the most difficult qualities of narrative inquiry to represent in research texts is the restorying quality of narrative. A written document appears to stand still; the narrative appears finished. It has been written, characters' lives constructed, social histories recorded, and meaning expressed for all to see. Yet, those engaged in narrative inquiry know that the written document, the research text, like life, is a continual unfolding in which the narrative insights of today are the chronological events of tomorrow. Narrative inquirers know in advance that the task of conveying a sense that the narrative is unfinished and that stories will be told and lives relived in new ways is likely to be completed in less-than-satisfactory ways. It is always a matter of experimentation with narrative form. Even when inquirers are personally satisfied with the result, they need always to remember that readers may freeze the narrative, with the result that the restorying life quality intended by the writer may become fixed as a print portrait by the reader. In works-in-progress groups, response from other participants is useful in helping sustain experimentation with form until the best possible text is composed.

Maintaining a Sense of Work in Progress

As narrative inquirers composing our research texts, we find ourselves at the boundaries in still another way. Students writing dissertations in reductionistic inquiry often complete their dissertations chapter by chapter. They write their introductory chapter, their literature review chapter, their methodology chapter, and so on, moving through their dissertation writing chapter by chapter. Each chapter is approved and checked off by supervisors. When the requisite number of chapters are written and approved, the dissertation is ready for final defense. This is frequently not so for narrative inquirers faced with writing their research texts. This is another tension of working at the boundaries. Frequently, students engaged in narrative inquiry expect to work through a similar process for their writing. Writing narrative inquiry research texts follows quite a different process. In our attempt to describe the process, we say it has a kind of "back and forthing" quality. We compose one chapter, share it with our response group, receive response, undertake revisions, and work through this process until we feel we have moved the text along as far as we can. We set it aside and begin another chapter. We follow a similar process with it until we set it aside. We read the two chapters together, looking for a sense of an aesthetic whole. Reading them together, we begin to revise both chapters, holding one up against the other, searching for a sense of what might make it seem a narrative whole with a sense of aesthetic completeness. This is more the process we engage in—a kind of back and forth writing, receiving response, revising, setting it aside, writing another chapter or section following a similar process, then holding it up against the other chapter, until finally there is a sense of a whole, a piece that feels like it could stand, at least for this moment, alone.

AUDIENCE AND THE COMPOSITION OF RESEARCH TEXTS

In Chapter Eight, we wrote of the importance of positioning each particular narrative inquiry within an ongoing scholarly conversation. The conversation, its substance, and its rules of acceptability are important to the form. Our discussions of the boundaries of formalistic and reductionistic ways of thinking make it clear that the kind of research text is shaped by the ways of thinking of those who read it. The issues at the boundaries often refer to the awareness and acceptability of alternate forms of inquiry within particular subfields or even, perhaps, universities or places in which we may find ourselves. As writers think about their audience as a source of narrative form, they need to think about the kinds of papers delivered at conferences for that particular discipline or group; they need to be aware of particular journals and the range of form of articles accepted for publication; and they need to consider books published in the area and inquiry forms expressed in these books. Of course, we are not suggesting that people not be creative in the construction of their research texts. If our work is to be accepted and to have influence, we need to shape our texts so that they have a chance to push the boundaries, yet not stretch them beyond audience belief.

CHAPTER TEN

Persistent Concerns
in Narrative Inquiry

‒⌇⌇‒ In this chapter, we discuss concerns that are first encountered as inquirers make preparations to enter an inquiry field.
These concerns remain with inquirers throughout the composing and
sharing of research texts. These are concerns that stretch across the
narrative inquiry process. We pulled them forward to this chapter in
order to discuss them in terms of all phases of an inquiry. We give a
sense of how these concerns are experienced throughout an inquiry
as we move from field to field text to research text, weaving our way
forward and backward, inward and outward, and always staying situated in place.

INTRODUCTION

Our focus in this chapter is to raise and discuss questions. None of the
questions have definitive answers. We raise the questions as concerns
that narrative inquirers need to be aware of, and thoughtful about,
throughout an inquiry. These concerns, persisting as they do, are ten-
tatively resolved in a series of interim considerations appropriate to
the particular inquiry at particular points in time.

The concerns discussed in the following paragraphs are ethics, anonymity (of both participants and researchers), ownership and relational responsibilities, how we are storied as researchers, the distinction between fact and fiction, and possible risks, dangers, and abuses. Finally, we take a look at something that for us is of major significance to the narrative inquirer—maintaining wakefulness.

ETHICS

Ethical matters need to be narrated over the entire narrative inquiry process. They are not dealt with once and for all, as might seem to happen, when ethical review forms are filled out and university approval is sought for our inquiries. Ethical matters shift and change as we move through an inquiry. They are never far from the heart of our inquiries no matter where we are in the inquiry process.

At most universities, and certainly at ours, before beginning research we need to obtain ethical approval for our research. In many ways, this process of obtaining ethical approval for our research proposals prior to beginning to negotiate our inquiries works against the relational negotiation that is part of narrative inquiry. However, as an institutional requirement, obtaining ethical approval is necessary. This places narrative inquirers in a catch-22 position. They should not approach participants until institutional ethical approval is granted. If they do approach participants first, they break institutional requirements. If they approach participants with ethical approval, then some aspects of the inquiry are no longer able to be negotiated. Furthermore, beginning participant negotiations with a set of already-approved forms and requests for signatures is a forbidding starting point.

Schroeder and Webb (1997), two doctoral students, wrote about the contradictions of needing to delineate the research clearly and in detail prior to establishing even preliminary relationships with participants. They raise several concerns about the mandated ethical review process. The one most relevant here is the interpretation of informed consent. They write:

> The university's expectation that participants who sign a research agreement at the commencement of a study are fully informed as to what they have consented to implies that the research project has been fully explicated prior to the commencement of the study. The reality

of collaborative research with participants, however, is that the research tends to change over time. The participant's role in the research may change during a study to include being a data collector, a data interpreter, and even a co-writer of the research reports. Such roles may not have been anticipated at the time the researcher initially approached the participant to participate in the study. [pp. 239–240]

As we reflect on our own work in schools, we are puzzled by how we could ever have obtained informed consent from all of the people with whom we came in contact. What does it mean to obtain informed consent in an institutional setting? What does informed consent mean in such settings? Who has the authority to offer informed consent? Is one individual, such as a principal or teacher, authorized to grant informed consent for others? Or do we, as researchers, need to obtain informed consent from every individual with whom we come in contact? There is, of course, such a thing as institutional consent, such as may be given by school boards and hospitals. But this consent does not constitute a response to the questions asked above.

Thinking about ethical approvals as meeting the university ethical guidelines for human subjects, although technical, detailed, and legalistic, does not, however, allow us to consider relational issues, which in narrative inquiry underpin the entire inquiry process. Elsewhere, we wrote that we needed to think of ethics in terms of relational matters: "In everyday life, the idea of friendship implies a sharing, an interpenetration of two or more persons' spheres of experience. Mere contact is acquaintanceship, not friendship. The same may be said for collaborative research, which requires a close relationship akin to friendship. Relationships are joined, as McIntyre implies, by the narrative unities of our lives." (Clandinin and Connelly, 1988, p. 281).

Understanding ethical approvals for informed consent from a relational point of view gives us another way of thinking about our questions. From a legalistic point of view, the questions of informed consent are insoluble and would, in a study of any degree of complexity, bring it to a halt. From a relational point of view, researchers are thrown back on their own ethical resources. For the research to proceed, narrative researchers almost inevitably find themselves in gray areas as far as the legalisms of informed consent are concerned. But from a relational point of view, they have to consider their responsibility as researchers with the participants. In much the same way that we consult our consciences about the responsibilities we have in a friendship, we need to consult our consciences about our responsibilities as narrative inquirers in a participatory relationship.

These relational ethical matters began to become part of our narrative inquiry as we heard and made sense of the stories told to us prior to our first meeting at Bay Street School. But they also began long before that, for as we noted, we were already in the midst of living our research stories. For example, as we noted in Chapter Five, both Bay Street School and Phil, its principal, were storied by others to us prior to our arrival at the school. This web of stories led us to the school and set a context for the negotiations of our relationship. We did not enter into a value-free neutral context. We had an overall research agenda that we felt would fit with stories we heard of the school.

Negotiation of ethical matters also began long before we first moved into the school. For example, Jean's stories of herself speak of an ethic of community, born of growing up in an isolated farming community in the years following the Second World War, a community where neighbors learned to depend on one another for their survival in what was often a harsh climate. As we narrate the ethics of an inquiry, then, we need to be awake to the ethics that emerge from our narratives of experience as researchers. Blaise (1993) writes: "The events in our lives, places we have been and the people we have known, keep coming back. Our life is one long novel and as we work our way through the second half it's a small wonder we never escape those crucial first pages, when the light was set for all time, when the world is an intimate place, and all its inhabitants were known by name. They were all at the dance and they got their hands stamped on the way out. They can wander back without paying, without warning, any time they want" (p. 43).

As Michael's story in Chapter Four suggests, his early childhood experiences flooded into his relationship with Ming Fang He and her inquiry of Chinese women in transition. Although the story, as told, does not explore the impact of Michael's "crucial first pages" on his relationship with Ming Fang and between her and her participants, we imagine how these stories initiated different conversations, attitudes, and responses in their relationship and how this might affect the ethics of, in this case, a supervisor-student relationship.

But our institutional narratives also speak of ethics, a kind of ethics born out of what we called, in the Prologue, the grand narrative, in which participants are seen as subjects in need of protection in research undertakings.

The ethics that emerge from our researchers' narratives of experience and those that emerge from the grand narrative via the institution were with us as we entered the inquiry field at Bay Street School. As we began that first meeting in Bay Street School, that first negotiation of who we would be in that narrative inquiry field, we were aware of negotiating narrative unities with our participants. Questions of who we would be in the field needed to be thought out and talked about. Were we to be positioned on the in-classroom or the out-of-classroom place? Were we to be more participant than observer? If participants, where and with whom? Were we teachers, researchers, women, men, friends, university students, teacher's aides, confidantes to the principal? Which of the multiple possible plotlines did we begin to imagine for ourselves and to talk to school participants about?

Later, ethical concerns emerged as we worked in the field and composed field texts. We were aware that our presence in the school made confidentiality and anonymity particularly difficult ones to negotiate. What was our response when visitors came to the school, saw us, and asked us what we were doing there? If we, or our participants, said we were there as researchers, anonymity would become clouded. If research participants let others know of our research relationship, then it also would make anonymity more problematic.

And what of our field texts? Should we use pseudonyms as we write our field texts? As we talk with supervisors and other team members, should we refer to our participants by their pseudonyms? When our participants asked that we not keep field texts of certain events, conversations, and documents, then of course we would not. But these events and conversations influenced us and may have led us to highlight or attend to other future events and conversations in more thoughtful and different ways. Even when we respected a request, we also knew that being witness to the event might influence us.

There were other ethical issues that began to emerge when we wrote interim research texts. In Chapter Eight, we wrote of the feelings of doubt and uncertainty as we took research texts back to participants. But there are ethical issues here as well, for it is our responsibility not to cause harm to our participants. As we composed our research texts, we needed to be thoughtful of our research participants as our first audience and, indeed, our most important audience, for it is to them that we owe our care to compose a text that does not rupture life stories that sustain them. But as researchers, we also owe our care and responsibility to a larger audience, to the conversation of a scholarly discourse, and our research texts need also to speak of how we lived and told our stories within the particular field of inquiry.

ETHICS AND ANONYMITY

Anonymity, one of the ethical concerns raised above, is a troubling issue throughout an inquiry. As we noted, it is a matter that, under the ethical guidelines for human subjects at our universities, we must guarantee. In most intensive qualitative research, and in narrative inquiry in particular, issues of anonymity appear and reappear. As we said, even when we guarantee anonymity, it is not at all clear that we can do so in any meaningful way. When we are in the field, visitors and others are aware that we are there as people with a long-term interest in that particular place. Even when we try to disguise what we are doing in the place, others may say that we are there as researchers. Our participants may say who we are and what we are doing there. For example, when we worked in Bay Street School, Phil, the principal, proudly announced we were his resident researchers and was quick to tell visitors and others that he was a participant in the inquiry. Stephanie, on the other hand, was reluctant to have senior administrators and consultants in her board of education know that she was part of the research. She was very careful to distance herself from the project when people from her board might learn that she was involved.

These matters shifted somewhat the farther we moved from the field site and as we began to compose research texts. Both Phil and Stephanie continued to have anonymity in the interim and final research texts that we produced. However, on occasion, Phil invited us to present papers and to participate in public forums about the research. On these public occasions, he identified himself by his real name and said that he was Phil in the research. Stephanie also shifted in her stance concerning anonymity when she moved off the landscape of her school and district. At the university, she was happy that people—graduate students and university professors—knew she was Stephanie, and she used her real name to introduce herself.

Concerns of anonymity as part of ethics often shift in other ways as participants take on other roles in other parts of the inquiry process.

For example, at initial stages in the research, participants may agree to anonymity, but as the inquiry process proceeds and participants take on other roles, they may decide that they want to be recognized for the work they see themselves coauthoring. Wendy Sweetland, for example, began as a participant in the Janice Huber and Karen Whelan study. As the inquiry progressed, she increasingly came to see herself as a coresearcher and coauthor of research texts, eventually throwing aside concerns about anonymity, as she coauthored a paper with Huber and Whelan. Often, teachers and other professionals ask that they be named, as did Pam in Phillion's research, so that their work can be validated as their own. Of course, this is necessarily troubling for participants and researchers because there may be risks when people—close up and in the home institutions of the participants—see participants as in some way not valuing or honoring institutional narratives. For example, criticisms they might have may not be welcomed; they may be seen as telling tales out of school; they may be seen as grandstanding.

Of course, there is the other possible outcome, in which people may say at the outset that they want to be named and say quite clearly that they choose not to be anonymous. Only later, perhaps when fieldwork is progressing or interim or final research texts are being written, do they begin to sense that they may be vulnerable if they are named. Then, they may request that they be given pseudonyms and that other fictionalizing methods be used to provide them with the safety of anonymity.

The ethical concern of naming children in research texts is also troubling. Often, children or adolescents who engage in narrative inquiry want to have their stories validated by having their names attached to the research texts. Sometimes, when parents agree, children's names are used. Always, in all of these matters of anonymity, we need to keep the relational at the heart of what we are considering. We need to work through with our participants, as clearly and in as many ways as we can, the possible future plotlines of the stories that may unfold from these decisions concerning anonymity.

What we are trying to make clear is that anonymity is a concern throughout the inquiry. As researchers, we need to be aware of the possibility that the landscape and the persons with whom we are engaging as participants may be shifting and changing. What once seemed settled and fixed is once again a shifting ground.

OWNERSHIP AND RELATIONAL RESPONSIBILITIES

Most novice narrative inquirers, as they compose their personal justifications as part of their thesis proposals, bump into the question of who owns stories. The question is usually framed quite directly in terms of whether the characters named in the inquirer's story own the story or whether the inquirer owns it. For example, students writing about their school experiences ask whether or not they need to get approval from teachers, students, siblings, or others mentioned in the story. Do they own the story because they tell it? Is it enough to make the characters anonymous? This becomes more complex when anonymity is impossible, as when one writes about a male parent or a sibling or a particular teacher at a particular grade level.

The question of ownership appears again during the writing of field texts. Narrative inquirers keeping field notes wonder if, for example, all field notes need to be shared with all participants. Do field notes belong to the researcher, who writes them, or to participants? The possibility of joint ownership, depending on participant-researcher relationship, may emerge. Do both participants and researcher need to negotiate the wording of field notes?

We remember the uncertainty we felt as we wrote our field notes at Bay Street School. What should Jean do about certain stories Stephanie told her? If some of the stories found their way into the field notes and if others, such as Phil (another participant), read them, they would be problematic. Sometimes, personal journals are written by the inquirer to separate material likely to be shared with participants from material the inquirer feels is inappropriate to share. This raises questions about whether material kept private at the field text stage can or should be made public at the research text stage.

Ownership concerns blur into concerns of ethics and negotiated relationships in the field. In direct terms, researchers are always aware of the possibility that relationships may be terminated, and they may be asked to leave the field.

Concerns of ownership emerge yet again in composing research texts. Master's and doctoral students feel this most keenly when they realize that their names will go on the finished research texts, and ownership is clearly theirs, not their participants'. These concerns are confounded with the likelihood that students will have read, by this point in their work, a critical literature on the co-optation of voice, a literature criticizing researchers for co-opting and using participant voices for researcher ends.

As we write this section, we realize that though the concerns are often framed in terms of ownership, ownership may not be the best way of thinking through the various dilemmas and questions that arise. We wonder if reframing concerns of ownership in narrative inquiry into concerns of relational responsibility is a more useful way of thinking about this matter. If we return to exploring the concern as it plays out in proposal writing, we think it more useful that novice narrative inquirers think not about who owns the stories of their early childhood and of their school experiences but of their relational responsibilities to others, such as their parents, their siblings, and others who cannot be made anonymous. Students frequently wish to honor the memory of their parents or to respect the values that parents stand for. Relational responsibility is a better way to think of this than thinking of it as ownership. Writers may decide that they own a memory and still conclude that they ought not tell a story based on it because of a feeling that the other person would not want it told or would be hurt in the telling.

Similarly, as we compose our field texts, questions of ownership are not as important as are questions of responsibilities to those with whom we are in relation. As trust develops, participants frequently give researchers carte blanche to say what they wish. Yet researchers, perhaps more aware of how texts may ultimately be read, may find themselves being more cautious about how participants are represented than are the participants themselves.

HOW WE ARE STORIED
AS RESEARCHERS

When we first began our work as narrative inquirers, we focused most of our energies on considerations of how we storied the participants in our studies. We were unaware that there would be stories told of us. Even as we write this, we realize that this was naïveté. It was something we could easily have imagined had we thought of the research as relational. Of course, the landscapes on which we work are storied. Of course, as researchers on those landscapes, we will be storied by those with whom we work. Stories of us are with us as we move from field to field text to research text.

When we first negotiated entry into Bay Street School as novice narrative inquirers, we slowly awakened to the stories that were told of us. At one point, Stephanie commented in an offhand way that Jean must be working on her master's and Michael must be working on his doctorate. The comment gave us some insight into how one of our participants storied us. Phil often storied us as his "resident researchers," people who were there to listen to his stories and to help him reflectively figure out future actions.

However, not only the participants with whom we work closely in the schools story us. In a later inquiry with Marie, a beginning grade-two Calgary teacher, we became aware that the children also told stories of us. One of the grade-two children, who had grown to like Jean's presence in the classroom, told her in a confidential whisper that the grade-three teacher was leaving, and Jean might be able to get her job and thus, finally, have her own class.

These stories of who we are as researchers are also evident in our field texts as we engage in interviews and conversations. The ways that participants talk with us tell us something about how we are storied. In work at Bay Street School, participants initially spoke to us in ways that let us know that they storied us as experts who had knowledge that could be given to them in workshops and professional development–day activities. Gradually, as they came to trust our working relationship, we were storied as trusted friends and colleagues. In a narrative inquiry with young girls some years later in Calgary, Jean learned, as she listened to the conversations with the girls, that they storied her as a kind of visiting teacher to the school, someone who was interested in their progress and school tasks.

The stories of who we are as researchers are also evident as we compose our research texts. Sometimes, as happened in our long-term work at Bay Street School, we learned how we were storied when one of the participants read our work and through others gave back his story of who we were.

Researchers need to be sensitive to these stories. Sometimes, they actively work to alter them. We found ourselves in this situation at Bay Street School when we were formally asked to put on a series of noon-hour workshops for teachers. We thought that if we did this, it would alter our relationships in the school and would institutionalize the story of us as experts. This, we thought, would undermine our participatory role and the story we told of ourselves. Running counter to others' stories can, as readers might imagine, create tensions. In our case, by not doing the workshops, we ran the risk of being treated as mere users of the school, as people who took but would not give.

FACT AND FICTION

In narrative inquiry, the distinction between fact and fiction is muddled. It is confronted as an issue most often in questions over research texts when we puzzle about, or are asked to puzzle about, the factuality and truthfulness of what we have written. But when we puzzle over these matters, we are puzzling over matters already evident in early stages of the work, matters that intensify as we come to writing research texts.

When a researcher is in the field and a story is told or an event is narrated, we may well wonder about the basis of the story. Did the events described actually happen? How do we know? How does the teller know? The answers to these questions, if the questions are asked at all, will vary depending on the story or event at issue. We may ask these questions yet again as we record them in field texts. Sometimes, we pose our wonderings in personal journals associated with other field texts. Writing a story or recording an event in a field text is conditional. It is conditional on our interests and surrounding circumstances.

As we ponder these questions, clear and certain answers become elusive. When pressed, what seemed like fact appears more and more as memory reconstruction, either ours or participants'. Are these reconstructions best thought of as fiction? Memoir writers and autobiographers, such as Torgovnick and Blaise, offer helpful comment on the insolubility of sorting out distinctions of fact and fiction. In an Afterword to her memoir, *Crossing Ocean Parkway* (1996), Torgovnick poses a question she was asked: What did your mother think? As a response to that question, she writes:

> In my book, my parents and brother appear as characters—by which I mean, representations, based on fact refracted by memory. As in any memoir, they . . . figure not in their own right but as actors in the drama of my life. . . . Did I intend to turn my parents into characters? I did not think about it until I was well into the writing process, but I had done it nonetheless. I realized this [when] . . . I casually mentioned

to my secretary that I was leaving my office to pick up my parents. She
replied, 'Oh, are they the same parents as in your Bensonhurst essay?'"
[pp. 175–176]

Being asked that question forced Torgovnick to think in terms of
fact and fiction. For her, they were the same people, her parents in real
life and her parents in the story. But for readers such as her secretary,
the parents in the story are all that is known. There was no history of
relationship, no memory, to flesh out the parental characters in the
book and to make it possible to avoid the question of fact and fiction.
For readers, the parents in the story are necessarily fictional characters. Yet, for Torgovnick, they are characters constructed out of real
life. Are they factual or fictional and for whom and to what extent?

The exchange between Torgovnick and her secretary compounds
the question of fact and fiction because when reading memoir, a
reader imagines events and characters to be real-life events and characters, the facts out of which the interpretations and narrative threads
that form the memoir are constructed. Yet, it is possible for a reader,
the secretary, to ask, "Are these the same parents?" For her, the factual
characters could have been, or probably were even assumed to be, fic-
tionalizations to some degree. Among other things, this story shows
how the relationship of readers to the text influences considerations of
fact and fiction. In this case, the question of fact or fiction appears to
be settled on the side of fact, by the author. The characters are her parents and thus are factual. Her secretary's question implies that the
parents in the story and the parents in real life are not the same. For
the secretary, a reader, there is a question of fact or fiction that could
be settled either way. But for the author, there is no easy resolution.
She says that during the writing of the memoirs her parents were fic-
tionalized as she created characters of them. Fact, in the text, is po-
tentially fictional both for reader and author. Do we then call it fiction?

Blaise, in what he calls a *Post-Modern Autobiography* (1993), argues
something similar from a starting point in fiction. He writes, "Everyone's fiction is almost completely autobiographical. What makes it fiction, usually, is its degree of disguise. So while most writers apportion
or ascribe their own experiences to other characters, I somehow claim
other people's experiences as my own" (p. 201).

For Blaise then, it might be said that everything, including autobiography and memoir, is fact because everything is autobiographical.

For him, as for Torgovnick, facts and fictions are matters of disguise, of fictionalizing.

For narrative inquirers, these writers offer some possibility for ways of thinking through issues of fact and fiction and for being able to move forward. As we continue to engage in narrative inquiry, these questions will remain with us. Although there may not be answers, we can continue our inquiries.

RISKS, DANGERS, AND ABUSES: "I, THE CRITIC"

Risks, dangers, and abuses of narrative are also concerns to be repeatedly considered over the entire narrative inquiry process. Though these concerns are woven throughout the book, we wanted in this final section to consider them once more. In this section, we do not give a complete listing of possible risks, dangers. and abuses. Rather, we simply remind novice narrative inquirers to listen closely to their critics as they enter the field and as they compose field texts, interim research texts, and final research texts. Our view is that every response is valid to some degree and contains the seed of an important point.

Take, for example, one of the central tenets of narrative, that is, the intersubjective quality of the inquiry. To dismiss the criticism that narrative inquiry is overly personal and interpersonal is to risk the dangers of narcissism and solipsism.

Another danger in composing narrative research texts is what we have called the "Hollywood plot," the plot in which everything works out well in the end. Such plots may be ones in which there is thorough and unbending censure, sometimes found in critical ethnographies, or they may be ones in which the good intentions of researchers and participants are found in every aspect of the study, a distillation of drops of honey, sometimes found in program evaluations and implementations. The hallmark of this plot in research texts is that they are not conditional, not tentative, not of the kind suggested by Geertz and Bateson in Chapter One. Spence (1986) called this process of creating these clean, unconditional plots "narrative smoothing" (p. 211). It is a process that goes on all the time in narrative while composing field texts and research texts. The problem therefore is a judicial one in which the researcher must make a series of judgments about how to balance the smoothing contained in the plot with what is obscured in the smoothing. To acknowledge narrative smoothing is to open another door for the reader. It is a question of being as alert to the stories not told as to those that are. We draw on Kermode (1981) to develop an idea of untold stories as narrative secrets to which a careful reader will attend. Narrative inquirers help their readers by self-consciously discussing the selections made, the possible alternative stories, and other limitations seen from the vantage point of "I, the critic."

One of the ways we learned to think about risks, dangers, and abuses throughout the inquiry is through our multiple "I's" as narrative inquirers. One of the "I's" is that of the narrative critic. Narrative inquirers cannot, as Welty (1979) claims fictional writers can, avoid the task of criticism. She writes, "Story writing and critical analysis are indeed separate gifts, like spelling and playing the flute, and the same writer proficient in both is doubly endowed. But even he can't rise and do both at the same time" (p. 107). Narrative inquirers cannot follow this dictum but need to find ways of becoming a kind of "I, the critic." The notion of critic picks up on Welty's notion from literary theory that doing and criticizing are related activities.

One of the problems of being too heavily into the notion of being "I, the critic" is that it has a negative, monitoring sense, the possibility of stifling inquiry. We need to find ways of being aware of what those on either side of the reductionistic or formalistic boundaries might think or say of our work, and we need to be alert and aware of the contexts for our work, and we need to be alert and aware of questions about field texts and research texts from the point of view of the three-dimensional narrative inquiry space. We call this awareness *wakefulness.*

We deliberately chose a language of wakefulness over a language of criticism in order to set a narrative inquiry working ground without crossing guards, gates, trap doors, and stop signs. A language of wakefulness allows us to proceed forward with a constant, alert awareness of risks, of narcissism, of solipsism, and of simplistic plots, scenarios, and unidimensional characters. This wakefulness is best fostered in response communities where diversity is cherished, where wondering about other possibilities is encouraged. Even with response communities at work during the research process, we encourage ourselves and others to attend closely to reviews of research texts, which inevitably raise questions about an inquiry. Our position, however, should not be misunderstood. Comments and criticisms can arise out of the plot-lines of formalism and reductionism. These comments need to be responded to in terms of narrative inquiry and, in particular, in terms of the particular narrative inquiry. We need to be awake to criticism but not necessarily accepting of it.

What we mean by responding to critics with a spirit of wakefulness is perhaps best illustrated by a story. In a recent conversation, a novice narrative inquirer described her proposed research into the experiences of rural Brazilian women. A Brazilian woman in the group asked what the inquirer could expect to obtain, being from outside the culture and not knowing the language. The inquirer responded that though she was not from the culture, she did in fact speak Portuguese. A discussion took place over the appropriateness of cross-cultural research being conducted by outsiders.

For us, interesting issues of another sort are raised. We see this conversation as part of wakefulness, as part of becoming wakeful on the part of the novice narrative inquirer, who does need to consider the question of language. She does need to consider what difference it makes for her to be inside or outside the culture. But her triumphant response—that she spoke Portuguese—masks the more general issue of being wakeful to working within the three-dimensional narrative inquiry space. We would not, for example, automatically assume that lacking the language would necessarily prevent her inquiry. It would depend. Her situation is so dramatic as to mask the more everyday, moment-by-moment ways in which people need to be awake to how field texts and research texts are positioned along the dimensions of time, the personal and the social, and place.

To take an opposite situation, suppose one is doing autobiographical work and reports a memory. Language is not at issue. The same question asked of the Brazilian inquirer applies to the person bringing forth the memory. What are the conditions contained in the three-dimensional space that condition the meaning that one might make of the memory? It makes a difference if the memory is an adult account of a childhood memory, or if it is presented as a child's account. Furthermore, a memory presented as a record from a childhood diary is, temporally, different from an adult memory, unaided by the diary, of the events. The conditions under which the memory is recalled make a difference as well—in a conversation, in a letter, in a research interview, and so on.

WAKEFULNESS

In Chapter Two, we characterized narrative inquiry as a kind of fluid inquiry, a kind of inquiry that challenges accepted inquiry and representation assumptions. It is a kind of inquiry that necessitates ongoing reflection, what we have called wakefulness. Narrative inquiry, positioned as it is at the boundaries of reductionistic and formalistic modes of inquiry, is in a state of development, a state that asks us as inquirers to be wakeful, and thoughtful, about all of our inquiry decisions.

As we move into the field, we face challenges from others, but also from ourselves, about what it means to do narrative inquiry. Others, and perhaps even ourselves, find comfort and a sense of ease within more stable forms of inquiry. We need to be wakeful about what we are doing as narrative inquirers, so we can continue to learn what it means to do narrative inquiry. As we stated, it has been helpful to us to engage in narrative inquiry from within sustained response communities, communities that help us question our living and telling of stories from the field.

In the above section, we noted the importance of maintaining wakefulness as we write research texts and receive response from others via critiques and reviews, others who work within more stable forms of formalistic and reductionistic inquiry. We imagine that these challenges will continue for many years. As we stay wakeful to these critiques, our responses will help develop criteria for judging the value of narrative inquiries.

In 1990, in our first major article on narrative inquiry, we wrote a section entitled "What Makes a Good Narrative? Beyond Reliability, Validity and Generalizability." In it we wrote, "Like other qualitative methods, narrative relies on criteria other than validity, reliability, and generalizability. It is important not to squeeze the language of narrative criteria into a language created for other forms of research. The language and criteria for the conduct of narrative inquiry are under development in the research community" (Connelly and Clandinin, 1990, p. 7).

We outlined several possible criteria being used, such as Van Maanen's (1988) *apparency* and *verisimilitude,* criteria that put the emphasis on recognizability of the field in the research text, and Lincoln and Guba's (1985) *transferability,* which takes the emphasis off generalizability. We wrote about the importance of avoiding *"the illusion of causality"* (Crites, 1986, p. 168), the apparent cause-and-effect relationship that appears to exist when narrating events in a temporal sequence. We wrote about good narrative as having an *explanatory, invitational quality*, as having *authenticity*, as having *adequacy* and *plausibility*.

These are criteria that continue to be developed and about which we encourage narrative inquirers to be thoughtful. However, as we look back on our 1990 question—What makes a good narrative?—we realize that we need to shift the question in order to more adequately address our concerns. Our question now is not so much what makes a good narrative—which we feel too often implies a question of what makes a good narrative research text—but it is rather a question of what makes a good narrative inquiry. This reframed question allows us not only to think through questions of research texts but also to attend to the whole of the narrative inquiry.

Within our own response communities, we ask ourselves and others to say which criteria they want to be used for judging their narrative inquiries. Sometimes, they develop new criteria that work for them, such as Conle's (1996) *narrative resonance* and Whelan's (1999) and Huber's (1999) *narrative interlappings*. Sometimes, our conversations circle back to the criteria named above, criteria that continue to make sense for judging the whole of a particular narrative inquiry.

As we continue to work at the boundaries of narrative inquiry, we attempt to develop criteria that work within the three-dimensional narrative inquiry space. However, it is *wakefulness* that in our view most needs to characterize the living out of our narrative inquiries, whether we are in the field, writing field texts, or writing research texts and wondering about what criteria to use in a particular narrative inquiry.

———— Epilogue

Living, telling, retelling, and reliving mark the qualities of a life. A book on narrative inquiry, one reflective of this ongoing quality of life, simply stops at some point or moment when the authors, and their most intimate readers, say, enough is enough, at least for now. Such a book starts in much the same way, not necessarily at an obvious point, but rather at a point that makes sense to the authors' stories of experience. And so it was for this book. We began with telling our researcher stories of experience. Other beginnings, other stories, were possible. We began in the midst. We end in the midst.

We try in these few end pages, which we do not see as conclusions, to look back at how we told our narratives of inquiry in this book. In so doing, we retell the narrative of the book. We hope to bring forward, for ourselves and for you as readers, a sense of how we, and perhaps others, have come to where we are in our doing of and thinking about narrative inquiry. This retelling may help us—we authors, our students, readers with a special interest—relive our work as narrative inquirers and move on in ways different from, yet connected to, where we began—retelling connected to telling, reliving connected to living.

In Chapter Four, we wrote that this is not a book on the definition of narrative nor of narrative inquiry nor even a book on how to do narrative inquiry. It is a book that tells stories of how we do narrative inquiry. We hope that it is a book on thinking narratively, a book that tells something of what it is that narrative inquirers do. We have not named narrative inquiry by its definable attributes. Rather, we tried to look at it as something that people do, and we tried to say something useful for others wanting to do something similar.

How do we go about our retelling? This task is easy because we simply retell the book bit by bit, and it is difficult because we want to highlight what we think is different and cuts across what we have called reductionistic and formalistic boundaries; that is, the boundaries that define in the broadest possible sense the social science inquiry world. Writing this, just as writing virtually everything in the book, helps us with our own reliving as narrative inquirers. We hope the same for our students and our readers, and we can only imagine that reading the book will somehow connect with their own narratives as inquirers and create narrative inquiry journeys that belong to them more than to us and to this book.

As we retell the book after the fact, we realize that we began by exploring our own stories of experience as inquirers. For each of us, our history as inquirers was told as a puzzle because we had both been trained in what we named the tradition of the grand narrative. However, as our stories helped us see, both of us felt that following the plotline of the grand narrative took us away from our central interest in understanding our own and others' experiences. As we tell our stories as inquirers, it is experience, not narrative, that is the driving impulse. We came to narrative inquiry as a way to study experience. For us, narrative is the closest we can come to experience. Because experience is our concern, we find ourselves trying to avoid strategies, tactics, rules, and techniques that flow out of theoretical considerations of narrative. Our guiding principle in an inquiry is to focus on experience and to follow where it leads.

We read a diverse set of authors who had also turned to narrative. We wanted to understand how our interest and experience fit, or did not fit, with the interests of these other narrative inquirers. We wanted to see what we could learn from their turn to narrative. Because we were able to read, either directly or by implication, a link to experience into the thinking of many of these others, we were able to refine our notions of narrative and to build what we referred to as a set of terms to bound a narrative inquiry space.

In Chapters Two and Three, we returned to our own work, to our own stories of experience as narrative inquirers, to try to see what we were doing when we pursued what we thought of as narrative thinking. As we engaged in this task, we found we learned much about ourselves and about what we thought was central to our inquiries. We focused on moments of inquiry tension—moments that we came to refer to as working at the boundaries with other ways of inquiry thinking. These tensions at the reductionistic (Chapter Two) and formalistic (Chapter Three) boundaries led us to a set of considerations about our inquiry life around matters of temporality; the place and balance of theory, people, action, certainty, and context; and the place of the researcher. For us, to think narratively, to have a narrative inquiry life, is to continually explore these matters.

In Chapter Four, where we came to grips with what narrative inquirers do, we turned again to our own stories of inquiry experience to compose a set of inquiry terms. Though they did not tell us what to do in detail, these terms created what we thought of as a space in which to carry forward our narrative inquiries.

In the succeeding five chapters, we mapped a continuum of narrative inquiry that stretches from being in the field to composing research texts. It is often believed that narrative research is the collection and subsequent analysis and interpretation of stories. We wanted to convey a sense of wholeness of narrative inquiry from the living to the telling and to the retelling of experience in narrative research texts. Collecting and analyzing stories is only part of narrative inquiry. It is in the living and telling of experience that we locate what represents our sense of our experience as narrative inquirers. Although we discussed several issues, on reflection, we understand that relationship is at the heart of thinking narratively. Relationship is key to what it is that narrative inquirers do.

Narrative inquiry is the study of experience, and experience, as John Dewey taught, is a matter of people in relation contextually and temporally. Participants are in relation, and we as researchers are in relation to participants. Narrative inquiry is an experience of the experience. It is people in relation studying with people in relation.

In Chapter Ten, we pull forward narrative threads such as ethics, ownership, and fact and fiction to show how experience lives with us throughout inquiry. Experience has a wholeness and an integrity about it that is neither left in the field nor on the pages of a field text but is alive at the end just as it is in the beginning.

The purpose of this retelling, like retellings in any aspect of the narratives of our lives, is to offer possibilities for reliving, for new directions and new ways of doing things. Our hope is that the book offers imaginative possibilities for other narrative inquirers to continue to work at the boundaries, to stretch themselves in new ways as they try to come closer to understanding experience.

In the book's introductory stories, stories lived more than twenty years ago, we saw ourselves as living out our inquiry stories in concert with the plotlines of the grand narrative. Although we were both troubled by how this seemed to take us away from studying experience, we both went along—Michael with assessing achievement cross-culturally using various test batteries, and Jean with measuring and predicting children's success in reading by correlating scores on two tests. There were few real alternatives available to us. This is how we had been taught to think about the topics we were addressing.

Now, we do have an alternative. We see ourselves working at the reductionistic and formalistic boundaries, finding ways to study experience narratively. We are fortunate in our current work to be able to return to our Bay Street School studies and to pursue the question of school reform from a narrative perspective. Bits and pieces of this inquiry are noted throughout the book. In our proposed work on the teaching-learning experiences of multiculturalism in elementary school, work that will begin in the fall of 1999, we return to the dual themes of children's and teachers' experiences and the influences of cultural narratives on those experiences. In this return, we work not from the plotline of the grand narrative but from the plotline of narrative inquiry.

~~~ References

Alvarez, J. *Something to Declare*. Chapel Hill, N.C.: Algonquin Books, 1998.

Anderson, K., and Jack, D. "Learning to Listen: Interview Techniques and Analyses." In B. Gluck and D. Patai (eds.), *Women's Words: The Feminist Practice of Oral History*. New York: Routledge, 1991.

Anderson, L. W., and Sosniak, L. A. (eds.). "Bloom's Taxonomy: A Forty-Year Retrospective." *The National Society for the Study of Education Yearbook*. Chicago: University of Chicago Press, 1994.

Bach, H. "A Visual Narrative Concerning Curriculum, Girls, Photography, etc." Unpublished doctoral dissertation, University of Alberta, 1997.

Bakhtin, M. M. *The Dialogic Imagination*. Austin: University of Texas Press, 1981.

Barone, T. E., and Eisner, E. W. "Arts-Based Educational Research." In R. Jaeger (ed.), *Complementary Methods for Research in Education*. (2nd ed.). Washington, D.C.: American Education Research Association, 1997.

Bateson, M. C. *Peripheral Visions: Learning Along the Way*. New York: HarperCollins, 1994.

Bernstein, R. J. "The Varieties of Pluralism." *American Journal of Education*, 1987, *95*, 508–525.

Blaise, C. *I Had a Father: A Post-Modern Autobiography*. New York: HarperCollins, 1993.

Bloom, B. S. (ed.). *Taxonomy of Educational Objectives*. White Plains, N.Y.: Longman, 1956.

Booth, W. C. "Pluralism in the Classroom." *Critical Inquiry*, 1986, *12*, 468–479.

Bowers, L. "Career Stories of Three Mothers as Teachers." Unpublished master's thesis, University of Alberta, 1993.

Bruner, J. *Acts of Meaning*. Cambridge, Mass.: Harvard University Press, 1990.

Carr, D. *Time, Narrative, and History*. Bloomington: Indiana University Press, 1986.

Carr, E. *Hundreds and Thousands: The Journals of an Artist.* Toronto: Irwin, 1966.

Chatman, S. *Coming to Terms: The Rhetoric of Narrative in Fiction and Film.* London: Cornell University Press, 1990.

Clandinin, D. J., and Connelly, F. M. "Studying Teachers' Knowledge of Classrooms: Collaborative Research, Ethics, and the Negotiation of Narrative." *The Journal of Educational Thought,* 1988, *22*(2A), 269–282.

Clandinin, D. J., and Connelly, F. M. "Personal Experience Methods." In N. K. Denzin and Y. Lincoln (eds.), *Handbook of Qualitative Research.* Thousand Oaks, Calif.: Sage, 1994.

Code, L. *What Can She Know: Feminist Theory and the Construction of Knowledge.* Ithaca, N.Y.: Cornell University Press, 1991.

Coles, R. *The Call of Stories: Teaching and the Moral Imagination.* Boston: Houghton Mifflin, 1989.

Conle, C. "Resonance in Preservice Teacher Inquiry." *American Educational Research Journal,* 1996, *33*(2), 297–325.

Connelly, F. M., and Clandinin, D. J. *Teachers as Curriculum Planners: Narratives of Experience.* New York: Teachers College Press, 1988.

Connelly, F. M., and Clandinin, D. J. "Stories of Experience and Narrative Inquiry." *Educational Researcher,* 1990, *19*(5), 2–14.

Connelly, F. M., and Clandinin, D. J. *Shaping a Professional Identity: Stories of Educational Practice.* New York: Teachers College Press, 1999.

Crites, S. "Storytime: Recollecting the Past and Projecting the Future." In T. R. Sarbin (ed.), *The Storied Nature of Human Conduct.* New York: Praeger, 1986

Cuban, L. "Curriculum Stability and Change." In P. W. Jackson (ed.), *Handbook of Research on Curriculum.* Old Tappan, N.J.: Macmillan, 1992.

Czarniawska, B. *Narrating the Organization: Dramas of Institutional Identity.* Chicago: University of Chicago Press, 1997.

Davies, A. "Team Teaching Relationships: Teachers' Stories and Stories of School on the Professional Knowledge Landscape." Unpublished doctoral dissertation, University of Alberta, 1996.

DeCarion, D. "A Narrative Inquiry into Home: A Space Called 'Anywhere.'" Unpublished doctoral dissertation, University of Toronto, 1998.

Denzin, N. *Interpretive Ethnography: Ethnographic Practices for the 21st Century.* Thousand Oaks, Calif.: Sage, 1997.

Denzin, N., and Lincoln, Y. (eds.). *Handbook of Qualitative Research.* Thousand Oaks, Calif.: Sage, 1994.

Dewey, J. *Human Nature and Conduct.* New York: Hart, Holt, and Company, 1922.

Dewey, J. *The Quest for Certainty: A Study of the Relation of Knowledge and Action.* New York: Paragon Books, 1929.

Dewey, J. *Art as Experience.* Toms River, N.J.: Capricorn Books, 1934.

Dewey, J. *Experience and Education.* New York: Collier Books, 1938.

Dewey, J. *Democracy and Education.* Old Tappan, N.J.: Macmillan, 1961. (Originally published 1916.)

Dietrich, C. E. "Narrative of a Nurse-Educator: The Interconnected Beginnings of a Daughter, a Teacher, a Friend, Family—A Personal Source of Practical Knowledge." Unpublished doctoral dissertation, University of Toronto, 1992.

Dillard, A. *The Writing Life.* New York: HarperCollins, 1987.

Dillard, A. *An American Childhood.* New York: HarperCollins, 1988.

Doyle, W. "Curriculum and Pedagogy." In P. W. Jackson (ed.), *Handbook of Research on Curriculum.* Old Tappan, N.J.: Macmillan, 1992.

Edel, L. *Writing Lives: Principia Biographica.* New York: Norton, 1984. (Originally published 1959.)

Eisner, E. W. *The Enlightened Eye: Qualitative Inquiry and the Enhancement of Educational Practice.* Old Tappan, N.J.: Macmillan, 1991.

Geertz, C. *Works and Lives: The Anthropologist as Author.* Stanford: Stanford University Press, 1988.

Geertz, C. *After the Fact: Two Countries, Four Decades, One Anthropologist.* Cambridge, Mass.: Harvard University Press, 1995.

Goldberg, N. *Writing Down the Bones: Freeing the Writer Within.* Boston: Shambhala, 1986.

Goldberg, N. *Wild Mind: Living the Writer's Life.* New York: Bantam Books, 1990.

He, M. F. "Professional Knowledge Landscapes: Three Chinese Women Teachers' Enculturation and Acculturation Processes in China and Canada." Unpublished doctoral dissertation, University of Toronto, 1998.

Hedges, G. "A Narrative Inquiry into Intuition: A Personal Development Process." Unpublished doctoral dissertation, University of Toronto, 1994.

Heilbrun, C. *Writing a Woman's Life.* New York: Ballantine, 1988.

Houston, W. R. *Handbook of Research on Teacher Education: A Project of the Association of Teacher Educators.* Old Tappan, N.J.: Macmillan, 1990.

Huber, J. "Negotiating the Interface of Embodied Knowledge Within the

Professional Knowledge Landscape." Unpublished doctoral dissertation, University of Alberta, 1999.

Jackson, P. W. (ed.). *Handbook of Research on Curriculum: A Project of the American Educational Research Association.* Old Tappan, N.J.: Macmillan, 1992.

Johnson, M. *The Body in the Mind: The Bodily Basis of Meaning, Imagination, and Reason.* Chicago: University of Chicago Press, 1987.

Kerby, A. P. *Narrative and the Self.* Bloomington: Indiana University Press, 1991.

Kermode, F. "Secrets and Narrative Sequence." In W.J.T. Mitchell (ed.), *On Narrative.* Chicago: University of Chicago Press, 1981.

Kroma, S. "Personal Practical Knowledge of Language in Teaching." Unpublished doctoral dissertation, University of Toronto, 1983.

Kuhn, T. S. *The Structure of Scientific Revolutions.* Chicago: University of Chicago Press, 1970.

Lagemann, E. C. "The Plural Worlds of Educational Research." *History of Education Quarterly,* 1989, *29*(2), 185–214.

Lagemann, E. C. *Contested Terrain: A History of Education Research in the United States, 1890–1990.* Chicago: Spencer Foundation, 1996.

Lagemann, E. C. *John Dewey's Defeat: Studying Education in the Research University, 1890–1990.* Chicago: University of Chicago Press, in progress.

Lakoff, G., and Johnson, M. *Metaphors We Live By.* Chicago: University of Chicago Press, 1980.

Lincoln, Y. S., and Guba, E. G. *Naturalistic Inquiry.* Thousand Oaks, Calif.: Sage, 1985

Lugones, M. "Playfulness, 'World'-Travelling, and Loving Perception." *Hypatia,* 1987, *2*(2), 3–19.

MacDonald, A. M. *Fall on Your Knees.* Toronto: Vintage, 1996.

MacIntyre, A. *After Virtue: A Study in Moral Theory.* Notre Dame, Ind.: University of Notre Dame Press, 1981.

Mallon, T. *A Book of One's Own: People and Their Diaries.* New York: Penguin Books, 1984.

Marcus, G. E., and Fischer, M.M.J. *Anthropology as Cultural Critique: An Experimental Moment in the Human Sciences.* Chicago: University of Chicago Press, 1986.

Mickelson, J. R. "Our Sons Are Labeled Behavior Disordered: Here Are Our Stories." Unpublished doctoral dissertation, University of Alberta, 1995.

Minister, K. "A Feminist Frame for the Oral History Interview," In S. B. Gluck and D. Patai (eds.), *Women's Words: The Feminist Practice of Oral History*. New York: Routledge, 1991.

Mishler, E. G. *Research Interviewing: Context and Narrative*. Cambridge, Mass.: Harvard University Press, 1986.

Molloy, S. *At Face Value: Autobiographical Writing in Spanish America*. New York: Cambridge University Press, 1991.

Oakeshott, M. *Rationalism in Politics*. London: Methuen, 1962.

O'Brien, T. *The Things They Carried*. Toronto: McClelland and Stewart, 1991.

Paley, V. G. *White Teacher*. Cambridge, Mass.: Harvard University Press, 1989.

Paley, V. G. *The Boy Who Would Be a Helicopter*. Cambridge, Mass.: Harvard University Press, 1990.

Phillion, J. "Narrative Inquiry in a Multicultural Landscape: Multicultural Teaching and Learning," Unpublished doctoral dissertation, University of Toronto, 1999.

Polanyi, M. *Personal Knowledge*. Chicago: University of Chicago Press, 1958.

Polkinghorne, D. E. *Narrative Knowing and the Human Sciences*. Albany: State University of New York Press, 1988.

Prince, G. *A Dictionary of Narratology*. Lincoln: University of Nebraska Press, 1987.

Propp, V. *Morphology of the Folktale*. Austin: University of Texas Press, 1968.

Richardson, L. "Narrative and Sociology." In J. Van Maanen (ed.), *Representation in Ethnography*. Thousand Oaks, Calif.: Sage, 1995.

Rist, R. "Blitzkreig Ethnography: On the Transformation of a Method into a Movement." *Educational Researcher,* 1980, *9*(2), 8–10.

Rose, C. P. "Stories of Teacher Practice: Exploring the Professional Knowledge Landscape." Unpublished doctoral dissertation, University of Alberta, 1997.

Rose, D. *Living the Ethnographic Life: Qualitative Research Methods Series*. Vol. 23. Thousand Oaks, Calif.: Sage, 1990.

Sarton, M. (ed.). *May Sarton: A Self-Portrait*. New York: Norton, 1982.

Schafer, R. *Retelling a Life: Narrative and Dialogue in Psychoanalysis*. New York: Basic Books, 1992.

Schön, D. A. *The Reflective Practitioner: How Professionals Think in Action*. New York: Basic Books, 1983.

Schön, D. A. *Educating the Reflective Practitioner.* San Francisco: Jossey-Bass, 1987.

Schön, D. A. *The Reflective Turn: Case Studies in Reflective Practice.* New York: Teachers College Press, 1991.

Schroeder, D., and Webb, K. "Between Two Worlds: University Expectations and Collaborative Research Realities." In H. Christiansen, L. Goulet, C. Krentz, and M. Maeers (eds.), *Re-creating Relationships: Collaborations and Educational Reform.* New York: State University of New York Press, 1997.

Schwab, J. J. "What Do Scientists Do?" *Behavioral Science,* 1960, 5, 1–17. (Reproduced in I. Westbury and N. J. Wilkof [eds.], *Joseph J. Schwab. Science, Curriculum, and Liberal Education: Selected Essays.* Chicago: University of Chicago Press, 1978).

Skinner, Q. (ed.). *The Return of Grand Theory in the Human Sciences— Althusser, the Annales Historians, Derrida, Foucault, Gadamer, Habermas, Kuhn, Levi-Strauss, Rawls.* Cambridge, England: Cambridge University Press, 1985.

Spence, D. P. *Narrative Truth and Historical Method.* New York: Norton, 1982.

Spence, D. P. "Narrative Smoothing and Clinical Wisdom." In T. R. Sarbin (ed.), *Narrative Psychology: The Storied Nature of Human Conduct.* New York: Praeger, 1986.

Stone, E. *Black Sheep and Kissing Cousins: How Our Family Stories Shape Us.* New York: Times Books, 1988.

Sweetland, W., Huber, J., and Whelan, K. *Narrative Interlappings: Recognizing Difference Across Tension,* in progress.

Thompson, P. *The Voice of the Past: Oral History.* Oxford: Oxford University Press, 1978.

Torgovnick, M. De M. *Crossing Ocean Parkway.* Chicago: University of Chicago Press, 1996.

Turner, V. "Social Dramas and Stories about Them." In W.J.T. Mitchell (ed.), *On Narrative.* Chicago: University of Chicago Press, 1980.

Van Maanen, J. *Tales of the Field. On Writing Ethnography.* Chicago: University of Chicago Press, 1988.

Welty, E. *The Eye of the Story: Selected Essays and Reviews.* New York: Vintage Books, 1979.

Whelan, K. "Toward Places of Community: Border Crossing of Possibility on the Professional Knowledge Landscape." Unpublished doctoral dissertation, University of Alberta, 1999.

Wittrock, M. C. (ed.). *Handbook of Research on Teaching: A Project of the American Educational Research Association.* Old Tappan, N.J.: Macmillan, 1986.

Wolcott, H. F. *Transforming Qualitative Data: Description, Analysis, and Interpretation.* Thousand Oaks, Calif.: Sage, 1994.

Zinsser, W. (ed.). *Inventing the Truth: The Art and Craft of Memoir.* Boston: Houghton Mifflin, 1987.

~~~ Index